FROM THESE ROOTS

FROM THESE ROOTS

BY

MARTHA EVANS MONTGOMERY

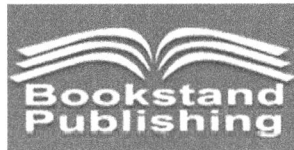

Bookstand Publishing

www.bookstandpublishing.com

Published by
Bookstand Publishing
Morgan Hill, CA
3484_4

The events and people in the book are described according to my perception and understanding of them and the events, based on my memories.

Unless otherwise noted, photos are courtesy of and from the personal files of the Author, Martha Evans Montgomery

ISBN978-1-61863-052-0

Printed in the United States of America

marthagem@gmail.com

FROM THESE ROOTS

This story is about the Carey-Evans family history from 1800 – 2011. It documents how, over a period of more than 30 years of research, a descendant of former enslaves ancestors, Martha Evans Montgomery, traced their roots, from the early 1800's, through their storms, and found sunshine during her journey. Along the way, she discovered how their dreams turned into the light of possibilities and new beginnings for the Carey, Evans, Spencer, Matthew and Wiley Families.

ACKNOWLEDGEMENTS

First and foremost I would like to thank God for his grace and mercy that brought me to this point. I thank him for being the guiding force with a plan for my life. I recently celebrated my 69th birthday, and I can truly say that I have learned that without him I would be nothing, but with him I can do all things, because he strengthens me when I am weak, and keeps me when I am wrong. I give all the glory to God, my heavenly father.

I am grateful for all the people who have been a part of this journey called "my life." I am thankful for my parents, Leonard and Martha Carey Evans, who loved me unconditionally and taught me to dream and reach for the top. I am thankful for my sisters, Hazel, Josephine (deceased), Bernice, and Dorothy, my brother Leonard, and their families, for all the love and support they have given me throughout the years.

I thank my husband William (Billy) for his love, patience and support. I appreciate his standing by and allowing me to work, without interruption, as I spent hours consumed with writing this book, often neglecting him. To my immediate and extended family, longtime friends and new friends, too numerous to name, I thank you for your support and encouragements. Without your support publishing of this work would not be taking place.

I offer a special thank you to Dr. V. Susie Oliphant, who willingly read and critiqued parts of this manuscript and provided such a heartfelt Foreword.

To all my ancestors, who paved the way, and many family members who contributed information, support and encouragement, to help me complete this book, you have my thanks and appreciation. I could not have done it without you. I love you all.

FOREWORD

Philippians 4:13, "I can do all things through Christ who gives me strength" is a scripture that exemplifies the persona of Martha Evans Montgomery as she struggled to visualize, research and write the historical information set forth in the pages of From These Roots. This book did not just materialize over night or appear instantaneously out of nowhere. Its very existence must be attributed to a gnawing need for knowledge about her ancestry and family history that just would not go away. This need has been satisfied through the manifestation of this written product.

Martha Evans Montgomery is a highly intelligent, committed and tenacious individual. When she grabs hold of an idea or project, she just will not let go. It becomes a passion that tends to consume her and forces her to keep working until the task or idea is brought to fruition. This book—From These Roots—was indeed a passionate pursuit. She has spent many long hours thinking about why she wanted to write, what she wanted to write and who would benefit from what she would finally write. Questions about her family fore fathers, who they were and where they came from, provided the driving force that kept her focused on this project for so many years. I am reminded of Proverbs 16:9, "In his heart a man (woman) plans his course, but the Lord determines his steps." God led and directed her steps as she encountered obstacles and overcame them in the genealogical research required to identify and authenticate her ancestry, as well as remembering and recording the details of her journey through her own life.

I was honored and excited when she asked me to write this foreword to her book. When I began reading the manuscript, I could not put it down. I found myself making genealogical charts in order to follow her family lineage. I found it to be well written and informative and I am sure that the reader will be equally stimulated and entertained through her exciting and revealing story.

Dr. V. Susie Oliphant
Retired College Professor and Public School Administrator/ Educator

INTRODUCTION

For many years I wondered about the early evolution of my family. I wondered how they managed to move into their new and unfamiliar environment, following their time living under the confines of slavery. I wanted to document their journey, for the generation of descendents who had not known them, to the best of my ability. My search was to see how they managed to survive and what they had accomplished. I wanted to know and share what I found out about their early existence. From oral histories, told by family members, it was evident that family unity was important to them. My research affirmed those feelings in many scenarios that found them interacting with each other, whether at family gatherings or in times of grief, when they had to support each other. This search has been filled with joy, frustrations and fulfillment as I have attempted to put my findings into words. This journey started over thirty three years ago when I began my search to find as many of my ancestors, as possible. I hope that, in some small measure, I have been able to connect the past with the present in a meaningful way.

As I wrote this book, especially when I wrote about my life, I discovered how much we all have in common, and even if no one purchases a copy, it was still worth it. It allowed me to reflect back on my life in a way that helped me understand who I am. Hopefully, someone can get the benefit and wisdom from my life experiences. I also found that writing can help you understand and confront events that haunt you and have power over you years later. Once you have confronted those things, they lose their power and free you to move on. Writing this book was truly a gift to me.

TABLE OF CONTENTS

Chapter 1

In Search of My Ancestors

As I sit here, starting my final draft, on the 13th day of October 2010, watching the raindrops fall from a gloomy sky, I feel truly blessed to be able to reflect back on my family's life and to see how far we have come. The time had come for me to complete what I started, October 2003, seven years ago, as an effort to write my story, and to link our ancestors from the past to our present families.

As I write this final version, the year 2011 is well into the seventh month. So many changes have taken place, since I began to write this book. Many of the people who were living at that time have gone on to Glory, including my parents. My mind is wandering back to the house that I was born in, located in a hollow, in a little coal mining camp called Ingram Branch, West Virginia (WV). I don't know what the weather was like on that day in July 1942, the day I was born. I can imagine that it was hot and sunny and that Mama and Daddy were anxiously awaiting the arrival of their seventh child. I imagine she and my father had spent many nights wondering how this new life was going to fit into their already large family of five living children.

Before I can tell my story, I have to recognize and honor the generations of ancestors, known and unknown, who provided the stepping stones I walked on to reach this point in my life. My knowledge of some of those early ancestors is pieced together from oral conversations, photos and historical documents. These bits of information have enabled me to weave a quilt of rich history that came together to form a picture reflecting who I am, and who we are today. For many years I felt this tug from someplace deep within to explore our family history. My older family members did not talk much about their parents, grandparents and great grandparents. I don't know if this was as a result of their not knowing much about them, or if the memories were so painful, they left them buried beneath the surface, as their way of coping with everyday life. The shoulders we stand on today have been bowed down, but they remained strong enough to lift up this new generation.

What I write about these ancestors is factual, as far as I know, from information given to me. I have been able to confirm some of this information through census, death and birth records. However, this book is written only to document my knowledge of our family history, and to pass on to other family member's information that may be a guide to help them further trace their ancestors. Some of this information may also shed a light on some inherited traits and genes, that may explain why certain patterns, continue to show up as part of our family's medical history. I have extracted this medical information from official death certificates of ancestors, whose records are officially open to the public, because the timeframe for confidentiality of these records has passed.

For further clarification, the information contained in this book is in no ways meant to be the only family history. I would hope that someone would take the lead and add to this research, maybe going back further than the 1800's. The information I share is my attempt to weave the six families into a living quilt of names, connecting us from the 1800's through the 21st century, through our maternal and paternal family members. In doing so, while writing about these ancestors, there was never an attempt to dishonor anyone or portray them in a negative manner. It is my wish that what I have shared will encourage each of us to be all that we can be. As we examine their environments, we will see how many of them overcame obstacles in their lives. Their accomplishments will show us that no matter how or where you are born, those circumstances do not necessarily determine what your future will be. I have learned from my missteps, and I am thankful that as I reflect back over my life, through the grace of God, I have been given a chance to do some things over. There is truth in the saying, "When you know better, you do better."

Although the early written documentation lists most of these ancestors as laborers, farmers or homemakers, their descendants went on to occupy every profession and occupation available. It is evident, through their early accomplishments, under less than desirable conditions, that these were and still are strong families. They held positions of honor in their homes and communities. Listed among my ancestors and their descendants are ministers, lawyers, doctors, midwives, scholars, farmers, landowners, builders, business owners, barbers, nurses, beauticians, administrators, homemakers, seamstresses, designers, teachers, coal miners, railroad and highway builders, steel workers, entrepreneurs and just about every other occupation you can name.

We stand on the backs of a people who instilled in us everything it takes to be successful so we could make a difference in our lives, our families and our communities. I am sure we had our share of unsavory characters mixed in also, and we acknowledge them as part of our great family history. It is my wish that the family pride, in who we are and where we came from, will be passed on to the younger generations so they can be all they desire to be.

My first real interest was sparked about 33 years ago. I watched the miniseries "Roots" as Alex Haley's slave epic story kept me glued to the television watching a part of history that I knew little about. I realized that I wanted to know about my ancestors and their struggles.

At the time, I did not know that the journey would take so many twists and turns. In the early 80's there was not much research available for African Americans to access. My first stab at researching began with asking my mother what she knew about her ancestors. She immediately said she was the youngest child in her family and did not really remember too much about the "old folks" back then. However, she told me to call her brother Joseph, who we sometimes called "Uncle Joe." She said he had a really good memory and knew a lot about who their ancestors were on her side of the family. Upon questioning my father, he said he remembered his Grandpa Jerry and said that his sister, Ethel, would be able to give me more information and the names of relatives she knew about and remembered.

When I first called Uncle Joseph to get information, he was very willing to share what he knew. However, he warned me that "it gets kind of messy way back then." I have since found this to be true. His first bit of information was interesting because he told me that our family name should really have been "Jackson." He stated that at some point during slavery, the family had been sold off to a plantation owner whose name was William Cary. I would later learn that not only was the family sold to William Cary but that some of the family was owned by another plantation owner named Esther Cary. This seemed to be the point where the family split took place. I don't know what the relationship between William and Esther Cary was.

I immediately realized that my work would be cut out for me. I knew that our family often talked about being "double" cousins. Later on you will see, as I start to connect family members, why this statement was made and has been proven to be true. I would later find one document that referred to an early family member with "Jackson" being their surname.

When I first spoke with Uncle Joseph on the phone, I wrote down with great excitement the names he was giving me. Some of the names he provided for my research were familiar, but most of them were names that offered little hope of ever tracing this family further back than my grandparents. With a little luck I would hopefully get the names of my great grandparents. I felt at that time the enormous weight of trying to do the impossible. Uncle Joe offered me encouragement and said he was so proud that I wanted to do this project. I would learn, through later research, that I had only scratched the surface with the information he passed on to me. I recorded the information on the four panels of a legal size folder.

After talking to Uncle Joseph about the Cary, Spencer and Matthew families, I phoned Aunt Ethel to get the information about the Evans and Wiley families, on my father's side. She too was excited about my new project and provided names to me I had never heard of. My excitement was once again tempered by the lack of accessible information.

I realized that someone had to take on this project so that the younger generation would have the knowledge of who their ancestors were. They could take pride in what they accomplished under adverse circumstances and limited resources. For me, this has truly been a "Labor of Love."

I have said all of this as a preface to the information that I will be sharing about those early ancestors. If you happen to see that your name was first used during the early 1800's, take pride in knowing that someone was probably thinking about an ancestor, and they were honoring them by giving you their name. I am honored that part of my name came from my Grandmother Martha Susan (Susie) Spencer Cary, and my mother Martha Susie Cary. I know some of you consider your name "old fashioned," but if you look at the big picture, in the African American culture and tradition, names were important because they were sometimes the only connection to the past. In the early days of slavery, names were chosen to give significance to the child, other than the one the slave owner chose, which was more than likely derogatory, in meaning. This was also a way to keep ties to family members who had died or had been sold off to other slave owners. The names passed on to family members were the invisible "ties that bind."

With the internet and so much information coming online, I found that I could trace the family to the earliest census records that actually listed African American, by name. My first research was done from the 1880 census made available by The Church of Jesus Christ of Later-day Saints, as part of their Familysearch.org website. I would later subscribe to the Ancestry.com website and would find that I could go back to the census taken in 1870. It was while during this research that I realized that the census is not just a means for the government to get into your business, but it is a valuable tool for documenting that you did spend time on this earth, that you had family and that future generations would know more about themselves by knowing who and where they came from. The census would also provide documentation that could be used to trace the migration of families, how they progressed economically, and how their families changed every 10 years. The Virginia (VA) Slave Birth Index was also helpful in finding names of children born on various plantations.

While looking at these early records of my ancestors, especially those in the 1870 census, I thought of how they must have felt just 5 years from being enslaved in a cruel system that did not even consider them to be human. It is interesting to see that the "race," which we now refer to as African American, had been, at the time of the census, "colored." Over the years we moved from being colored in 1870, black in 1880 until we made it to the 1910 and 1920 censuses where we became mulattoes and black again, only to become Negroes in the 1930 census. I guess you can say some people were born colored and died black or born black and died as a Negro. And what about those of us born since the 1930 census, most of us were labeled Negro, until recently, but will probably die as African Americans. I have also looked at many marriage and death certificates and they too reflect our ever evolving race designation. As they say everything old is new again and vice versa. Thankfully, your racial designations do not determine who you will be, or what you can accomplish during your life time.

I need to digress a little here because for the young people who may be reading this book, I just want to say that I chose to see my ancestors, not as slaves, but born into slavery. I believe that we all come on this earth free. It is society that places a label on you. Our ancestor's conception was not unique from any other child conceived at that time. The circumstances were truly not ideal or right, but in the sight of God, they were just as precious. God sees us all as being the same, created in his own image. They were born free spirits, but enslaved by an evil society that condoned inhumane treatment of those who were different. There are many forms of slavery. Even today in the 21st century, people are born everyday into negative circumstances that sometimes prevent them from excelling to their highest potential. However, the will to do better can still change the outcome.

Some individuals born in the year 2010 will not be as free as our ancestors, who were born in this country more than 200 years ago. Their lack of pride and freedom is self-imposed by their failure to set high goals for themselves, but rather to be content with the status quo. The testament to the survival of our ancestors is great because they were still able to make great strides, even though they lived under adverse conditions and unsafe environments.

Daddy Sam Evans
Cheerque Indian
Grand Pa.

From what I know about our ancestors I can attribute their early roots to the continent of Africa, as evidenced on some of their 1918 WWI Draft Registration cards, and my Native American great-grandmother, Louisa Evans, on my paternal side, who I was told was a full-bloodied Cherokee Indian. Since Indians were often listed as "colored" that part of the bloodline is harder to trace. The only documentation is written on the back of the only photo that I have of her son, Sam Evans, which bears the handwritten notation on the back that says "Daddy Sam Evans Cheerque Indian Grandpa." Some of the physical features, attributed to Indians, are prominent in the Evans descendants. My cousin Ernest Womack, who knew Granddaddy Sam, described him as having different physical traits from the other blacks in the community.

I don't know what influence my early ancestors would have had on me as an individual, because I was not fortunate to have known many of them. However, I do know the influences passed on through their children must have been very strong. The early family survived through adverse living and social conditions, and environmental elements, unlike the ones that were associated with their native land. Out of all of those adverse conditions, the cruelest one they survived was "Institutional Slavery." They managed to pass down their customs, traditions, and their love of family, because they kept these things in their heart, locked away from the ugly world they were forced to live in. I am thankful for their strength and will to survive. Because of my faith in God and them, I am who I am today.

As I search for a comparison of the historical significance of their heritage and birthplace to the land they ended up in located in the State of Virginia, I see none. The unfamiliar cultures they were forced to adapt to caused them to become silent participants in their own destruction. Their identities were forced into their subconscious in order to survive in a cruel and foreign land called the United States of America. They were denied the choice to immigrate; instead they were forced on crowded slave ships to become captives in a foreign land.

Through it all, they suffered the indignities and trauma of being ripped from the familiar and forced to endure treatments of being less than a human being. Their sense of dignity was stripped from them; their names were beaten from their memory and changed to reflect that of their slave owners and masters, and their history destroyed, through their separation from all that was familiar. Their life was made worse and their safety was no longer guaranteed.

Because of the way our ancestors entered this country, many would never tell the story of their homeland to future generations. Even today, those who had the knowledge refused to talk about the suffering they saw in those early years during and after the abolishment of slavery, at least in theory. In most cases their connections to their birthplace and family beginnings was severed and destroyed by their masters, with hope that it would never be remembered or shared. Many years after the end of slavery, and some wanted to tell their story; they were often admonished and told not to discuss those things in front of the children.

Their bodies had been crushed but their spirits could not be killed. In spite of everything, when the time came, they rose up through the storms, their lives improved and they became empowered to try to make things better for those who would come after them. Their spirit rose again in the generation of children born after 1865. Some of our grandparents were the first beneficiaries of this new lease on life. This spirit continues today in the lives of the descendants of the mighty generations that could not be destroyed.

Our family story and journey began long before the 1800's. It began with all the generations before them. Our story will not end with us, but will continue through all the generations that come after us. There is not a lot of physical documentation about my early ancestors and their early life, but it is evident that there was always a lot of love, dedication and success following them throughout history that produced descendants exemplifying that same willingness to push forward. The greatest gift they left was Love of Family. My story seeks to expand on the ones they left behind and those who continued to fulfill the early dreams of our ancestors.

In May 2005 I had the privilege of recording a CD, with the assistance of the Library of Congress's American Folk Life Center, through the National Public Radio's Story Corps Project. This forty (40) minute recorded CD will be housed in the Library of Congress for eternity. With the assistance of my friend, Virginia Reynolds, who acted as my interviewer, I was able to answer a set of questions I had prepared; to cover what I felt would be relevant information for future generations to know. That recording was my attempt to tell my story and theirs as part of a family's history.

The official recorder interrupted only once. He asked how it made me feel knowing the fact that my family had been split, and their names changed, as the result of a sale to a new slave-owner. My response was that there were many ancestors I would never know. That link had been broken. There is no knowledge of anyone who could tell the story of who those early Jackson families or their descendants were.

For those who did not get a copy of it at the 2005 Family Reunion, it is a part of the Story Corps Archive. It can be located at the Library of Congress, in Washington, DC, under Martha Montgomery – MBY000024. I hope this book will supplement that project in an expanded version of our family history. Since 2005 I learned much about our early beginnings. As I try to complete this final version, and prepare to have it published, I will be ever mindful of how important this information may be to future generations. Of course, as in all things, everything cannot be proven. This is not an attempt to say that all my findings are true and that they are the only ones. What I was privy to, I have tried to share and incorporate into this narrative. I also solicited input from various family members to tell the story about their family. If your immediate family is missing, you must not have responded to my request.

My inspiration for this project was made more urgent, and the completion more pressing, when in April 2006, I visited my beloved mother. The occasion was her 92nd birthday celebration. I carried home, for her viewing, two DVD recordings of significant events in her life. The first was the celebration of her and my father's 60th wedding anniversary in 1992. Dad went home to be with the Lord in February 1995. The second DVD was the celebration of her 90th birthday in 2004. The look of joy on her face as she watched those important events was so precious. At the time she had been in failing health during the previous 8 months period.

After viewing those DVD's she looked at me with such love and pride and said "you really know how to cheer me up." We hugged and I told her she had always been there cheering us on and that it was time for us to do the same for her. She thanked me with that sweet smile and I knew then I had done something special for her, and realized the effort of sharing memories is so important.

Mom celebrated her 92nd birthday on April 30, 2006, surrounded by all of her children, and most of her grandchildren, and many family friends. She held her youngest great grandchild for the first time took pictures with all of us and waved goodbye to us from her favorite chair, as some of us returned to our respective homes. I did not know, at that time, this would be the last time I would receive a good bye hug and kiss from her. Looking back, I think she knew. She insisted on leaving her sick bed and walking into the living room so she could see us drive off.

My mom and I were able to talk nearly every day, after she took ill, sharing as we always did. Mom went home peacefully to be with the Lord May 17, 2006. Shortly before her oldest child, my sister Hazel, departed the hospital, after spending the day with her, Mom looked at her with that same love she had shown all our lives, as she walked out the door. The first child she bore, whose face she saw for the first time, was also the same child's face she saw for the last time on earth. I dedicate this book to my Mother and Father and all my ancestors, known and unknown. I also take the liberty to mention, by name, many persons who have been a part of my life throughout the years. By doing so it is an act of honor and appreciation for all you have been to me. I hope you consider it an honor as well.

Rev. Anderson Carey

Law Carey

Russell Goldman/Lukinsey Carey

Emma White

Dora Rice

The late Mrs. Sallie Pryor
Former Choir Member

Gladys Womack
Dickerson

Anna Womack Gamble

Whitfield Matthew

EARLY CAREY ANCESTORS 1800's - 2011

Chapter 2

(Jackson)Carey Families

My official research will begin with the 1870 census records which document the existence of my family through the following surnames: Jackson, Cary, Spencer, Matthew, Evans and Wiley. Because I have not found documentation of my paternal great-grandmother Louisa's maiden name, that part will be left for some future generation to research and add to this rich history. Prince Edward County, Virginia, is the location where I found my early ancestors.

I will start with the family history on my mother's side of the family through her father, Joseph Sanker Cary, Sr. I have noticed that the spelling of the surname was changed in later census records. An "E" has been added, so some of the records will reflect the spelling "Cary" and others will reflect the spelling "Carey." Where available, I will share photos that will add faces to familiar and some unfamiliar names.

In the four pages of notes from my conversation with Uncle Joseph, he informed me that his grandfather's name was Ralph and his grandmother's name was Amy. He also gave me the names of Ralph's children. To illustrate his memory, I will list these children's names, and at a later time identify them in the official census records I found. During later years some of these names may have been changed as they are reflected in later census records. Sometimes the first name has been switched to the middle name and vice versa. When looking at census records, you have to keep in mind that these records were taken by census workers, who sometimes were not that educated themselves, thereby making many mistakes, in the spelling of some of the names. They often used the name that the person was called by on a daily basis, even if it was a nickname.

The names that Uncle Joseph gave me about his father's siblings were: John Robert, James Anderson, Ellen, Par, Fannie, Ralph Alexander, Joseph, Cornelia, Nicey, and Agnes.

According to Uncle Joseph, Ralph Cary had one brother named Anderson, and two sisters – one named Agnes, who he said was our Cousins Anna and Bea Womack's great grandmother, and Nannie, who was Uncle Nelson Carey's grandmother. Nannie Cary was married to Sam Cary. I don't know anything about Sam Cary's family, prior to the marriage between him and Nannie. Maybe Sam's family lived on a different Cary plantation. Remember earlier I talked about being "double cousins," - well this is one of those instances. I will just state for now that Nelson Carey, the grandson of Nannie Cary, who was my great aunt, would marry Florine Evans, the daughter of Sam Evans, my grandfather, on my father's side of the family. This is only one of the unions that show the marriage of relatives from both sides of the family. Since the Evans and Carey families were not related, this marriage is not considered interfamily.

When I started the research, my first information would come from the United States Census taken in 1880, because that was the only one available. As years passed, I would be able to go back and do additional research using the 1870 census and some slave indexes.

The 1880 census was taken fifteen (15) years after slavery was abolished. I was led to believe that this was the first census that listed ex-slaves, with names. However, there was a census taken in 1870 that also listed the heads of household, along with all persons residing in the household at the time the census was taken. This census was very significant because you could see how many families had stayed together in the same communities, where their slave owners had resided, or if they had ventured off to other parts of the United States. This 1870 census also showed the names of children, who were not listed in the 1880 census, thereby giving you a clearer look at the earlier family picture.

In searching the 1880 census for Ralph Cary, I found him but with a wife named "Annie." As I stated earlier, names were often misspelled or given differently from birth names. I have found, on some of their children's death certificates, her name listed as Amy as well as Annie.

Additionally, Amy's maiden name on records is sometimes listed as Bolton or Bouldin, and on one what appears to be (Amy) Snead. Each informant was different, thereby causing the confusion. I am thinking that sometimes the informant did not know the exact name themselves. It was possible that they were repeating what someone had told them, without documented proof. However, there is enough proof to confirm their family relationship.

Because I had prior information provided to me, by Uncle Joseph, researching the 1880 census, I was able to confirm, by the children's names, that these were indeed my great grandparents.

The 1880 census did not list all of the children that I was told were in the family. After further research, it was determined that some of them had married, moved away, living in other family households, or sometimes in a former slave owner's home, as a domestic or farm worker.

For clarity, I will just list those children on the 1880 census at this point so if you chose to do your own research, you won't be misled. I will return to the 1870 census later. The post office for the Cary family was located in Farmville, Virginia.

In 1880 Ralph Cary was listed as a black male, who was a farmer married to "Annie" They lived in Hampden, Prince Edward (County) Virginia. He was listed as the Head of Household, his birthplace was Virginia, and his year of birth was 1830. This was an approximate year because he was listed as 50 years old. The record stated that the birthplace of his father and mother was Virginia. The children listed were: Agnes, 18, Thenia, 16, Fannie, 12, Leila, 10, and Alex, 8, Joseph 6, and Wash, 2. Virginia death records reported that Agnes and Cornelia both died in 1880, presumably after the census had been taken. Ralph Carey died before the 1900 census.

It was harder for me to find Ralph in the 1870 census because his name was spelled differently. When I put Amy Cary's name in, bingo, I found the Cary family. Ralph was spelled "Rolfe."

Some of the handwriting, on the original census records, was better than others. In the later census records taken in the 1900's, it seems that the enumerators, in some areas where the blacks lived, did not try to make their entries legible. I have to give credit to the transcribers at Ancestry.com because they have done a great job of deciphering what was written. Ancestry will also put alternate spellings and will allow you to make corrections to entries where you have knowledge that a name is incorrect. I made the correction on my father's name and it was accepted.

The 1870 census listed Rolfe (Ralph), who was born about 1828, and Amy, born about 1835, with their children as Robert, 14, Henry, 16, Anderson 12, Ellen 8, Agnes, 6, Parthenia, 4, and Fanny 2.   My grandfather, Joseph Sanker was not born until 1876 or 1878, so he was not listed in the 1870 census. They also had a daughter named Nicey. I don't have a record of her year of birth. Tracing the female children in later records was made more difficult without knowing married names. The three females I was able to trace were Ellen Cary Morton, Fannie Cary White and Nicey Cary Goldman.

According to the record I found, Ralph Cary died in 1889, from consumption, what we know today as Tuberculosis.

Amy Cary was found again in the 1900 census living with her son, Joseph and daughter in law, Susie. According to the death certificate, Amy died February 25, 1915, from a malignant tumor in the womb, with a contributing factor of anemia.

Ellen was the last child born into slavery to Ralph and Amy Cary. In the 1880 census I found Ellen Cary, 18 years old, working as a cook, in the home of George Claiborne. In the 1900 census, 20 years later, at the age of 36, Ellen was married to Anderson Morton, who was 61 years old. She had a son named Joshua, 19 years old, a daughter named Annie, 17 years old, and in the 1910 census, she is listed with a son, 10 years old, named Henry Wesley. They are found again in the 1920 and 1930 census. Ellen passed away November, 1945. I was three years old and I remember going to Virginia with Mama when Aunt Ellen passed. I remember sitting on the bed, early in the morning with my new white shoes on, waiting for time to catch the train to Virginia. Since I was the baby and not in school, Mama took me with her. Mama said she got a kick out of seeing her brother carrying me around in his arms. I don't remember the funeral, but I can remember the train ride and sitting eating fried chicken out of a shoe box.   Cousin Wesley, was a farmer, and lived down the road from the family home, and passed away in June 1975. Joshua's 1917-1918 WWI draft registration shows him living in Baltimore, MD, working in a steel mill as a brick layer helper. My mother said I reminded her of Aunt Ellen, because I had a little head and mouth like hers and we both had dusty brown hair.

Fannie Cary was the first child born to Ralph and Amy after slavery was abolished. She was born in 1867 or 1868. She is one of the first children to be listed in the 1880 census as being in school, at the age of 12. I found her next in the 1900 census married to John White, born in 1868. They were living in

Worsham, Prince Edward County, Virginia, and were the parents of Asco, Emma, Lucy, Samuel, Thomas and Rollo.

Fannie Cary White passed away in June 1904. Her death was written up in the Farmville, Virginia Herald. It read: "Fannie White (colored) died at her home three miles from here last Monday morning at 9 o'clock. She was the wife of John White. Deceased will be greatly missed by the white people among whom she had been a servant from childhood. The white people were faithful to the last in providing for her during her sickness. She leaves six little children. It is believed that she was a faithful Christian. She said a few days before her death that she was ready and willing to go." I make note of this because it was unusual in 1904 to find a write-up on regular colored people in the newspaper, unless they were well thought of or meant something special to the "white folks."

Sometime after the 1910 census was taken, John married Betty and he had six additional children, whose names were Minnie, Alberta, Clarence, Florence, Lora and Ernest. They lived in Hampden Township, located in Prince Edward County, Virginia.

I found a Henry Cary born about 1853 who was 25 years old, in the 1880 census, working as a laborer and married to Ada Cary, 18 years old and they were living in Hampden, Prince Edward County. In the 1900 census Henry is 47 years old, now married to Nannie, 25 years old, with a 11 year old son, named Richard and a 4 year old daughter, named Maud.

Robert or John Robert Cary born about 1855 is found in the 1880 census working as a laborer in the home of John Franklin. He is found again in the 1900 census living in Worsham, Prince Edward County, Virginia. There is no mention of a wife in the 1900 census, but records show he had children named, Robert, Lincoln, Cornelia, and Claiborne. In the 1910 census Robert is married to Mary. When the 1920 census was taken he was married to someone named Rachel Frost. They are also mentioned in the 1930 census. Robert or John Cary as he was called passed away on December 8, 1936 in Farmville, VA., at the age of 80.

James Anderson or Anderson James Cary was born about 1858 according to the 1880 census. I did not find him again until he was located at the age of 40 years old, in the 1900 census records. He was living in Madison, Charlotte County, Virginia, with his wife Anna (Annie) Thomas Cary. Their children were Mary

A., Annie Belle, Anderson Booker, Lukengus, who was a lawyer, and Landon (Cabell). The 1910, 1920 and 1930 census shows him still living in Walton, Charlotte County, Virginia, with his wife Anna and a grandson named Lesley Haskins.

An interesting fact came to light when I located the 1918 WWI Draft Registration Cards for Lukengus and Anderson Booker Cary – they identified their race as "African." Their brother Landon Cavil identified his race as "Black." Lukengus was a student in college, in Virginia and Anderson Booker, a farmer, said he was in bad health and working for his father, and Landon was married and working for the railroad.

Anderson Cary was an ordained minister, who served as one of the early ministers in the family church, New Hope Baptist Church, which had strong Cary ties from its beginning in 1867.

The church was organized in the year 1867, two years after slavery ended, when a small group of believers began prayer services in their homes. When the group grew too large to meet in their homes, a decision was made to establish a permanent place centrally located for worship. The Grandfather of Deacon Nelson Carey, and Sister Leila Jordan, William Scott, gave enough land to establish the first permanent place of worship and called the church Brush Arbor.

Later Brother William Scott extended the gift of land enough for the cemetery, at that time called a burial ground. Rev. Peter Carey was the first pastor. In 1885 a tract of land was purchased from the Carey estate of Booker and Ann Carey, and others to build the new building which was completed in 1886. This historical building would later become the community school for colored children, known as New Hope School. It was still standing and years later it would be moved to become a part of the new sanctuary, where the families still worship. Most of the family members, who moved away, from their birthplace, are still carried back for their final home going service and burial in the same cemetery as their ancestors.

Rev. Anderson Carey passed away on August 28, 1939, at the age of 78, or 81 depending upon which year of birth used. His death certificate lists the cause of death as having something to do with his gall bladder with gastritis, an inflammation of the stomach, a contributing factor. He is one of a small group of family members that are not buried at New Hope Cemetery. His death certificate lists his father as Ralph Cary and Annie Bolton as his mother. The mother's name on the siblings various death certificates varies depending on who is giving the information. I guess some things will remain a mystery to our generation.

There was a family story told to me by Uncle Joseph and Mom about the home that my grandfather and grandmother lived in, before he passed. It seemed that my great grandfather Ralph and his son Anderson bought 10 ½ acres of land for the family. The land was to be divided between all the children, after his death. When my grandfather's house was built, his name was never put on the deed to the house they lived in, instead only Anderson, his brother's name was on it. Anderson's son Lukengus, the lawyer, was supposed to have recorded a new deed. He never added my grandfather's name to the deed and that information was not known to my grandparents.

When my grandfather, Joseph, passed, my grandmother thought she had a home, but, she would later find out that the property was never transferred to my grandfather's name. She was assured by Anderson, her brother in law, after my grandfather's death, that she would have a home "as long as she did not remarry." I understand as the story was told to me that my grandmother did not appreciate this turn of events and she later had the best part of the house moved to another piece of land that had been purchased by her daughter, Amanda and her husband Willie (Buck). The house became a part of the new house that Uncle Buck was building. In the end she had her house and it is still standing many years later. I don't know all the facts but I heard it from more than one source. The latest source was as it was told by Aunt Amanda in a taped interview in 2003, when she was asked about the home she lived in. I understand that as a result of this family dispute, the family was very stressed out after my grandfather passed, and it was a sad time where many feelings were hurt. Those bad feelings among various family members would last for many years.

Ralph Alexander (Alex) Cary was born about 1872. He was born seven years after slavery ended. He is found in the 1880 census and the 1900 census. In the 1910 census he is listed as the head of the household at 34 years old married to Elizabeth, who was born in 1889.

The 1910 census lists them with children named Hassick, Caleb, and Melville. Their son Lathion was born around 1911, and he is listed on the 1920 census as 8 years old in the home with his mother and other siblings. Ralph Alexander's 1917-1918 WWI draft record show him as being a self employed farmer, living in Darlington Heights, Virginia. Ralph Alexander passed on December 7, 1918, at the age of 40. His death certificate list his cause of death as suffering with kidney and bladder trouble for a long time with a contributing factor something like "Bright's" disease, chronic nephritis, inflammation of the kidney. His death certificate lists his occupation as a farmer. His death certificate also lists his father as Rafe (sic) Cary and his mother as Amy Snead. Once again, we have conflicting information regarding the maiden name of the mother.

There is a record of a son named Wash, in the 1880 census, born about 1878, but I could find no additional information on him in any of the records I was able to research.

Nicey Cary was married to Frank Goldman. Recent information was given to me by Russell's wife, Nannie. The names of their children were Parthenia (Polly), John Otha, Edward, Lucille (Patty), Russell, Ralph, Carey, Lloyd, Garland, and a son named Samuel, who either died at birth or at an early age. I don't have any additional information about her or her family, other than one of their sons, Edward, who passed in 2004, was a professor at Saint Paul College, in Lawrenceville, Virginia and Ralph, who passed in 2011, served for 20 years in the military, and retired from Burlington Industries in Drakes Branch, Virginia. Ralph was married to Elsie M. Smith, and they had three children, Ralph, Jr., Francine and Cheryl. Russell is a minister and the only surviving child. The photo of Nicey was taken from the recent obituary program for Ralph, Sr. The families resided in Cullen, Virginia.

Parthenia Cary is the mystery because I couldn't find any information on anyone by that name, after the 1880 census, other than some one named Parthenia Cary had a child who died in 1899.

Joseph Sanker Carey, my Grandfather, was born February, 1876. He was born 11 years after slavery ended. He is listed as 2 years old at the time the 1880 census was taken. Joseph is found again in the 1900 census, married to Susan Spencer, who was born April 1879. They were married March 10, 1899. It was my understanding that Susan's full name was Martha Susan. I have only found one record with Martha in her name. That record is the name my grandfather put on his WWI draft registration card, as the next of kin, which by the way was signed by him, with his own signature, not with an "X," as was the custom for those who could not read or write.

Joseph and Susan's residence was in Worsham, Prince Edward County, in 1900. They were living with his mother, who is now listed as a widow. The first child born to Joseph and Susie was named Estelle. She was born in 1899 and died on October 23, 1899. The 1900 census show them living in Hampden, Prince Edward County, in Virginia, with no children. Interestingly, the 1910 census only lists Joe and Susie Cary, and does not show them having any children. We know from the 1920 census that there were three children born before 1910.

The 1920 census shows the family still living in Hampden, but the family has now grown to include six children. Also we are now seeing the name Cary being spelled with an "E" in it. The children were Albert, born 1902, Willie Wallace, born 1904, Joseph Sanker, born 1907, Amanda Edna, born 1910, Tom Henry, born 1912, and Martha Susie, my mother born in 1914. By the time the 1930 census was taken, there were only three children, Willie, Amanda and Martha, still in the household. Albert and Joe had relocated to Baltimore, Md. The name is continuing to be spelled "Carey," on the census record and death certificates.

Joseph Sanker Carey passed on June 4, 1932 at the age of 54. The cause of death is listed as cancer with anemia as a contributing factor. On his death certificate, his mother is listed as Amy Boudine and "Sam Cary" is listed as his father. The information on the death certificate was given by his brother, Rev. Anderson J. Cary. I haven't been able to figure out the discrepancies on the death certificate as to who his parents were. The only thing I can say after doing so much research is that the recorded information is only as good and true as the informant thinks. Not to say this particular death record is correct or incorrect. The official birth record I found for Joseph listed Ralph and Amy (Annie) Cary as his parents.

My grandfather Joseph's occupation was a farmer. The name John Franklin appears on his death certificate as his employer. This is probably the same John Franklin family that Joseph's brother, John Robert, was living with as a laborer in the 1880 census record.

I never knew my grandfather but my mother talked lovingly of him. She said he had a mild personality and always liked to sing spirituals. In addition to working the farm, he was a barber. She shared that her father, who she called "Papa," had a favorite saying that "You are a fool and a liar too." She remembered how he would sometime fuss when Grandma Susie went out to deliver babies, because he knew she might not get paid. However, she would go as soon as someone came for her. Sometimes she would have to sit up all night and day waiting for the baby to come. For each baby she delivered she was to receive $5.00 for a single child and $10.00 for twins. She was always ready to go because; she knew if she did not go, the black families especially would have no one to deliver their babies. She delivered babies for the white women in the community, as well.

Mama said her sister, Amanda, never learned how to cook until after she got married. She never wanted to eat the biscuits Grandma made after she had just returned from delivering a baby, and would always ask Mama to make up the bread.

Susie Spencer Carey was a dedicated midwife for 33 years. She turned her license in on June 16, 1952, and was presented her Midwife's Certificate of Retirement from the Virginia State Department of Health. During the time my grandmother was a midwife, she did not have to be accompanied by a doctor when she delivered her babies. Aunt Amanda said she remembers one incident where a white family was traveling in a horse and buggy when the wife went into labor down the road from where they lived. This was the lady's first child and they heard her screaming and hollering and the husband was so excited that he did not know what to do. She said Grandma started gathering up quilts and towels and hurrying out of the house. At the time they did not know what was happening, but when Grandma came back to the house she told them that she had delivered a baby on the side of the road. The lady would spend the next month living in the home of my Aunt Ellen, where Grandma would go daily to take care of the mother and baby.

As a midwife, Grandma would have to leave home early some days and be gone until late at night. When my grandfather became sick, Aunt Amanda was left home to take care of him.   Grandma delivered three of her grandchildren, Fannie, James and my sister Hazel. Because she was so dedicated, shortly after she delivered her grandson James, she had to leave her own daughter, Amanda, to go deliver someone else's baby. She would train her daughter Amanda to carry on the family tradition, with the same dedication. Two summers ago, while visiting the old home place, we came across her black midwife bag and a book used in her practice. Some of the items in the bag had been destroyed by the elements under the house, but there was a book detailing what the law passed in 1918 required midwives to do when delivering babies. Also there were some old blank Live Birth Certificates that had not been used, along with a pair of her eyeglasses. I have those items and will cherish them because they are things that were touched by her loving hands. Those items belonging to her are special to me because they were items that meant something to her.

Mama said "Grandma Susie was very lively and very feisty." I guess that is why she moved the house that should have been hers in the first place to another piece of land. Although she worked as a domestic for the white families, she would speak up for herself and would not let them run over top of her. On one occasion she was asked to wash down walls and she refused and told them they would have to get someone else to do that because she did not do that type of work. Mama said Grandma was a good cook and she would spend her time in the kitchen watching and learning from her. This early homemaking training would serve Mama well when she started her own family. She said she remembers walking up and down the road, along side Grandma, as she was churning milk into butter, by shaking the milk inside the jar.

Mama said she also remembers walking in the room, when Grandma and Aunt Mandy would be talking, and they would stop and say she was too young to hear what they were talking about. Being the youngest, she said she used to get so mad when she wanted to go someplace or do something and Grandma would listen to Aunt Mandy and not let her go. She said she sometimes was allowed to tag along with her sister and brothers to the parties they went to. I guess even then you had sibling rivalry. She said Aunt Mandy would get upset when she was teased by those who would tell her that Mama was the youngest, but had the prettiest legs.

My older siblings were blessed to know Grandma Susie personally, as young children. I can only listen to them as they recall specific memories of her. When I visited her, I was very young. My sister Dorothy went back with Grandma, after one of her visits to West Virginia, and stayed for a period of time attending school with her cousins there, while Mama was recuperating from childbirth. Grandma didn't mind leaving her home to take care of her family in West Virginia.

Susie Carey went to be with the Lord the summer of 1953. I do remember when Mama received the telegram that she was gravely ill and how sad she was when she left for Virginia. Mama wrote a letter back to Daddy telling him about Grandma's passing. I was the one to read the letter to him. Her death was the first family member I associated sadness and loss with.

I will spend time talking about each of the children of Joseph and Susie Carey in a later chapter. However, I want to finish up with the family history of Ralph Carey's children, at this time.

With the information on Ralph Cary, I started to wonder who his parents were and what their names were. My curiosity sent me into additional research. I wanted to see if I could find out something about his parents. This puzzle would not be solved until I was able to search the 1870 census records under "Cary," and I found a listing for a Rachel Cary. I later found a death record for Rachel Cary, who died in 1871.

Interesting enough Rachel's parents were listed as Ralph and Amy Cary. Upon further research, I found that Ralph and Amy could not have been her parents, because she was born in 1803, and Ralph was born in 1830. I also knew then that I would have to research Ralph's brother and sisters to get additional information on their families to complete the puzzle. You are probably asking how I can make this assumption about Rachel being their mother. Well I am glad you asked.

The 1870 census shows Rachel Cary, born in 1803, living in Hamden, Prince Edward County. She is listed as about 67 years old living with a daughter named Sarah Cary, who was born about 1820 and age listed as 50. This information leads me to believe that Ralph had another sister that Uncle Joe did not know about. If this is true, then Sarah would have been the eldest child in the Cary family. This information was found on the census records on the page following information for Ralph's sister Nannie, under Sam and Nannie Cary's household.

The 1880 census records also showed that Anderson was born about 1825, Ralph, about 1828, Nannie about 1830 and Mary Agnes about 1834.

To further substantiate that Rachel was the mother of these siblings, I found on the death certificate for Anderson Cary, who was 91 years and 5 months old at the time of his death May 14, 1915, his mother and father listed as Sancho Cary and Rachel "Jackson." This information was provided by Anderson's wife, Elizabeth Cary. This is the only record that I have been able to locate showing that someone in the family had at one time used the "Jackson" surname. Uncle Joe's oral information from family members said the name was changed to Cary when they were sold. This death certificate lends some support to that statement. It shows that Rachel's name had at one time been Jackson, either by marriage or slave owner.

As stated previously, I found a death record for a Ralph Cary who died September 15, 1889, from consumption. His parents were listed as unknown. The last census record he was found in was 1880. The 1890 census record were destroyed in a fire so if he were still living, he would not have been in that census. The 1900 census does show Annie still living, in Worsham, Prince Edward County, Virginia, as the head of the household, which included her son, Joseph, my grandfather, and Susie, her daughter in law. Amy/Annie died February 25, 1915. I was told that Amy had one brother named Gilbert, but I have not been able to document any early information on them for the lack of a surname, that is consistent.

At the time of Amy (Annie) Cary's death she was listed as a widow. Her death certificate states that she had been under the care of a doctor from September 12, 1914 until February 27, 1915. She was last seen by the doctor on February 18, 1915. It seems odd that the doctor said he had seen her through February 27th but her date of death is listed as February 25, 1915. I wonder if it was the custom back then that the deceased stayed in the home until a doctor finally came by to pronounce them dead. The cause of death was cancer.

One thing I found to be consistent is that most of the family members were all buried in New Hope Cemetery. The informants are not that knowledgeable about the parents of the deceased. This is just another example of how records were kept. The State of Virginia did not have death certificates until June 14, 1912.

They kept no state death records at all for the period from 1897 to June 13, 1912. Some counties kept their own records. I have not been able to locate any online for Prince Edward County during that time period. If families did not keep records in their Bible, I guess there was no documentation. If we consider the fact that most blacks coming out of slavery could not read or write, they would not have had those records anyway.

I guess they were too busy trying to adjust to their new freedom to be concerned about death or birth records. I am sure that the plantation owners kept records, since they were considered property. While we are on that subject, I want to write about some of those property records. Since I started this research, many years ago, I have from time to time found other sources to back up oral records.

One such document is called "Virginia Slave Births Index – 1853-1865," authored by Leslie Anderson Morales as part of the Alexandria Library/Special Collections.

When I stumbled across this document, I could not wait to get my hands on the volume that could give me information on the William Cary family, who I was told, owned our ancestors. The 1860 census listed a William H. Cary living in Dwelling #469 and Esther Cary living in Dwelling #470, in Prince Edward County, Virginia.

On page 457 and 458 of Volume 1 – A-C, I found listed under Esther Cary, the slave-owner's plantation in Prince Edward County, Virginia, the names of Booker, born October 1856, Peter, born September 19, 1859, and Betty, born March 14, 1854. All of these children had listed as their mother, Nanny. Nannie was the sister to Ralph, Anderson, and Agnes Cary. There is no name listed for the father, which was the custom, but the name Sam has been confirmed through the Census records of 1870 and 1880.

Nannie Cary was born about 1829. The 1870 census shows additional persons living in their household. This is where I was able to locate Rachel Cary, who I am led to believe was Nannie, Ralph, Anderson and Agnes mother. At the time the census was taken in 1870 and 1880, Ralph, Anderson, Agnes and Nannie were all living in houses next to each other.

The other names I was able to locate in this book were under the slave-owner William Cary. I will only list those names who I feel have a connection through the name of their mother. There was a Henry born in January 1853 that could have been the son of Ralph and Amy Cary. There is no name listed for the mother.

Elizabeth and Anderson had a daughter named Ella who was born in 1859, and the slave index list a child by that name, with a mother named Elizabeth. There was the name of a Mary Susan also born to Elizabeth on December 25, 1861, and Anderson and Elizabeth had a daughter by that name.

Upon further searching I found the names of Martha, born 1865, with no mother's name, and Richard, born September 28, 1853. Following those births were Isham, born June 24, 1858 and Peter, born August 21, 1860, both having the same mother named Agnes. Agnes was the other sister to Ralph and Anderson Cary. They were found in the 1870 census records under Charles and Mary Agnes Womack. In the 1880 census, the children are listed under Agnes Womack and she is listed as divorced. I was unable to positively connect any of Amy Carey's children to the Cary slave-owner.

The information following is what I extracted from the 1870 and 1880 census records for the families of Anderson, Agnes and Nannie Cary.

We will start with Anderson since he was Ralph's older brother. Anderson Cary was born about 1825. When I found him in the 1870 census, his name was transcribed as "Auaerson Cary," who was married to Elizabeth, born in 1844. At that time they had one daughter named Mary. We see them living in Hampden, Prince Edward County, in the state of Virginia. He was a laborer and she was a housewife.

After researching the census records for Anderson, I hit a brick wall until talking to someone I had known since childhood, Betty Baker Miser, who enlightened me about that side of the family.

It seems that Anderson was her great grandfather and that my great grandfather was Ralph, who was his brother. I knew that her father and mother, Charlie and Nora Baker, like mine, had migrated to West Virginia in the early 30's, from the same area of Virginia. The families had always been close, but it was not until recently I found out the connection. The elder Bakers had always referred to my aunts as cousins, but my mother never said anything about the family connection. As a child we called elders either cousin or aunt, sometimes with no blood relationship, so that in itself was not uncommon. Also since Nora was 13 years older than Mom it is possible that she did not know the family connection. Their paths did not cross again until 1934 when they once again lived in the same community, in West Virginia. Betty said that she had always known growing up that we were related, because as a child she used to sit on her father's lap and question him about his family. During those early years, my family never sat and talked about who was related and who was not. In the little coal mining town we were born and where we spent the first years of our lives, not much was said about relatives from Virginia. We just knew that our parent's families lived there.

I grew up thinking that we had no close relatives living in Ingram Branch, West Virginia, where all the other families there were related to each other, by marriage or birth. In a conversation with my oldest sister, Hazel, she said she remembers Betty telling her at school that they were cousins. However, when she asked our mother if this were so, she said not as far as she knew. Maybe Mama did not know the connection herself, because she has always said that she did not know much about her early ancestors. Betty helped me connect our families together through over 200 years of separation, first by slavery and later by silence and a failure to share family history. I am happy to include them in this family history story.

As Betty and I have talked in recent times, we speak about how close our families were when we lived in Ingram Branch. She said her mother always liked to garden and would always send fresh vegetables to our house and when they slaughtered the hogs, we always were the recipient of some of the meat. Funny how little things stick with you and how when you look back you can make connections that before were not clear. She said when she moved to Virginia as an adult, my Aunt Amanda told her not to call her Ms. Carter, because they were cousins and she should call her Cousin Mandy. I guess Grandma Susie was okay with Mama moving to West Virginia because she knew there would be family there to look after her. Anyway, I was finally able to put some faces on that part of the family tree and give information, although limited, on his descendants.

The 1880 census records for Anderson Cary, born about 1824, listed him as a laborer, married to Elizabeth, who was born in 1842. At the time of the census, they lived in Hamden, Prince Edward County, in Virginia. He is identified as the Head of Household, and stated that his parents were born in Virginia. The household was rather large now with ten children listed from ages 20 to 4. Anderson is about 22 years older than Elizabeth, which probably explains the young ages of the children.

The children of Anderson and Elizabeth were Ella, *Mary, who I will show her connection in the Baker family later, Pattie, Wash, Lee, Willie, Lucy, Mittie,

James and Bettie. Anderson and Elizabeth Cary were found again in the 1900 Census and in the 1910 census. He is listed as 86 years old and she is 68 years of age.

Anderson Cary's death certificate gave me the information about his parents. His father is listed as Sancho Cary and his mother as Rachel Jackson. This was the information that confirmed that at one point the family name had been "Jackson," and that what Uncle Joe had told me about the name change to "Cary" was probably true.

On May 14, 1915, Anderson Cary died at the age of 91 years and 5 months as the result of "failure of all vital organs." He was buried in New Hope Church cemetery. Elizabeth Cary was the informant and her knowledge of his parents is the only clue we have to who they were. There are probably other family members from that side of the family that can provide additional information, for further research, about whom they were and where their descendants are now. I was just happy to make this one connection.

The one family member that I have the information on was Anderson's daughter, Mary, born about 1862. The Virginia Slave Birth Index list a female child born in December 1861 on the plantation of William Cary, whose mother is listed as Elizabeth. Coincidence, I think not.

Mary Cary, the daughter of Anderson and Elizabeth, married Tom Baker. Among their children was a son named Charlie Baker. Charlie married Nora White, pictured in the photo to the left, the daughter of Archie and Maggie White. Once again this union leads to another "double cousin" scenario through the earlier Anderson Cary family line and the White family line. Charlie and Nora would also move to Ingram Branch, West Virginia, where my parents would later move. It was there that the Baker/Evans families lived on either side of the railroad tracks for many years. Nora was very active at Ingram Grove Baptist church. When Charlie retired from the coalmines, they returned back home to Virginia. She united with the family church, New Hope Baptist, and served as a Sunday school teacher, Member of the Missionary Society and the Choir. One of their children was a daughter named Betty. So the moral of this story is you should try to know who your family members are. Good friends can sometimes turn out to be good family.

In addition to Betty, Charlie and Nora's other children were, Elizabeth, Rosa, Charles, Lila Mae, Maggie, Thomas, Phyllis and Jimmy. A daughter names Mary died at birth. Out of the family of Charlie and Nora came many descendants. Betty said that two of her sisters, Elizabeth and Rosa had 12 children each. She said at the time of her mother Nora's death, in 1973, she had 49 grandchildren and 40 great grandchildren. That family has increased probably five folds since that time, as evidenced in the picture below.

The Family of Charlie and Nora Baker

The next branch in this family tree is that from Ralph Cary's sister, whose name was Nannie Cary.

The 1870 and 1880 census for Nannie Cary, listed her as being born about 1829/1830. She is married to Samuel Cary, who coincidently has the same surname as her maiden surname, "Cary." At this point, I don't have any information on Samuel Cary or his family. For this reason I will focus on the family that Nannie and Samuel created from their union. In the 1870 and 1880 census they are listed as living in Hampden, Prince Edward County, in Virginia.

Sam Cary is listed as a laborer and Nannie as a housekeeper. Their children were either listed as at school or laborers. The names and year of birth of their children were listed as Bettie born in 1852, Booker, 1855, Peter, 1857, Ann, 1858, Hannah, 1859, Mary, 1861, Nancy, 1863 and Anderson, 1865. Another child, Sallie was born in 1873, but I could not find her on the 1880 census records, which is not unusual. Also living in the house hold is their 22 year old niece named Annie Cary.

I don't have enough information on all of their children to really delve into their descendants, but I will trace the lines that came from their son Booker and daughter Sallie. This "double cousin" scenario plays out once again in the family through Booker Cary and Maria Scott Cary's descendants.

First of all, Booker, Peter and Betty were the children I could readily identify as part of the family when I found them listed in the Virginia Slave Index under the slave-owner Esther Cary. Booker Cary was said to be born in October 1856, Peter born in September 1859, and Betty born in 1854. Each was born in Prince Edward County, Virginia and their mother's name is listed as "Nanny." As I stated before there is no mention of the father's name in any of these slave records. These were the only three children I identified listed under Esther Cary, who was the slave-owner. The discrepancies in the year of birth are not significant because often times the census records listed the "age" of person, rather than year of birth.

Booker was the second child born to Sam and Nannie Cary.

The 1890 census records were destroyed in a fire so the next census we find Booker listed in is the 1900 census. Booker is the head of the household and is now married to Anna M. Scott. Betsy Scott, the mother of Anna is also living in their household. In the census record, they are living in Hampden, Prince Edward County, Virginia.

The Booker Cary family is now populated with seven children in 1900. They are Samuel J. 1881, Bethe A., (which is probably Bettie Ann) 1883, Lulie B. (which is probably Lelia) 1888, Augustavus, (probably Gussie) 1891, Belle, 1893, Mary L, 1896, and *Nelson J, 1898, pictured below. Some of the names may not be as you and I know them today, but these are the names taken from the official census records. The photo to the left is of Booker's daughters, Lelia, Nancy and Bettie Ann. In the 1880 census record, his wife's name is now listed as Maria. At some point, the Anna has been dropped. There are now additional children in the 1910 census. They are: Lenard, 1901, Pearly, 1904, and Nannie, 1907. I am told here was also a son named William but I did not find a record for him in my research, and he may have been listed in the 1890 census records that were destroyed by fire.

Booker Cary can be followed through the census records, with various other family members, in his household until the 1930 census. He is listed as being 74 years old at the time. Booker Cary passed away on September 13, 1931. There is a plaque on the New Hope church that bears his name.

The Cary family would once again become "double cousins" with the marriage of Nelson Cary and Florine Evans, who will be mentioned again in the Evans family tree as she was the sister to my father, Leonard Evans.

The 1930 census found Nelson and Florine Cary living in Hampden, Prince Edward County, in Virginia. They have one daughter, Mattie. They would not stop there, for in the years to come their family grew by leaps and bounds.

The additional children were daughters: Irene, Mary, Ada, Alto, Anna, Josephine, Maxine, Kay, Emma, and finally two sons, James and Samuel. These are the cousins that we grew up knowing from my father's side of the family. Needless to say, their descendants are many and I will leave it to someone else to do their family tree. They are doubly loved because "we are double cousins."

The photo below is of the family of Nelson and Florine Carey. It was taken at one of our annual homecoming Sunday service, where the Carey family provided the music for the worship service at New Hope Baptist Church. Their talent as gospel singers has been passed down to their children who are carrying on the tradition of singing for the Lord.

The Family of Nelson and Florine Carey

At this time, I am also able to include another of Sam and Nannie's children into this history, Booker's sister, Sallie Carey, was born about 1873. She married Matthew Pryor and their daughter Dora, pictured to the left, was the youngest of thirteen children. Dora had been a part of the family gatherings for many years. Dora was born on May 8, 1914 and she and my mother were always close cousins. She was married to James Rice. At the time of her death, on May 7, 2009, she was survived by two sons Clarence, his wife Ann, and Earl, his wife Mary, four grandchildren, seven great grandchildren and one great-great grandchild.

The final branch of the Cary family is that of Mary Agnes Cary. She was the sister of Anderson, Ralph and Nannie. Agnes was born about 1834. The 1870 census listed her name as Mary A. Womack and she was married to Charles Womack. The family lived in Hampden, Prince Edward, Virginia, with the post office identified as Farmville.

From the oral history passed on to me by Uncle Joe, Agnes Womack was the great grandmother of James Richard and Malinda's children, through her daughter Rachel, who was James Richard Womack's mother. His father is unknown. James Richard and Malinda's children were James, Anna, Beatrice, Charlie, Gladys, and Raymond. Gladys passed away on March, 12, 2011 at the age of 92. Beatrice is the only surviving sibling.

The information listed in the next paragraph was mentioned earlier, but because there is sufficient data to suggest that we are talking about the children of Mary Agnes and Charles Womack, it is being repeated to support the existence of their being part of the William Cary plantation. (Upon further searching I found the names of Martha, born 1865, with no mother's name, and Richard, born September 28, 1853. Following those births were Isham, born June 24, 1858 and Peter, born August 21, 1860, both having the same mother named Agnes.)

The 1870 census for Mary Agnes and Charles Womack listed their children as Richard, 1854, Martha, 1856, Johann, 1858, Peter 1860, and Rachel, 1863. When we find Mary Agnes Womack again in the 1880 census, she is listed as Agnes Womack, a farm laborer, divorced and with two children, Richard age 20 and Rachel, age 19. They are now living in Madison, Charlotte County, Virginia. There is no other mention of Charles Womack.

*From what I have been able to piece together, Rachel Womack had a son named James Richard Womack, born about 1877/1879. She would later marry James Johnson, and to this union, Elijah and William Morton Johnson would be born, as seen in the 1910 census. It is my understanding that Rachel owned a store in Virginia before she relocated to Baltimore, MD to live until her death. Elijah's family still lives in the Baltimore area.

The 1910 census finds James Richard Womack married

to Malinda Spencer Womack, pictured to the left, living in Hampden, Prince Edward, Virginia, with two children, James A., 2 years old and Anna, 2 months old. The 1920 census shows James Richard Womack and Malinda Spencer Womack with three additional children: Beatrice W. 6 years old, Charlie, 4 years old and Gladys O, 1 year old. Another son named Raymond was born after the 1920 census. Anna was married to Samuel Gamble, and later to William Duck, Beatrice was married to Joseph White, Charlie Womack was married to Viola Edwards, and Gladys was married to George Dickerson.

James Richard Womack passed in 1968 and Malinda Spencer Womack passed away March 31, 1959. As we look at the families we will see how the Womack family and Spencer families became woven into this quilt.

Ernest Womack was raised first by Susie Carey, and after she passed, by Amanda and Willie Carter. When Ernest left Virginia and moved to Arlington, he met and married Bertha Williams, pictured on the left with Bertha's sister, Arlene, on the right. Their children are Diane, Patricia, Ernestine and Ernest, Jr., and grandson, Halston. His birth mother, Beatrice Womack White, is now 98 years old and lives with them in Virginia along with her nephew Jasper Gamble.

Chapter 3

Spencer/Matthew/Carey Families

Albert Spencer, Sr., who was born about 1820 and Sisley Spencer, born about 1830, were found in the 1870 census living in Hampden, Prince Edward County, Virginia. The children living at home at that time were Jacob, 1852, Angelina, 1860, Mary, 1863, Dennis, 1866 and Elva, 1869. This family was confirmed as being the correct Albert Spencer family Uncle Joseph had provided names for, since they had the same names as those children he told me was in the family. The 1880 census finds Albert, Sr. and family living in Walton, Charlotte, Virginia. He is listed as working as a farm laborer. In the household are his wife Sisley, and a 9 year old daughter, named Maria. Mary is also still in the household at the age of 16. Albert Spencer, Jr. born about 1854 and Lacy Spencer were living elsewhere when the census was taken. They were living in the household of Jack Thompson, working as farm laborers. The census record does not show where Mitzi was living.

Sisley Spencer, my maternal great-great grandmother was the first midwife in the family. The profession was passed down from generation to generation. She passed this mantel down to her daughter in law, Amanda Spencer, my maternal great grandmother who in turn passed it down to her daughter, Martha Susie, my grandmother ending up with her daughter, Amanda, my aunt, carrying on the tradition.

Albert Spencer, Jr., is found again in the 1880 census living in Madison, Charlotte, Virginia with his wife, Amanda Matthew Spencer, who had a brother named Whitfield, pictured on the left. At the time of the 1880 census Albert and Amanda have a one (1) year old daughter (Martha) Susan Spencer, born in 1879. They lived on land owned by the Cary family, who were slave-owners. Albert Spencer, Jr. and Amanda Matthews Spencer had three other children. Ciceley Spencer their first daughter died August 1878, from "thrash." Although Ciceley's name was spelled differently she was probably named after Albert's mother.

I was told that they also had a son named Jack Spencer. I have not been able to locate a record on him. The family tells the story that Jack either went off with a woman and was killed and never came back or the other story is that he was killed in a race riot. In the 1900 census, Albert Spencer, Jr. and Mandy Spencer are listed as living in Worsham, Prince Edward County, Virginia. The youngest child born to Albert and Amanda about 1884 was Malinda, who was 16 years old and still living at home.

Malinda would later marry James Richard Womack and their descendants, James, Anna, Beatrice, Charlie, Gladys and Raymond were born. They were discussed earlier under the Mary Agnes Cary Womack section. Malinda Womack died March 31, 1959.

My mother told me what she knew about her grandfather Albert. She said he was regarded as a "tough old man" and had a fondness for cursing. He was a farmer and sharecropper. I was told by another relative that he dabbled in witchcraft and knew how to work spells. He told people he could place his hands on a table and make it rise. He also knew a lot about herbs for medicinal purposes. He wasn't a church man and I was told he would say things like "he is the preacher of somebody's shit house." Mama said that Great Grandma Amanda was very religious and was always trying to get him to go to church. When that failed she would have church at home around him and would sing to him trying to, as she would say, "Get the devil out of him." She called him Bro. Albert and would be singing "Do You Feel the Spirit." She would then ask him if he felt anything. He wouldn't say anything and when she continued to ask him, "Bro. Albert, do you feel anything?" He would finally say "No and neither do you." The other story told about him was that he skinned a black cat and threw the bones in the creek. Instead of the bones flowing downstream with the flow of the water, the bones flowed back towards him. After that incident, the story was that he had sold his soul to the devil and was known as the "witchdoctor." I think Mama said he worked at Sparrows Point in Baltimore, MD before returning to live in Virginia.

Aunt Amanda was asked in her taped interview if Great Grandma Amanda, who was a slave, ever talked about being a slave. She replied that whenever she would try to tell them about what it was like; Grandma Susie would get angry and tell her "don't be putting all that stuff in the children's head." From my research that seemed to be the typical response about talking about that difficult time in their lives. It was too painful and ugly that it was not something that they wanted to share with their off springs.

Albert Spencer, Jr. is listed in the 1930 census records with a new spouse named Mary Liggs Spencer. He is said to be about 85 years old at the time. Mary is listed at 79 years old.

Albert Spencer, Jr. died November 16, 1931 according to his death certificate from natural causes. There was an additional note that said the related cause was "senility."

As stated previously, Martha Susan Spencer was the second child born to Albert and Amanda Spencer. She was married to Joseph Sanker Cary, Sr. They were discussed at length under Ralph Cary's family history, but now I will focus on the family they created. Joseph and Susan's first child, Estelle, died shortly after birth. They had six additional children. Pictured at left is Susie, with daughters Amanda and Martha. Photo below is of the Carey boys in the family.

The Cary family was deeply religious people and they were brought up in a Christian home. The four sons in the family left home at an early age to seek employment in the north. They would eventually settle in Baltimore, MD. The only children of Joseph and Susie that I got to know during their life time were Joseph, Jr. and Amanda. For that reason, I am able to talk more about them and my relationship with them. I have very fond memories of both of them and really appreciate the information they gave me when I was in search of my ancestors. Uncle Joseph was considered the family patriarch who sort of took on the responsibility for the family after their father passed.

Albert Carey was born in March 1901. For some reason the 1910 census does not record any children on the form for Joseph and Susie Cary. Albert would have been about nine years old. In the 1920 census Albert is listed in their household as 18 years old and single. Sometime after the 1920 census, Albert relocated to Ingram Branch, West Virginia, and worked in the coal mines. He would later return to Virginia for a period of time. In the 1930 census, Albert has relocated to Baltimore, MD, where he is living as a boarder in the household of General A. Jesse and working at Sparrows Point. He was never married and had no children of record. Uncle Albert passed in 1982. He was a great guitar player, and played at the parties held in the neighborhood.

Willie Wallace Carey was born in June 1903. He was married to Nannie Carey, in 1926, whose father was Booker Hill Carey. His second wife was Beatrice. Willie also moved to Ingram Branch, West Virginia sometime after the 1920 census and worked in the coal mines. He returned to Virginia and would be found living at home again with his parents in the 1930 census. Growing up he loved to play the guitar at house parties and play cards. Mama said Willie was a big tease. He learned how to cuss from his granddaddy. She said when he played cards, he would cheat by stealing cards and that one of Daddy's cousins used to say "that SOB will steal the doors of hell off its hinges." Mama said Willie was always the jokester and the guitar player. At some point he relocated to Baltimore, MD., where he worked at Sparrows Point and he passed away May 1980. Uncle Willie's third wife was named Mary and they had daughters named Cassandra and Bertha Mary.

Uncle Willie and Nannie had one daughter named Isabell who was married to James Clarence Thompson. They had one son named Charles M. Thompson. He had a daughter named Sheila and when he married Joan Baisey, they had three children: Brigitte, Lisa and Charles, Jr. Pictured below is me, with two Cousin Brigitte Brown, on my left, who I recently met while doing the family research and my Cousin Denise Roseborough.

Willie had one son, William Henry, whose mother was Pauline Evans.   William Henry, who was nicknamed Hambone, was married to Elizabeth Johnson, and their children were Denise, Patricia, William Henry, Jr., Christopher, Jacqueline and Renee. William Henry's other children were Henrietta, Larry and Shelia.

Joseph Sanker Carey, Jr. was born in April 1906. The 1920 census shows Joseph, 13 years old, still home in Virginia with his parents. At the age of 16 Joseph moved to Baltimore where he obtained employment at Bethlehem Steel Company. Joseph married Nancy White, in April 1928. She was born in Charlotte County, Virginia, in August 1904, to Samuel and Frances Venable White. Their union lasted 48 years, ending when she passed in June 1976. Two of Nancy's brothers were Richard and William White.

In the 1930 census, they were boarders in the home of Inruard Taylor. Joseph had one son, Joseph Martin Carey, born late in his life. Joseph married his second wife Mary Jennings on her birthday, January 6, 1979. We always spoke of Uncle Joseph as what we referred to as "well off." Although he did not get much formal education, he was very smart with what is known as "mother wit." Uncle Joseph had a good memory and he was the one that provided me the information to make it possible to document our early ancestors. He educated himself by reading, studying and intelligent investigations of the problems that affected the society we lived in. He was active in his church for over 50 years serving as trustee, church treasurer, Sunday school officer, and choir member at St. Paul Baptist Church, in Baltimore, MD.

Uncle Joseph was a Past Master of the Mt. Lebanon Lodge No. 22 of the Most Worshipful Prince Hall Grand Lodge, F. and A.M. of the State of Maryland. He used his membership in this organization to broaden his intellectual growth. He always took an interest in all of his nieces and nephews, because he had no children of his own when we were growing up. He was very proud when his son Martin was born late in his lifetime.

We all looked up to him and he had a special place in all of our hearts. We always looked forward to his visits to West Virginia when we were children because he always gave us some money before he left. Since we did not have a lot growing up it was a real treat when he visited. Out of all of my mother's brothers, he was the only one I remembered visiting us. He always treated Mama special and would always send her money to help out when things were hard in our family financially. My second oldest sister, Josephine, was his name sake.

Uncle Joseph was very successful. He owned his own home in the city and he always saved his money. He worked for Bethlehem Steel Company for over 40 years. It was a pleasure to visit their home because Aunt Nancy loved to cook and was always willing to lend a hand, day or night to help others. As grown ups visiting him, he always brought out his home made wine for us. Uncle Joseph was always the one hanging out with the nieces and nephews when we would go down to Farmville, Virginia for family reunions in the summer. It was always fun to go the reunions, but it was also scary, especially when he started telling the ghost stories. We always felt that the old house was haunted and would sleep with our heads under the covers. When all the lights were out you couldn't see your hand in front of your face.

My mother said that growing up Uncle Joseph always looked out for her. She said she always wanted a wagon when she was little and her brothers were always trying to build one for her to ride. They all spoiled her, even after she married and left home. She said when people would ask him why he did not have any children; he would say "if I want children I'll go to West Virginia and get one of Martha's," and she would say, "Oh, no you won't."

Uncle Joseph was very adventurous and loved traveling. He was the first in the family to visit the Holy Land, and when he talked about it, I knew that one day I would go there for myself.

When Uncle Joseph married for the second time, he and his new bride, Mary Jennings, went to Hawaii on their honeymoon. They shared more than ten years of wedded bliss, caring for each other, worshiping together, and experiencing a kind of bliss and joy which enriched their golden years. He departed this life in August 1989.

I will be eternally grateful for all the valuable information he shared about our ancestors, even the family secrets. I know there are a lot of things that will never be known but it is good to know that we had some characters in the family and that they enriched our lives by being part of the family circle. Family was very important to Uncle Joseph and I know he would be very proud to know that I am putting this information in print so all the present and future generations will know where they came from and be inspired to keep the family traditions alive.

Amanda Edna Carey was born in May 1909. She was the last surviving member of her immediate family. We find her first in the 1920 census at the age of 10. In the 1930 census, at the age of 20, she is still living in the home with her parents and siblings. Aunt Mandy as we affectionately called her spent all of her life in Prince Edward County, Virginia, where she would go to New Hope Elementary School. She said in an interview taped in 2003 that she did not like school at first but learned to enjoy it after making new friends. They walked to school every day and along the way they ran and played with their new friends. She went to the 7th grade but dropped out when her father got sick and she had to stay home to care for him while her mother went to work.

In July 1932, she married Willie Anderson "Buck" Carter, the fifth of thirteen children, born in Buckingham County, Virginia in September 1909 to Willie and Sallie Epperson Carter. They met through one of her cousins, after a family member's funeral, and she said they just fell in love right away. He and Aunt Amanda spent fifty seven years together as husband and wife. Willie departed this life in October 1988. Her union with Willie Carter produced a daughter, Fannie Mae and a son, James Anderson. When Grandma passed they continued to raise Ernest Womack, who was the biological son of her first cousin, Beatrice.

Willie (Uncle Buck) was a kind considerate person who involved himself in the community, civic affairs, including the Prince Edward County School Desegregation dispute, and church, where he was an ordained deacon. He was a lifelong member of Oak Grove Baptist church where he served as Chairman of the Board of Deacons. He served for many years as the President of the Prince Edward Chapter of the NAACP. He was also a Mason with Lodge #146. He enjoyed hunting and was a carpenter by trade. He also was a successful farmer, who owned eighty acres of land in Prince Edward County. Uncle Buck would later find work in Baltimore, MD, at the shipyard, to help support his family. Upon his return to Farmville, he once again became very active in his church and the community. He was well known for his community service and was active in the early voter registration drives in the county. He told them how to exercise their rights to vote and drove them to the polls to vote and to the registration sites. He was one of the few who did not fear the whites in the community, because as a landowner, he did not live with the threat of having to move off of their property.

During those early days of voter registration and school desegregation, he and the family lived under constant threats of physical harm, but that did not deter him from his civic duty. There were many harassing phone calls made to the home where the family was told that if he continued in his efforts the house would be blown up, with them in it. With those threats hanging over the family Aunt Mandy and he devised a plan so that, if a strange car drove down the road towards the house she would know it was not him and she could be prepared, as she sat on the front porch with her shotgun. If it was him coming home, he would stop the car and then cut his lights off and on a certain number of times before turning onto the road to their house. She said there were many blacks in the community who snitched to the white folks about what was going on in the meetings. Because so many of them were sharecroppers, they did not have much choice but to tell or run the risk of losing everything they had managed to acquire.

At an early age, Aunt Mandy joined the family church New Hope Baptist where she remained a faithful member. She served with the Missionaries, the Willing Workers and sang in the choir. She also had the distinction of being honored as one of the Mother's of the Church because she had cared for so many in the church and community.

Aunt Mandy's career choice was to be a mid-wife. This choice of occupation dated back three generations before her, beginning with her great-grandmother, Ciceley, who as a mid-wife traveled in an ox cart. Ciceley had trained her daughter in law, Amanda Matthews Spencer, to be a midwife to continue the family tradition, after she passed. Amanda Spencer provided the training for her daughter Susie Spencer Carey, to take over when she could no longer provide the service. In 1925, Amanda's mother, Susie accepted the calling and received her mid-wife permit. At that time, there were little if any differences in the delivery of babies. Amanda and her mother traveled together for the delivery of black and white babies.

It was during one of those deliveries, where the town doctor had to be called in, because the afterbirth did not come out, and Grandma asked him if he would help Aunt Mandy get her permit to be a licensed midwife. When Grandma Susie and the others became midwives, they were not required to be certified or licensed. The black doctor who helped Aunt Mandy get her license was Dr. Rollins, who had a general practice in Farmville. There were times, if the mother lived too far away, Aunt Mandy would bring the mother to live in her home until after the baby was delivered. Amanda had already been an intricate part of that process while caring for sick family members and others in the community.

When her mother, Susie, decided that she could no longer continue her work, Amanda decided to continue the family's legacy on a full time basis and became a mid-wife in 1952. She spent the next 35 years as a mid-wife in the same manner as the earlier women in her family had done. She was one of two African American women in Prince Edward County registered as a mid-wife. Over time her work included the counties of Cumberland, Buckingham, Hanover, Louisa, Charlotte, and the Cities of Richmond, Charlottesville and Lynchburg, Virginia.

Amanda was very proud of her work through the years. She had many unique experiences as a midwife. She tells the story of being called to Richmond to deliver a baby for a white couple and being asked to wait, until it was time for the baby to be delivered, in a room where they kept their dogs and cats. As she sat there, in that room, listening to them drinking, laughing and having fun, she decided that she was not going to stay there. When she told them she was not used to being in a room with animals and that she was going to leave, they told her that they could not take her home because the baby had not been delivered. She asked if she could use their phone and she immediately called Uncle Buck to come get her. When he got there and realized that they had her waiting in a room with animals, he was angry and told them she was leaving and would not be coming back. He grabbed her bag and they headed for home. He was very supportive of her being a midwife, but was not going to see her mistreated.

There was only one occasion where there was a stillbirth that she had to deal with. She said the girl would not help the baby come out and that only the head was exposed for about an hour. She said she was upset and Uncle Buck was telling her they were probably going to charge her with the death of the baby. The girl having the baby was unwed and the family did not want the neighbors to know that she had been pregnant so the boyfriend and parents came out and held up a quilt until they got into the car with the baby. They carried the baby to the coroner's office and told him what had happened. There were no charges, however on another occasion she had to go to court to prove that she had not written the name of the father on the birth certificate of a white woman's baby. She said that they were told very explicitly that they were never to put the name of a father on a birth certificate unless the couple was married. It seemed that the lady had put the father's name on the certificate after she had left. The child's father went to court and in order to prove that she had not written it, they took her fingerprints and found that hers were not on the birth certificate, but the fingerprints of the child's mother were.

That incident was another example of the "system" trying to blame a black person for what a white person had done. She said that it was doing those times it was easier to blame a black person and most times you could not prove you were innocent. In 1984, while being honored by Longwood College at a conference entitled: Feminist Self-Expression: Portraits of Private Lives, for her mid-wife work, she stated that she had delivered approximately 500 babies. By the time she retired the obstetrical system had changed. Patients had to be referred by the Public Health Department or a private doctor, and have a written statement saying the mother could have a home delivery. Not only was Amanda one of 118 Licensed in Virginia, she also trained women in the art of being a mid-wife. She retired from this family profession in 1987.

I am so proud to report that the great contributions that my ancestors provided, as midwives in Prince Edward County, is being recognized in an exhibition that will be housed in the Smithsonian Institute's new National Museum of African American History and Culture. This museum is under construction, and will be opened in the near future. A member of the staff has collected, for preservation, from my cousin Fannie, artifacts including the log book of births, photos of my grandmother and Aunt Amanda, the white uniform she wore, a photo holding a baby shortly after birth, a bottle containing the solution that was put in the baby's eyes, pieces of brown paper bags that names of children delivered were written on, and the interview recorded on June 2, 2003, by Dr. Amy Tillerson, as part of her Thesis Project. These items belonged to my Grandmother Susie Carey and Aunt Amanda. The honor of an exhibit in the Smithsonian is one the entire family can be proud of.

Aunt Mandy always opened her home to us on a yearly basis where we all gathered for family reunions. Mama laughingly told me how growing up Aunt Mandy was afraid of frogs and how her brothers used to chase her with them. Her home was the place that my older siblings went to during the summer to help out on the farm. Since I was the youngest, I never got to go away during the summer months. Now I know it was no picnic so I really was the lucky one. Aunt Mandy had a great sense of humor and would make you laugh until you cried. She had a way with words and because her life was filled with service and love to others, she was a true missionary. Although growing up she never wanted to learn how to cook, she turned out to be a great cook and I can still taste those egg custard pies she made. Mama said Aunt Amanda was the one who would throw a rock and then hide her hands. Her work here on earth ended peacefully in October 2007, at the age of 98. She was the last surviving member of her family.

Fannie Mae their oldest child, born in 1934, moved to Baltimore after graduating from Robert R. Morton High School. She graduated from Morgan State University. She had a long career working in the health care field. She retired and moved back to Farmville, to help take care of her mother, and where she became very active in the community she was raised in. She was a devoted daughter and loved to entertain family and friends. Fannie has been most helpful to me in providing information.

Fannie spends a lot of time quilting, making homemade jelly, and making dolls. She is married to Claude Silver. She and her husband Claude continue to work tirelessly in New Hope Baptist Church. She is an usher and he is a deacon. They also do catering for family gatherings. She also contributed information for this book. Fannie and Claude have been a very important part of our family's life for as long as I can remember. We have shared good times throughout the years at family reunions and gatherings. Their home has now become the home where visitors find a welcome mat at all times. Fannie was instrumental in assisting my sister Bernice in going to Cosmetology school. She offered her a place to stay while visiting Baltimore, MD for a two week vacation 50 years ago – Bernice took her up on the offer and stayed. That is the kind of love that this family has been able to share- unselfishly.

Their son, James Anderson Carter, was born two years later in 1936, in Prince Edward County, spending his early life there and completing his education, graduating from Robert R. Morton High School in 1955. James was full of laughter and joy and he loved people. James moved to Arlington, VA and Baltimore, MD, where he spent much of his adult life, until he decided to move back to Virginia. I remember how he loved to drive fast and hit those winding roads going back to the homestead. He was quick to share the truth and cared enough to express criticism as well as to give praise. James loved to have a good time and didn't care who was around, he always acted the same. If you did not know him you would think he was mean by the way he talked. James was married to Josie and they had one son, James, Jr., and one daughter, Diane.

James passed away August of 1990. Photo on the right is of James' son and grandchildren.

Ernest Womack, the child Aunt Mandy and Uncle Buck raised, was born in 1930. He attended school in Farmville before moving to Arlington, Virginia where he met and married Bertha Williams. They had four children, Dianne, Patricia, Ernestine and Ernest, Jr. Ernest, Sr. worked and retired from the United States Postal Service. He and family live in Springfield, VA., along with his birth mother Beatrice Womack White, and first cousin, Jasper Gamble.

The Carter home was a warm and loving place, always open for family and friends, and known as "The House by the side of the Road." To honor the work that Willie Carter did in his lifetime, the street they lived on was officially given the name "Carter Road" by the Town of Farmville, Virginia.

Tom Henry Carey was born in November 1911. On the 1920 census he is eight year old. He relocated to Baltimore in the early 30's and worked at Sparrows Point. He was married in the early 40's to his first wife Dora and in his later years he and his companion Bertha had one child named Jean. Bertha's other children were Pearl, Mary and Keith, who have always been considered part of his and our family. In his early years, Tom was a guitar player for the parties held in his youth and I understand he could be kind of mean. He passed in 1965.

My mother, Martha Susie Carey was born in April 1914. She is first listed in the 1920 census, at the age of 5, with her mother and father and all of her siblings, living in Prince Edward County, Virginia. The 1930 census would list her at the age of 15 and in school.

Mama attended New Hope School for colored children and went to the seventh grade, which was as far as their education in that county went for the majority of black children. The site where the school was located is a historical site. In the 19th century it was called the "Midway Inn" because it was located midway between Charlotte Court House and Worsham. Travelers on their way to Farmville spent the night there and completed their journey the next day. The school was closed in the late 1940's and the students were sent to Mercy Seat School in Hampden Sydney, Virginia. In 1953 the school was purchased from the Prince Edward County School Board for $500.00. In 2001, the school was moved to the site of New Hope Baptist Church and attached to the church. When we were attending a family reunion there in 2002, Mama stood proudly in front of the school, which has been named a historical building. She said standing in front of the historical building brought back many old memories. At that time there were seven former students living, all women, including her sister, Amanda and cousins, Beatrice and Gladys.

Mama was a good student and prided herself on her beautiful handwriting. Her knowledge would serve her well when she became an adult and needed to make adult decisions. She enjoyed school and stressed education as a priority for each of her children. There was no such thing as staying home from school or quitting without graduating, at the least, from High School. Her dream was fulfilled and she was proud when each of her six children graduated from high school. She said if she had been given the chance to further her education she would have. I would probably not be here years later writing about her life and my history if her life had gone in another direction. I was joking with her about her old boyfriend and she said "if I had married him, you wouldn't be here." I saw him once when we were at a reunion. It was so funny because he kept following Mama and trying to say something to her, and Daddy was keeping an eye on him. Mama got a kick out of that and when I teased her later, she had a good laugh.

From a historical standpoint, Prince Edward County was the only place in the country that closed down their schools, rather than desegregates them when the Supreme Court ruled in favor of Brown in its lawsuit against the Board of Education.   Many people are not aware that before there was a Brown vs. Board of Education, there was a Davis vs. Prince Edward County breaking new ground on the school front. I had many cousins who were denied an education in Prince Edward County and who had to be sent away to stay with relatives in the north, to continue their education. Some were fortunate, while others never did get that chance.

Martha Susie Carey was the youngest child born to Joseph and Susie Carey. My mom did not talk much about growing up but in conversations, she has shared snippets, without knowing that I was taking notes. She told me they lived on a farm and that her father was a farmer and a barber. Her father died when she was quite young and she said it was a sad time for the family. When he was sick, he told her mother that he thought she was afraid of him. She didn't like going in his sick room alone. Before her father became ill and passed, the men used to come over on the week ends for him to cut their hair and then play cards.

Although her father died when she was young, her maternal grandfather, Albert Spencer, was still living with them until he married for the second time at the age of 80. He lived until the year of 1931. She said he liked to curse and was known for his unique ability to swear, at the slightest nod. The young men would do things in the card games to get him riled up so he would start cussing. They got a kick out of it. She said Grandma Susie would threaten to put Great Granddaddy out of the house if he did not stop cussing. After her father passed, Mama said Grandma became the head of the household. I don't remember her very well, but when I was very young, I would go to Virginia with Mama when she went to visit. That was one of the benefits of being the baby in the family.

My mother told me that as a child she had a love of rings. The rings only cost ten cents in those days and she said every time she got a dime she would go to the store and buy a ring. She wore rings on all of her fingers. I guess that is where I got my love for rings. Her other fantasy was for a wagon. Years later she bought one for my brother for Christmas.

She said she bought him the biggest wagon she could find and on that Christmas morning, when he received it, she was just as excited as my brother. I remember we rode her all over the house until she had enough. She said that after that she was satisfied. She finally got to ride a wagon and the wheels did not fall off. She said as a child her brothers had tried to teach her how to ride a bicycle and she would always fall off so she never learned how to ride.

Mama was a good cook and a great housekeeper. The lessons she learned watching Grandma, as she grew up, paid off after she was married with her own family. She said she remembers, as a child, walking up and down the road with Grandma as she churned milk in a jar to make butter. Her best friend growing up was Nannie Hall. When they were about 14 years old, the two of them got all dressed up and took a picture together. Mama taught herself to sew when she was twelve years old. The first item she made was an apron for her mother. She said she used to tell her mother that she could sew but she did not believe her until she made that first apron for her. After that she made clothes for herself, her mother and also for her cousin Ernest, who was living with them at the time. She said she did not have any patterns but would look at the clothing in the Sears and Montgomery Ward catalogs and then make her patterns out of newspapers and design her own. I can say now that she was a fashion designer and did not know it at the time.

I will continue to tell about her life when I tell about the union of the families through her marriage to my father, Leonard Evans, the son of Sam and Norma Wiley.

Chapter 4

Evans/Wiley Families

The family circle is once again broadened with the connection between the Carey and the Evans/Wiley families, through the marriage of my mother, Martha Carey and my father, Leonard Evans.

The 1870/1880 census records were the first place I could find documentation for the makeup of the Evans and Wiley families.

I will explore the Wiley family first as I make this connection, only because my information on them is limited. The Wiley family branch became a part of this family through Norman Wiley, who was the daughter of Charles and Margaret Wiley.

In the 1880 census Charles Wiley, born about 1852 was married to Margaret Wiley, born about 1853. They were living in Madison, Charlotte County, in Virginia. He was listed as a farmer and she as keeping house. The children in the family at that time were Mattie, 5 years old, Thomas, 4 years old, Munchie, 3 years old, and a baby, no name listed, 2 months old. The names of the other children, I was told were Anna, Ethel, Will and Norma sometimes spelled ending with an "n," who was my grandmother.

Because there are no records for the 1890 census, I did not make another connection to the Wiley family until 1900. In that census, I found Orman (sic) Norman Wiley, who was 15 years old at the time, born about 1885, living in the household of Mattie Wiley Crute, her sister, who was married to Miller Crute. She is identified as the sister in law of Miller Crute. The other people living in the Crute household were the children of Mattie and Miller Crute; Emmett, Margaret, Addie, and Alice.

Tom Wiley, the brother of Norma was married to Galley Morton. Their children were Lee, Amos, Tossie, Willie, Thurman, Moses, Mertha, Charlie, and Mattie.

Tom Wiley's second marriage was to Bessie Harvey Mack. Their children were Margaret, Ann and Ida. I don't have information about the Wiley family, but I did know Cousin Margaret Wiley Wesley and her daughter, Ida Wesley Young. Cousin Margaret passed on July 4, 2010.

The Register of Marriages for Prince Edward County shows Norma Wiley, daughter of Charles and M. Wiley, married Samuel Evans, the son of Jerry and Louisia Evans, on March 28, 1906, at the age of 22. They would have nine children, among them Leonard, my father.

The Evans family history was traced back to the early 1800's, with the birth of Jerry Evans who married Louisia. I have no records of Louisa's family, or her maiden name, but was told that she was a Cherokee Indian. Aunt Ethel described her as being a lady of short statute.

As far as parents for Jerry Evans, on his death certificate are the names of Beverly and Mary Anderson. This information was provided at the time of his death by Tom Davis, who was married to Jerry's daughter Mamie Evans.

On a March 24, 1900 marriage license for Jerry Evans and Vinnie Evans, his parents are listed as Beverly and Polly Evans. The only name carried on both documents is "Beverly" as his father.

In the 1870 census, I found the family of Jerry and Louisia Evans. They were living in Buffalo, Prince Edward County, in Virginia. The 1870 census records stated that Jerry Evans was born about 1835 and Louisia was born about 1844. The post office for them was located in Prospect, Virginia.

Jerry Evans was listed as a farm laborer and Louisia as keeping house. At the time the census was taken in 1870, the children in the household were Darkus, age 8, Emma, age 5 and Francis, age 1. Also listed in the household was Jerry's brother whose name was Booker, who was age 14 at the time.

Booker Evans, Jerry's brother is found once again at 20 years old still living in the home of Jerry and Louisia. He is single and working as a farm hand. I think the next time I find a Booker Evans, born about 1856, was in the 1920 census, at the age of 58, married to Anne. Their children were: Annie, Lizzie and Helen. I am assuming this is the same Booker Evans from the 1870/1880 census.

The 1880 census would find the family of Jerry and Louisia (Lou) living in Hampden, Prince Edward County, Virginia. In addition to the previous children listed in the 1870 census, there are four additional children. They are Willie, 8 years old, George, 6 years old, Mary, 4 years old and Thomas, 3 months.

Since there are no records remaining for the Virginia census taken in 1890, the last child known born to Jerry and Louisia was my grandfather, Sam, who was born about 1883.

The Prince Edward County, Virginia Deaths, 1880-96 records the death of Louisia, whose parents were unknown, and who was married to Jerry as dying from Bright Disease, on June 10, 1896. The next time Jerry Evans is found is in the 1900 Census he is married to Vinnie Carter. Their marriage license lists her father as Caleb Carter, with no name for her mother. They are last found in the 1910 census, still living in Hampden, Prince Edward County, in Virginia. When I searched the Virginia Slave Births Index 1853-1865, under the slave-owner Evans name, I could not find any children in Prince Edward County that could be connected to my great grandfather's family, through his wife, Louisia.

The death certificate I secured for Jerry Evans is interesting. He was living in Darlington Heights, Virginia. His race was listed as "white." He died on April 10, 1918 from Bright Disease. He was buried in New Hope Church cemetery, as were most of my other ancestors. The person doing the research for his death certificate told me that this was the only one she could find for a "Jerry Evans." I guess that is a mystery that someone else may be able to solve. I never had the chance to ask my father much about his grandfather. He and Uncle Thomas did tell me that they remembered him as Grandpa Jerry and that he stuttered. My father would have been about 7 years old when Jerry Evans died. Another family member told me that Jerry Evans was mocked by a sheep and that was why he stuttered. There are many old wives tales that are used to support some of the things that could not be explained logically.

There is not much known by me about my grandfather's siblings. The records I could find were for William (Willie), George, and Mamie. Daddy talked about an aunt named Dorcas (Nelson), who I think either had a son named Leroy or was married to someone with that name. That information is rather sketchy. Of course I have the information for my grandfather.

I found a William and Salina Evans in the 1900 census, living in Worsham, Prince Edward County, Virginia. No children were listed.

I found a George and Mary Clark Evans in the 1900 census. One child was listed as John Clark. I also was able to locate the marriage license for George and Mary Evans. They were married January 18, 1897. His parents were listed as Jerry and Louisia Evans. Her parents were listed as Richard and Elizy Clark. They were married by Rev. Hugh Harvey, a Presbyterian Minister, at the home of Samuel Harvey, the bride's uncle.

The marriage license I found for Mary Evans and Thomas Davis showed that they were married at New Hope Baptist Church, on December 26, 1894, by W. L. Fowlkes. Her parents were listed as Jerry and Louisia Evans. His parents were listed as Charles and Ann Davis.

Mammie (Mary) Evans is found in the 1900 census married to Thomas H. Davis. The children in the household were Belle, age four, and George E., age one. They were living in Worsham, Prince Edward County, VA.

The 1910 census found the Davis family living in Hampden, Prince Edward County, VA with seven children. They were Belle, age 14, George E., age 11, Mattie S., age nine, Charles H., age seven, Walter C., age five, Willie, age three, and James one year and four mos. Tom Henry Davis and Mammie Davis were found again in the 1930 census, the last census released to the public.

Thomas Evans's, born March 1880; birth record was found in the Prince Edward County birth records, for 1862-96. He was not located after the 1880 census. Family members said he left Virginia to go to Massachusetts and was never heard from again.

This is where it gets interesting. As stated before, we have several instances of "being related on both sides of the family." Nelson was the son of Booker H. Carey, whose parents were Sam and Nannie Carey. Nannie Carey was the sister of Ralph Carey. There were many families with the last name Carey. Nelson's other grandfather was Peter Carey, according to early church information, who I assume was Sam Carey's father. I still have to do some research on the "Peter Carey/Sam Carey" side of the family. Some information is just coming to me, so further research will be necessary.

I insert this information here because we will eventually connect the Evans family together with the Carey family through the marriage of Sam and Norma Evans daughter, Florine, to Nelson Carey, the grandson of my great uncle and aunt, Sam and Nannie Carey.

Sam Evans, my grandfather was born somewhere between 1883 and 1884, depending on the records you find. His official birth, when he registered for the WWII draft, is listed as April 22, 1883. He is described as being 6 feet tall and weighing 170 pounds. There are no records available for the 1890 census, because they were destroyed in a fire in Washington, DC in 1920.

The 1906 Register of Marriages for Prince Edward County sated that on March 28, 1906, Samuel Evans the son of Jerry and L. Evans and Norma Wiley the daughter of Charles and M. Wiley were married. Their ages were both listed as 22 years old. The first census Sam is found in is the 1910 census. He is listed as 26 years old and the head of the household. He is married to Norma (Wiley). She is said to be 22 years old. They are living in Hamden, Prince Edward County, VA. At that time they were the parents of Shirley, born about 1905, Florine, born about 1907, and Otis born about 1908.

The next record for the Evans family would be found in the 1920 census. The census record has most of their names incorrect. I point this out so that anyone doing further research will not be misled as to the validity of this being the correct family. They are now living in Buffalo, Prince Edward County, VA.

Sam and Norma Wiley Evans were now the parents of Shirley, born 1905, Otis, born 1907, Florine, born 1908, Leonard, born 1911, Thomas, born 1913, Henry, born 1917, and Alto, born 1918.

By the time the 1930 census was taken, the older children had left home. The additional children in the family were Ethel, born in 1920 and Julia born in 1924. They had moved again, this time back to Hampden, Prince Edward County, in Virginia.

A note of interest, they had gone from their race being called black in 1920 to now being called Negroes, ten years later.

In 1942 Sam registered for the WWII draft listing his occupation as a self employed farmer. He listed his next of kin as Ms. Sam Evans, whose address was RFD 3, Farmville, Virginia. He signed his name with an "X."

I never got to know my grandfather. From those who knew him, they said his nickname was "Pie." He was a horse trader and was a self-employed farmer who had a large farm. I was told that he did not look like most "colored," which was probably contributed to the features he inherited from his Cherokee mother. He had high cheek bones, which is a characteristic shown in many of the Evans family members.

Since I did not know my grandparents, one day I asked Mama to tell me what she knew about Daddy's family. She said she always heard that Granddaddy Sam was a woman's man, but was very jealous of Grandma Norma. He liked to tell jokes and have a good time. Their house was the gathering place where all the parties were held. She said she used to go over there and that Grandma Norma would cook up lots of chicken, and when it was all gone, she would cook up more and holler out "hot chicken."

Also Grandma would make sweet potato pies. Mama was the youngest in her family so she was not always allowed to "tag along" with the other siblings. She said her brothers Willie and Albert would play the guitar and there would be lots of dancing, drinking and fighting.

She recalled one time when Uncle Nelson, who would later marry Aunt Florine, came to a party and found his "then girlfriend" there with another man and wanted to fight. She laughed as she said she remembers Uncle Nelson chasing the other man all throughout the house, out one door and then another. It was evident from early accounts, the Evans boys loved to party, even into their later years. Granddaddy was a fun loving person and passed that on to his children. She said there would always be fights over the young ladies before the party ended. My sisters, Josephine and Bernice, visited and stayed with our grandmother Norma, when they were little.

In 2003, after my father had passed, with only one sibling still living, I had a long conversation with Uncle Thomas. His memory was fading but he was able to share some information about his father and siblings. He told me that during those early times, his family was considered well-off, for Negroes. His family's farm had plenty of farming equipment and tools, a truck, a car and lots of horses that his father bred and traded. For some unexplained reason I have always been fascinated by horses and wanted to learn to ride them, but never got the chance. Maybe this was coming through my grandfather's love of horses. They lived in a big house that his father had built from the ground up. He said they did not get much education because they all had to work on the farm. He said Aunt Ethel wasn't old enough to work on the farm but she was the one who had to bring the water out to the fields every day for the workers.

Uncle Thomas said Aunt Florine complained about how hot it was in the fields and would always try to get out of the fields as soon as she could. Aunt Julia was the youngest so she did not have to work in the fields. He said that Granddaddy spent some time working in Baltimore in the steel mill at Sparrows Point. Granddaddy Sam died, August 2, 1942, less than a month after I was born. He said he remembers riding back to Virginia with Granddaddy's body on the train. He was described as being tall and stout.

Grandma Norma died in 1953, while living in New Jersey. We were still living in Ingram Branch, and I remember when Daddy came back from her funeral. The only thing he bought back that belonged to her was a pair of her eye glasses. We used to play with them by trying them on and trying to look down and walk. It was like walking off a cliff. The one photo that I have seen of Grandma Norma showed her as a very elegant looking lady. My older siblings knew her. I did not.

The children of Sam and Norma Evans would spread out across the country from New Jersey to West Virginia and Maryland. Some of them would become long shore man at the shipyards in Baltimore, Md., while others would seek work in the coal mines of West Virginia, and the state of New Jersey. They

would also work building the highways in Virginia and West Virginia. I am not sure what occupations the ones who relocated to New Jersey held, but they lived there raising their families until the time of their death. At some point their children relocated to the West Coast and have not been in close contact with their families back north for quite some time. Hopefully, one day we will all be reunited.

Sam and Norma's eldest child was Shirley. He was

born in Prince Edward County in May 1904, but would spend his adult life in Newark, New Jersey. He was married to Frances and they had one son whose name was Walter. I understand his nickname was "Old Red." Shirley died in October 1975. When he died, he was brought back to Virginia and is buried in New Hope Cemetery, where his parents are buried.

Otis, born in 1905 died sometime between 1920 and 1931 in Newark, New Jersey, from pneumonia. Mama said she remembered when he died because Grandma Susie met Grandma Norma walking up and down the road crying saying that Otis had died. She said he was the tallest of the boys and had a really good grade of hair. I found him listed in the 1910 census.

The next child born to Sam and Norma was Florine, born March 1907. She lived in Prince Edward County, Virginia all her life. Aunt Florine attended public school in Prince Edward County and became a wife and homemaker when she married Nelson Carey, in December 1927. Uncle Nelson was a farmer who enjoyed music and playing the guitar. His favorite hymn was "The Unclouded Day." He joined the family church at an early age and worked faithfully as a teacher for the Junior Class, treasurer of the Sunday school and president of the Senior Choir. He was an ordained deacon at New Hope Baptist Church. During the first years of the school in the 1940's Uncle Nelson donated cut wood and made fires for the school. During that same time Aunt Florine cooked the food that was donated for the students free of charge. From what I was told, Uncle Nelson, in his youth days, was quite the "ladies" man. He also was one of the guitar players at the famous Evans family gatherings.

Florine and Nelson Carey had 13 children. They are found first in the 1930 census with one child, Mattie (Walter Hall). Their family would be blessed with additional children: Irene (Benton), Mary (Barksdale), Ada (Mack Williams), Alto (Stokes), Ann (Eddie Stubbs), Josephine (Herman Huitt), Maxine (Joseph Salters), Nannie Kate (Kay) (McLellan/Glen Bynes), Emma (Frank Gaines), and Samuel (Marie) Carey, and James (Naomi) Carey.

They were all born in Prince Edward County. They would remain there until they were ready to leave home, to go away to school or to work. As a result of the miscarriage of justice, when the schools were shut down, many of the younger children would move to New Jersey to live with family members. They would continue their education in the school system in the north. Those that were left behind would eventually return to the Prince Edward County School System.

I have had the pleasure of knowing these cousins over the years and we have really been able to share great family memories. Their descendants are so numerous, that it would take another book to list them all. The love that we have shared over the years had been a source of great strength. Our families look forward to the times we spend together at family reunions and when we must meet under sad circumstances, we still find time to enjoy each other's company. I truly love them for being a part of my life and they have contributed so much to this family history.

When I first started writing this book, I asked my cousin Irene to tell me something about growing up in her family. She was so willing to do so and now I will share what she wrote about her family in 2004.

"My name is Irene Carey Benton and we grew up on a farm in Abilene, Virginia. We worked on the farm growing up. We did not live too far from school and church so we could walk to Sunday school every Sunday. The school we went to only went as far as the seventh grade."

"Sometimes my mother would cook hot food for the school. She was a homemaker and housewife. Mother worked very hard cleaning, cooking and washing for us. She also sewed for us. Since there were a lot of us, we would almost fill the school bus up. When they closed the school down, we went to another school.

"I remember as a little girl going to grandma and grandpa's house on a wagon filled with hay. All of us would be riding in the wagon. Sometimes when we got older, we would walk to grandma and grandpa's house. They would always have something good to eat. I remember the upstairs and downstairs of the house. They had a big yard, and I would go to the spring sometimes with my aunts to get water. I remember that Grandpa's nickname was "Pie."

"My father liked to hunt and he used to hunt animals and sell the fur to make money. Our main farm crop was tobacco. We worked hard on the farm for a living. We raised all of the food that we ate."

"My oldest sister Mattie was the one to help Mother take care of us when we were little. As we got older, we took care of each other."

"Cousin Susie Carey was the midwife for all of my mother's children, except the last one, James. James was born in the hospital. I used to wonder why Cousin Susie would be bringing all of those babies to my mother in that little black bag. I said to myself one day I wish she would stop bringing Mom all of those babies. Every two years she would bring Mother a baby (smile). Now I know why and I thank God for my family. It is not too many of us."

Florine Evans Carey passed in October 1976. Nelson Carey passed in May 1987. The Carey family had many descendants to carry on their heritage. When Aunt Florine passed in 1976, they had twenty five (25) grandchildren and four (4) great grandchildren. When Uncle Nelson passed in 1987, he had twenty seven (27) grandchildren and twenty one (21) great grandchildren. It is now 2010 and the numbers have increased to include great- great and I am sure great- great- great grandchildren.

Thomas Evans was born in July 1913. He stayed in Virginia during his early years. He worked on building highways through Charlotte Courthouse and South Boston in Virginia, and the highways in Lynchburg, Virginia. However, when he turned 21 years old he followed my father to West Virginia to work in the coal mines. He would later move to Baltimore, Maryland, where he would work as a long shore man, until he retired. Thomas was married to Fannie Reed. He had one daughter, Betty Cornish, who we got to meet just a few years ago. He also had two stepdaughters, Carolyn and Izena Reed and a stepson, Marlon Reed. In his final years Betty helped to take care of him before he passed.

Uncle Thomas was always a snappy dresser and loved to wear his big hats and drive big cars. He was a player all the way around. His nickname was "Slick" and if you knew him, you knew why he was called Slick. He loved the good times and the women who went along with the good times. He was a ladies man, but I understand as a child he was scared of the dark. Uncle Thomas stuttered like his grandfather. When he had a few drinks in him and he was trying to make a point, it was more noticeable.

Uncle Thomas and my father were probably the closest of his brothers. They looked alike and had a lot of the same ways. He never stopped having a good time, even when he ended up in the nursing home. He was still trying to flirt and see how he could get out of the nursing home long enough to go to the neighborhood bar. Uncle Thomas was the last of the siblings to pass away. He passed in February 2003, in the town he loved, Baltimore. It was doing one of the worst snow storms and the weather did not permit the Memorial Service we had planned for him. His daughter, Betty, her pastor and my sister, Bernice, were there to bid him farewell in a private service.

Henry Evans was born in April 1916 in Prince Edward County, Virginia. He would spend his early life in Prince Edward County and then relocate to East Orange, New Jersey. He lived there the remainder of his life. Uncle Henry was married to Ada and they had four children. They were Ada, Mary, Henry, Jr., and Dorothy. He also had a daughter named Mary Lean. His second wife was Rosa. He passed away February 1976 and was buried in New Hope Cemetery, Farmville, VA. His children moved to the west coast and have been living there every since.

Virginia Alto Evans was born in 1918. She grew up in Prince Edward County and lived there throughout her life. She was married to Charles Patterson and they had one daughter, Norma Bernice. She later married Charlie Taylor and they had five children. The children were Dorothy Mae, Charlie, Jr., James Arthur, Robert and George.

I remember my older siblings talking about how much fun Aunt Alto was. She liked to party and they always went to her house, as adults, when they were visiting Virginia. Her home, as her parent's home had been when she was growing up was the party house and the place to be. Aunt Alto died the summer of 1962. I do remember traveling from Hampton to attend her funeral. She was the first of my father's siblings to pass.

Over the years, the Taylor cousins have been very actively involved in our family reunions. They were a family of boys that had such musical talent. They had a singing group and they went all over the area singing in churches and at family affairs. Although the boys moved away, they all ended up back together in Virginia. They were very close and dedicated to each other. For boys, they were unique in their relationship. There was no sibling rivalry, just Love. Daddy always talked about them when he came back from his visits and always carried presents for them when he visited. Daddy also liked to hang out at Aunt Alto's house because he liked to party too.

Children of Alto Evans (Patterson) Taylor

Ethel Evans was born in July 1920. She spent her early years in Prince Edward County, and like her brothers before her, she would relocate to New Jersey, where she made her home. She was married to Walter Cummings and they had one daughter, Frances Cummings Claytor. She moved to New Jersey at and early age and spent most of her adult life there. She opened her home to the family from down south when they were visiting in New Jersey.

Aunt Ethel enjoyed playing the piano and singing. She was the historian of the family and gave me all the information that enabled me to research our ancestors. I think she was sort of the leader in the family. She seemed to have control over all the boys. She would visit Daddy in West Virginia, and was always in Virginia for family gatherings. She became the surrogate mother for all of my cousins that were relocating to New Jersey from down south. Aunt Ethel was the photographer in the family also, because she had the only photo of her father, Sam, and on the back she had written, Cherokee Indian, to document his heritage. Aunt Ethel gave me the history of the family that she knew. She told me about two brothers of Sam, George and Tom, and his two sisters Dorcas and Mammie. Aunt Ethel passed in August 2001, in New Jersey. Her husband, Walter Cummings preceded her in death.

Aunt Ethel's only child was Frances who had the gift of a beautiful singing voice. She used it to sing gospel and she also wrote poetry. She wrote the following prayer:

"Dear God, as I begin this day let me turn my thoughts to you. And ask your help in guiding me in everything I say and do. Give me the patience that I need to keep my peace of mind, and with Life's cares, I hope, dear God, some happiness to find. Let me live but for today, not worrying what's ahead, for I have trust that you will see I get my 'Daily Bread.' Give me courage to face Life's trials and not from troubles run, let me keep this thought in mind, 'Thy will', not 'mine', be done. And if some wish I do not get though I have prayed to Thee, Help me believe and understand you know what's best for me. I've failed you many times, I know, but when tonight I rest, I hope that I can kneel and say, 'Dear God, I've tried my best."

Frances daughter, Ethel (Neicy), was so kind to send photos of family members for my records. I am grateful to her for this gesture. In addition to her daughter Ethel, Frances had three sons, Henry, Willard and Stanley. Frances passed in 1995.

Frances pictured with her three sons below.

Julia Evans the youngest child was born in 1924. She spent her early years in Prince Edward County Virginia, and would also follow her family to New Jersey. Julia had one daughter, Lucille, who still resides in New Jersey and one granddaughter. When Julia passed she was brought back to Virginia for her final resting place, in the family cemetery to be among her ancestors.

Pictured below cousins wearing official Carey-Evans T-shirts, designed by Gladys Yvonne Harris: Top L-R, Rev. Walter Hall, Constance Lambert, Andrea Berry-Roberts, Laseanda McLellan, Bottom, L-R, Shirley Hinton, Pamela McDaniel, Edith Benson, Shearrain Benton-Bullock

Chapter 5

Family of Leonard and Martha Carey Evans

Leonard Evans, my father, was the fourth child born to Sam and Norma Wiley Evans. He was born in June 1911 in Prince Edward County, Virginia. He spent his early years in Prince Edward County, Virginia. He is first found in the 1920 census at the age of 11. The census record has his name incorrect. They have him listed as Bernard. I put a notation on the record to change it to Leonard. In 1920 they were living in the township of Buffalo, in Prince Edward County, Virginia. Of course birth certificates must have been still rare at that time because when Daddy tried to get one later in life there was no record of it. During those times, births were recorded in family bibles.

Daddy is found again in the 1930 census they have him listed as Lenvard, 17 years of age and living in Hampden, Prince Edward County, in Virginia. There are also two additional children in the family at that time, Ethel and Julia. In 1920 they were listed as black and in 1930 they are listed as Negro.

Daddy was educated in the Public Schools of Prince Edward County. He did not get much formal education because they had to work on the family farm as children. Although his formal education was limited, he had what we called "mother wit." He stayed in Virginia working on the family farm until he had the opportunity to relocate to West Virginia, at the urging of a friend of the family, Mr. Hall, who had moved there earlier to work in the coal mines. He was a hard worker and the ties between the Carey and Evans families led him to the girl who would become his beloved wife, Martha. Years later, Leonard and Martha would be blessed with six children and my story is a continuation of their story.

Since Daddy's home was the house that everyone gathered at, it was fate that they would get together at some point. They attended the same church, New Hope, where he was baptized at an early age. Daddy never talked much about growing up other than the fact that they had a big farm to work on and they had fun growing up as a large family. He did say, as a child, he remembered his Grandpa Jerry. He was also the only sibling who moved to West Virginia (WV) and liked it well enough to spend more than 60 years there.

Daddy and Mom were married in 1933. They were together for 62 years. Early in their marriage, Daddy relocated to Ingram Branch, West Virginia first; with the promise of going back to get Mama after he was settled. In the meantime their first child, Hazel was born. Daddy would seek work in the coal mines of WV. Once he was settled and Mama and Hazel were able to travel, he went back to get them. They traveled by car with the Hall's to their new home, one owned by the coal company that employed him, with the added benefits of shopping at the company store and having the company doctor serve their health needs.

The work in the coal mines was very dangerous but it provided a better living for his family than farming in Virginia. Soon after they moved to West Virginia, WW II started. Daddy registered for the Selective Service in 1940. Because by that time there were five children, he was exempted. In 1942, he applied to be a member of the United States Civil Defense Corps. He was accepted and satisfactorily completed the prescribed and approved courses of training and instructions. After demonstrating the necessary knowledge and abilities to carry out his duties, on December 18, 1942, he became a member of the Auxiliary Police Unit of the United States Defense Corps, in Ingram Branch, West Virginia, where he served with pride. He was a patriotic citizen willing to serve his country.

Daddy spent most of his time working to care for his ever growing family. He joined Ingram Grove Baptist Church and encouraged all of his children to do well in school. Daddy was a wise man and insisted on the best for his family, especially educating his children. He took great pride as each one of us graduated from High School. He was a self trained barber and for many years cut the hair of the men in the community who were sick and shut in. My brother always cried when Daddy cut his hair.

Daddy's nick name was "Kingfish." He was always a great dresser, loved his hats, and like his siblings loved to have a good time. When he became able financially, later in life, all of his suits were tailor made. He loved to dance and looked forward to meeting up with his friends on the week ends at the juke joint. Most of the miners worked so hard during the week that the week end gatherings were the only social life they had. Daddy also, like his siblings, loved to have a drink to relax. He was never a heavy drinker and it never interfered with his everyday life, but he indulged just enough to feel good. He never missed work because of drinking and never drank during the week. Daddy would make his own "home brew" in a large ceramic crock pot that sat behind the stove. He also made homemade wine and white lightning, moonshine. He never sold it; it was for his friends and his personal use. Once he took a hit, he used to sit around and pick on his guitar. He taught himself to play and enjoyed it.

Daddy was never one to take a back seat on an issue. He and Mama had heated "discussions," especially when he had been out on the week end with his drinking buddies, and decided to come home late, after a few drinks. As I look back at those times, I think a lot of his anger came from pent up frustrations from work that carried over into the home life. Also some of it could be attributed to his up-bringing where his father was very dominant in the household.

Although my father liked to hang out with his drinking buddies on the weekends, he never missed a day's work because he had had too much to drink on the weekend. He never neglected his family due to the use of alcohol. There were many instances in his family, where there was an excessive use of alcohol. Sometimes it was to the detriment of the user. I would hear Daddy and Mama talking about how some of them drank too much. I am fairly certain that some of their health issues were made worse with the excessive use of alcohol. I never knew of their being hard liquor kept in our home, except for home made wine and homebrew, but it was always readily available at the juke joint, or someone else's house.

It was not until years later, as an adult, that I realized the damaging affects of alcohol on the body as any other disease. Recent scientific reports have stated that the genetic trait can be transmitted through your inherited genes. As I look back, I can readily see many instances where existing health issues were made worse through the excessive use of alcohol. There are many family members, on both sides of our family tree, who evidently had this genetic trait, going back to some of our early ancestors DNA. We know now that it is nothing to be ashamed of and should recognize it for what it is, a disease, and to seek treatment. We were told as adults that Indians had a low tolerance for alcohol and that we must have inherited that low tolerance from our Cherokee Indian ancestors. I don't have medical facts to back that statement up, but if it is proven medically that you do have this genetic trait, being aware can help prevent future health related issues.

In the early 40's, 50's and 60's specifically, there was little professional help, especially for blacks, with limited access to professional services, to deal with any problems connected with drinking. Sharing this knowledge, about the family's bouts with drinking, is not set forth to condemn anyone or their lifestyle. You should consider this as a source of family health history information, the same as you would consider family health history knowledge about diabetes, heart problems, hypertension, and certain forms of cancer. Make no mistake alcoholism is a disease. Upon reading the causes of death listed on some of our ancestor's death certificates, it has given me greater insight into some of the diseases and health issues that have affected our family. After saying all of that I want to also say that genes are just a weakness in your body – you can control your health issues and be the generation to break the cycle.

Daddy loved hunting and looked forward to hunting season. He would bring home his catch and show it off with pride. I was always afraid of the squirrels and wild game he brought home. When he and his friends went hunting for deer, they would share the meat from the kill.

During all those years in the coal mine, Daddy suffered many injuries. His back was broken, legs broken and he ended up, like all long time coalminers with Black Lung Disease. I remember being afraid of his crutches. None of the accidents he suffered kept him from returning to the coalmines. I guess they say once a coalminer – always a coalminer. In those days, with limited education, there weren't too many jobs for unskilled workers. As children, we would race to meet Daddy when he got out of the mines so we could get the lunch that he had left in his lunch bucket. His coal mining career spanned over 30 years. He was a loyal member of the United Mine Workers of America, Local #7086 and he thought there was no president like John L. Lewis, because he did so much to improve the benefits for the miners and their families. He was a life long member of the NAACP, and always had an interest in politics, never neglecting to vote. When the polls opened, he would be right there.

Daddy was a good provider for his family and when he was out of work, it was not a happy time for him. Daddy was one of the best checker players around. He also spent time playing dominos with us. Playing games were special times the family spent together. He always insisted that we were home for dinner and we always ate dinner together. Daddy sat at the head of the table and was always the one to bless the food. You did not dare pick up your fork before he sat down at the table.

Daddy was a member of Ingram Grove Baptist Church in Ingram Branch, and when we relocated to Beckley, West Virginia, he joined Welcome Baptist Church. He was a faithful member and he was always the first one to get to the church to help bring the body in for a funeral, because they did not have official pall bearers then, and they depended on the men in the community to just come and help out.

Being the great family man that he was, he looked forward to our reunions and the ones his family held in his home place of Virginia. Whenever someone in his family was sick, he was always there to see what he could do. He took a great interest in his nieces and nephews and never failed to take gifts to them when he went to visit. He shared his money with his family also. He was a generous man. He loved being around his grandchildren and cherished each one of them in a special and unique way to them. He let the grandkids get by with things that if we had done would have been cause for use of the belt. Daddy usually left the discipline up to Mama to do. If the offense called for it, he did not shrink from it though. When Mama was away, we were always on our best behavior.

Daddy loved to eat chitterlings and I remember when the weather turned cold and the pigs went to slaughter, we knew it would not be long before the house would have the pungent smell of chitterlings. Mama always cooked them for him and none of us, other than Hazel, would eat them. Mama said when she was pregnant with Hazel, her craving was for chitterlings, and she did not even like them.

Not only did Daddy speak his mind to friends, but he did not have any problem telling off a "boss" when he felt there was a need to. This sometimes led to having to take unpaid days off from work, threats of being fired, and walking off when he felt the need to do so. One particular time the "white" boss thought he was getting the upper hand by telling Daddy he did not have to come in the next day, threatening to take a day's pay, and not to be outdone, Daddy told him what he could do with the shovel he had in his hand. He could shove it and told him "you can't fire me because I quit." At the time it happened we as children did not know why Daddy was not going to work, but I guess that was the time when he felt like it was more important to stand up for himself and worry about a job later. I guess that was also some of that "hot blood" from his Indian ancestors coming out. He never advocated violence to us but he taught us to always take up for ourselves and not to let people push us around unnecessarily. I guess I learned that lesson well and had no problem acting on it, when I felt there was a need to handle a situation that was getting out of hand.

Daddy and Mama always tried to shield us from the hard times and although we were poor, we did not know it. All of the families in the community had about the same thing, so we really did not know what it meant to have luxury. What we considered luxury was a clean home, clothes to wear, food to eat and parents that loved us.

Daddy did not own a car until later in his life. He could drive but never had a driver's license. When they bought their first car, Daddy could not wait to get behind the wheels of the car. Mama would nearly have a nervous break down when he took the car out. It got so bad that Mama had me get a friend to call and pretend to be calling from the police department about a complaint that he was driving without a license. I solicited the help of my friend, Shirley Brown from Maryland, and when she called to question him he was so polite to her and said that someone must have been jealous that he had a car and reported him for no reason at all. He assured the police that he had not been driving and would not drive. When I went home the next time after the incident, he proceeded to tell me about the phone call and what had happened. I had to chuckle to myself as he relayed the conversation to me because I had been on the other end when the call was made. He kept saying those old nosey bodies need to mind their own business. He kept repeating his favorite saying, "By Jinx Coe", if I knew who called I would show them a thing or too. It is a good thing we did not have caller ID at that time.

Daddy did not like nosey people and once when someone made a comment about them buying their home and spending so much money for it, he told him not to worry about it because he had enough money to make them a full length coat out of hundred dollar bills. I guess that statement shut the nosey neighbor up for a long time.

Daddy retired from the coal mines in the early 60's and spent the remainder of his life enjoying what he had worked hard for. He was able to do anything he chose to do and did everything first class. It was nothing for him to go to his favorite tailor and order two or three suits at a time. He said he had earned everything he had and wanted to enjoy it. In later years, when their finances increased significantly, he also was good at saving money and did not squander his money on useless things. Although they may have lacked financial resources early in their married life, they were blessed in their later years to be financially independent. Although Daddy had a lot of health issues, caused by his many years working in the coalmines, he enjoyed a good life until he got sick the last year of his life. He kept up his faith until the end.

He still was the first one up and dressed, as he had been when we were growing up. During those times he was always the first one up and dressed and had made the fire long before we got up and dressed. He never lay around in bed. When I would go home for visits and sleep late, I would hear him say to Mama, "Gearl's not up yet." It wouldn't be long before I made my way out of bed. Daddy enjoyed sitting in his favorite recliner and looking out the window as the people passed by. In the summer he took such great pride in keeping up his property. He would cut the grass and then go out and sit under the big shade tree to marvel at his work. Daddy was a cigarette smoker but also enjoyed smoking his pipe.

Daddy had the privilege of giving all of his daughters away at their wedding, except Josephine. We always waited to see what he was going to say, when the minister said "Who gives this woman to be married." He always said "I do – Leonard Evans." We would then wait to see what else he was going to say.

When he met me at the bottom of the steps to give me away, he made me so proud of him and I knew he wanted the best for me, his baby girl.

In 1933 my mom, Martha Susie's, life would change also when she begun her new life with Daddy. For the next 62 years they would nurture and care for each other and their family, which included five daughters and one son. They lost their first son in a miscarriage in 1939.

The children added to their family were Hazel Mae, Josephine Arletha, Bernice Sue, Dorothy Marie, Leonard Irie, and me, Martha Geraldine.

In 1934, before Mama would join Daddy in West Virginia (WV).   After the birth of their first child, they had their first crisis when my oldest sister, Hazel, had to be hospitalized. Mama said it was touch and go for a while, but they made it through while Daddy was in West Virginia working. She said Hazel's stomach had swollen up and they did not know what had caused it. The doctor said they got her to the hospital in the nick of time. It seemed she has been picking up beans off the floor and eating them without their knowledge.

When Hazel was well enough to travel, Daddy went back to Virginia to bring them to West Virginia with him. Mama said she was so excited to be leaving Virginia and that a family friend, Mr. Hall, had drove down to get them. Mama started a new phase of her life being a wife and mother, raising her children and keeping house. She said she was happy to be leaving Virginia and never looked back. She had lots of friends that had relocated there so she was surrounded by people she knew and met many new people, who would become lifelong friends. She said she never got homesick for Virginia.

She said Grandma Susie came to visit her on three occasions after she moved to West Virginia. Her visits usually were when Mama was getting ready to have a new baby. Mama continued to nurture her childhood dream for a home of her own. She said she used to daydream about owning her own home and she even drew up the plans for it. In 1956, she started purchasing a piece of land to build it on. It would be many years later before the house would be built. She never gave up on that dream and in 1971, she and Daddy moved into the home filled with the pride of accomplishing another dream.

In the early days, after moving to West Virginia, there were some good years and some not so good years. Times were hard in the 30's during the depression and of course segregation was still in existence. They had moved from the segregated south in Virginia to West Virginia, which was not as south as Virginia, but prevalent with the same problems. Work for blacks was scarce; they were still being treated like slaves and second class citizens and knew that the communities were separate, and not equal. The photo on the left is of my Mom posing on the steps of their first home. I was probably about five or six years old. She did not know I was standing behind her. Don't ask me why I am dressed like I am wearing a jacket and short set, with a scarf covering my head in the summertime. We only took pictures in the summertime because with the brownie camera we had to wait for the sun to shine. Their house was located on the other side of the railroad tracks, further back up into the hollow, close to where the mines were. They got all of the soot and cold dust first. The water they drank came from a spring in the woods and of course the outdoor toilets were close by the houses. They would live through a war that would put even more strain on their economic situation. She had left a home where food was readily available from the farm, and there were plenty of families living close by who shared whatever they had. During the 40's they used ration books to purchase sugar, milk, flour, and other necessities, because there was a war going on, and the government used the best they had to feed the troops overseas.

Mom always took everything in stride and did what she could to help out with the family finances. With all the difference in the culture from her birthplace, she still was happy to be there. She was experiencing her first taste of independence from the family she left behind in Virginia.

To supplement their income, she started to sew for others, making clothes for people in the community where she got paid .50 cents for clothes for children and .75 cents for grownup dresses. She said when the people stopped paying her for making the clothes; she stopped sewing for them and concentrated on sewing for her family.

She learned how to stretch food so that there was always enough to go around. She canned vegetables and fruits in the summer and we ate them in the winter. We also raised chickens that we played with during the week and probably ate one of them on Sunday. I can still taste the good bread pudding that she used to make. No one could hold a candle to her cooking. She taught us how to cook and of course, who could forget those mouth watering rolls that she made. That was one of the treats we always looked forward to upon returning home for special visits. At one point she gave away her recipes but then said she was giving away her hand at making these dishes so she was going to keep them to herself. We are still trying to figure out how she made her famous goulash. I believe my sister Hazel and Dot ended up with the cooking skills more so than the rest of us.

Mama was raised in a very religious family, worshiping in the family church, New Hope Baptist, so naturally when she moved to West Virginia she joined the local church. The church was named Ingram Grove Baptist Church and the pastor was Rev. C.E. Ellis. He was the same minister that baptized all of her children. Mama made sure that we went to Sunday school and church weekly. She made sure we were involved in any activities sponsored by the church or school. Mama was one of the most loving, caring people that you would want to meet. She never made an enemy and she treated everyone with respect and love. She really lived by the Golden Rule and the teachings of the bible. Don't get me wrong, she had a feisty side also and was no push over, as evidenced in some things she would do and laugh about many years later. One thing you did not do was mess with her family.

She told of the time when she and some of the other women in the community went down to picket at the company store because the owners of the coal mines were taking all the money the men made and not leaving enough for them to live off of. In addition, they went down to support their husbands as they carried out a miners strike for better working conditions and better pay. Daddy did not want her to participate, but she did anyway.

Mama continued her love for sewing by making most of our clothes. She loved being a mother and always put us first in her life. She did without a lot so that we could have what we needed. She made many lifelong friends in Ingram Branch, first as a new wife and mother, being involved with the education of her children and always looking after some child in the community that needed care.

Mama had a great appreciation for music and boy did she love to dance. She would show us how to do some of the old dances, like the black bottom and swing. She and Daddy would sometimes go to the juke joint on the weekends. Mostly she stayed at home with us and we learned to play lots of board games as a family.

Mama was the disciplinarian in the family. She believed if you spared the rod you would spoil the child. I don't think any of us nor were her grandchildren spared her loving discipline. We were not spoiled and we knew what our place was in the household. She taught us respect for all, especially our elders. We were given the best that they could afford and none of us were ever treated differently. She made sure that we all had chores to do and that they were done. As the baby in the family, there were things that I could not do, or at least I pretended that I could not do them. I hated washing dishes and knew if I waited long enough she would wash them for me. She knew what my game plan was before I put it into play.

There were times when work was slow in the coal mines or when Daddy had been injured, that really called on her to make do with little or nothing. Because she was so nice to other people, there was always someone around willing to help out. I can think of two families right off the bat that I am sure Mama would agree with me about their love and care for us. They were Ms. Essie Burger and Ms. Rosa Hill, who lived at Ingram Branch and sort of adopted all of us. They remained friends for their life time. Those were two of the houses that we were allowed to stay over night in.

When the coal mines were shutting down Mama was so concerned that we would get stuck in Ingram Branch. Daddy was no longer working in the mine and we lived in the company's house. I think that was the time Daddy was fired for speaking up about something wrong he saw in the mines. It would be just a matter of time before we would have to move anyway. She worked tirelessly trying to find a place for us to move to. Ingram Branch was becoming a ghost town with families moving away as the mine was letting workers go and fathers were leaving to find work in other places. Mama said she felt that "her children would be doomed" if she did not get us out of that hollow. The walls were closing in and the bridge that led out of the hollow was in danger of collapsing because needed repairs had not been made. She wondered if she did find a place would the bridge hold up long enough to carry all of our belongings packed in a pick up truck across it. Things were looking pretty bleak.

Because of her constant drive not to be deterred, she found a house for us to move to in a place I had never heard of, called Beckley, West Virginia. She did not tell Daddy before hand how small the house was for fear that he would not want to move. As I alluded to earlier, Daddy let Mama handle the household affairs. We moved sight unseen and ended up with eight people in a two bedroom house.

On Halloween, October 31, 1953, she moved her family to another phase, with new challenges that she was determined to face and overcome. Mama said she was thinking that the older children would soon be moving out and that we could make it for a little while.

After moving to Beckley, before Daddy found work in another coalmine, Mama went to work outside the house for the second time. She still continued to be the main housekeeper at home, but was willing to help out while Daddy looked for work. Daddy never wanted Mama to work outside of the house, but she said that he had allowed her to work one day a week for a white family living in Oak Hill, when we lived at Ingram Branch, and that she used to do laundry for a white family to supplement their income.

Daddy wanted to still be the breadwinner while she was the homemaker. In Beckley, she once again supplemented their income by working in a restaurant as a kitchen helper. She also did the laundry for the owner.

By the end of the late 50's Mama had just about finished her job of raising children, because one by one they started to leave home. She had joined Welcome Baptist Church in Beckley and supported all of their endeavors. Her last pastor, Rev. David Allen, was so fond of her that he called her "Mom." He would later say at her home going that she was the type of person who did something for you and never talked about it. He shared how she had helped him and his family on many occasions, and never expected anything in return. That was the kind of Christian spirit she exhibited all her life and whatever she did for you she did it with a smile.

Mama was a homebody and never got that involved in things other than church and our schooling. She did not visit too many people in the community, but she made some friends who she shared common interest. She always offered a helping hand whenever it was needed. She consistently used her skills of sewing for children in the neighborhood where there was a need. She was always the babysitter to the grandkids in the summer months. She would continue to sew, making quilts for all of us, and she always had some child in the neighborhood she made clothes for, in addition to her grandkids. Mama had an old Singer Sewing Machine with the metal foot pedal, refusing to upgrade or sell it to the repairman when it needed to be fixed. She used the metal foot pedal to exercise her legs. She taught Hazel and me how to sew and we used that same sewing machine. We were the only two interested in sewing. The sewing machine is one of our few family heirlooms and it has to be over 70 years old.

Mama always looked forward to our coming home to visit. We started a family tradition of returning every 4th of July as a way of celebrating the love they had instilled in us as children. She always taught us to be there for each other and we were never allowed to fight among ourselves. We were taught to defend ourselves though and to take up for each other when someone else was picking on us.

She was feisty and not afraid to get up into Daddy's face when she felt the need to make her point. She stood a little over four feet tall, but her size did not deter her. We were never abused but she always corrected our wrongdoing. Her psychology was not called "talking" it was called "the switch." I am glad that I learned how to raise children properly from my mother. It has helped me to be the type of person who would rather have your children angry at you, than spending time in the school principal's office or the courtroom. I am grateful for all the love and care she poured into all of us.

She never forgot a promise of a whipping that she owed you either. We are probably what we are today because she cared enough to do what she felt was necessary to teach us how to behave. Oftentimes only a look was required. The mothers in the community were also given permission to correct us if they found us doing something wrong. "A village raising a child" was the code of the day for the time during our childhood.

Mama was not the type of person to complain. When you said something bad about the weather, she would just say "I am just glad to be here to see whatever comes." She told me about the big snow storm in 1941 before I was born, while they were living in Ingram Branch. She said it was so cold and so much snow that the trains could not run for days and you couldn't get the doors open to the house. She said as she was looking out the window at the snow, she saw the men walking down the railroad tracks from work, and they looked like little boys.

Mama was not the type of person who wanted to travel a lot. She was satisfied to go back to her home place on a regular basis to visit with her family. Her visits to us were rare but always enjoyable. She had the sweetest smile and no one believed she was the age she was. She had never been in a hospital until in 1999 when she had to have major surgery. Her doctors were amazed at how well she recovered. The Lord had blessed her with good health and she never failed to give God the praise for all he had done for her in her life time.

She was able to live by herself until the last eight months of her life. She took care of all of her business affairs in an efficient manner and only told you what she wanted you to know. She and I did become confidants in her later years because she always felt that I could handle her affairs the way she wanted things done.

She still only told me what she wanted me to know and if I asked too many questions, she would let me know if I had crossed the line. I did not take offense at that because I knew that she would ask for help if she needed it. If there was something she wanted to discuss with someone on the phone she would call me and I would do a conference call and help out with whatever issue was at hand. I am thankful that she had enough confidence in me to trust me with her wishes. I learned to listen when she was trying to make a point because if you tried to talk she would talk over you. Her disposition was quiet, but you did not make the mistake of ruffling her feathers or getting her wrong. She laughed as she told us of one incident, after we had all left home, where she used her umbrella to make that point. It seemed that when she happened to make a surprise visit at one of the houses Daddy and the men used to hang out at in the neighborhood, one particular woman was paying too much attention to Daddy's conversation. She kept the umbrella to show us how torn up it was. I don't think she had any trouble after that. I guess I inherited my feistiness from her.

Mama went through a lot in her 92 years and 17 days on this earth. The photo on the left was taken at her 90th birthday celebration. She still kept a smile on her face until the very end. She loved to listen to her spirituals and she had favorite ministers that she never missed when they came on the radio. She taped sermons preached by her last pastor Rev. David Allen. She always made sure she did not miss her religious programs when Rev. Thomas Steelman, Rev. Philip Copney, Elder James Denson, (who she had no idea would one day be her son in law), were on the radio. I think she must have recorded a lot of the ministers who preached on the radio in the early 70's and 80's, as evidenced by the boxes of tapes she had in her possession. When she was spending time by herself, after Daddy passed, she said those message uplifted her spirit.

Mama had a collection of old 78 rpm records and guarded them closely. She enjoyed pulling them out and listening to them as she went down memory lane. She collected everything and never threw away anything. Growing up during the depression, she always felt that she might need it at a later date. She knew where everything was and would go behind you to make sure that you put it back where you found it. I guess she was the modern day "pack rack" but in an orderly way. I also took that trait from her. I am trying to break it though. Continue to pray for my deliverance from being a "hoarder." Mama kept every card that was ever given to her. She said they were too nice to throw away and cost too much money.

I am glad that she did keep some things because as the family historian, I am now the proud owner of memorabilia belonging to family members that would have been lost had she not kept it. She also kept every grade card we received while going to school. I bet some of my siblings are not anxious for their children to see how "well" or "not so well" they did in school.

Mama refused to get an automatic washer while she was able to continue using the wringer washer she had from the 40's. She did get a dryer and in the end she agreed to purchase an automatic washer. She told me about one of the last times she tried using the old wringer washer and how the water overflowed and she had such a hard time mopping it all up. In her last year there were a lot of things going on in her life, but because she wanted to remain independent, she kept a lot of things to herself.

Mama was always an inventor and she spent hours trying to figure out how to build a trash container to burn things in. She figured it out, made a cover for it and showed it off with pride. We made the mistake of leaving it outside, unsecured, after she passed and someone saw a good thing and stole it. I hope I never see it in their yard, because if I do they will have hell to pay. She should have been an inventor because she had great ideas and made many things around the house for her personal use. I have a picture of her standing by her trash container invention, with pride, satisfied that she had solved her problem.

Mama was a homebody and her travels centered on her family visits. She preferred that we visit her and she looked forward to those visits. She never flew on an airplane and use to tell me "you had better stay out of them planes." We talked about my many trips and when I found out she would worry whenever my travel involved flying, I started to just tell her where I had gone after my return. When I traveled to the Holy Land and Egypt, I had to tell her I was going because I knew I would be gone for an extended period of time and she would wonder why I was not calling her. We talked on a nearly daily basis in her later years. She was more concerned because I would be gone for a long period of time. She didn't want me to go but I convinced her that I would be alright. I reminded her that Uncle Joe had gone to the Holy Land and that from listening to him talk, I had wanted to go. She said "well just be careful and I will try not to listen to the news if I hear about something happening over there." I am happy to say that the trip was great and I enjoyed sharing the pictures with her and giving her a bottle of water I had dipped out of the Jordan River. I did not trust the water they were selling which was already bottled. I wanted the real thing. We did not have all the airline security then that we have now or I would have been stopped and it would have been taken away.

Mama was present at all of our weddings, except Leonard's and Josephine's, and had a good relationship with all of her sons in law and daughters in law. She treated them as if they were always a part of her family, and welcomed them as her new children.

Mama kept God as the head of her life. She read her bible daily and had many favorite scriptures. She supported many local charities, but preferred to give directly to those she knew were in need. She taught her children to love the Lord, be good to people, get an education and go out into the world and make a difference. Each child and grandchild had a special place in her heart. She always told each one "you are my favorite."

Mama touched the lives of all of those around her. Until the end her heavenly smile was the first thing you saw when you approached her. She was unselfish in her giving and she always saw the good in everyone. She never spent time in idle gossip. She was a proud independent woman who walked with her head held high. She was blessed and a blessing to others.

Beyond her immediate family, Mama became a surrogate Mom to the Morton children, Henry, Melvin, James, Vernell (Lefty), Sam, Viola, and Robert. She was a surrogate grandmother to Joe Webb, who affectionately called her "Granny." She spoke so well of her caregivers, who we considered as part of our family, Roxanne Taggart, Jacquetta Johnson, Patricia Banks, and Rosetta Swain. During those last months of her life, she was never left alone but surrounded by family and friends. I once said to her when I had to give her a bath, and in her pride, she did not want to be a burden, that she should think of it as being my baby. I assured her everything was going to be alright. I know The Lord and her family welcomed her as her heavenly journey begun.

My father and mother left behind a generation of descendents that they could be proud of. From their humble beginnings in Prince Edward County Virginia in 1911, and 1914, their marriage of 62 blessed years, the leaves are still growing on the tree and the seeds they planted so many years ago, have roots that run deep and wide.

We are proud to be called the children, grandchildren and great grandchildren of Leonard Evans and Martha Susie Carey Evans.

Hazel Mae their first child was born in 1933.

Hazel was born in Virginia and was the only sibling delivered by our Grandmother Susie, who was a midwife. My mother said she had a difficult birth with Hazel and that she came here sickly. Hazel ended up in the hospital during the first year of her life and Mama said they almost lost her. She had major surgery as the result of crawling around on the floor and eating dried beans without anyone knowing it. When her stomach started to swell, she was rushed to the hospital and had emergency surgery upon her arrival there. Because of her early stomach surgery she has had to be very careful about what she eats. She could not eat anything with small seeds in it, like tomatoes.

Once Hazel had recovered from her surgery she made the trip to Ingram Branch, West Virginia with Mama and Daddy. As the oldest child in the family, Hazel had additional responsibilities placed upon her, mainly helping with the younger children. She always tells us that "she raised us." She had always been the "mother" figure when Mama was not around. She cooked and cared for us and she also had no problem whipping us when we acted up. There were times when she took on all five of us at one time by herself. As you can see she was "Bad." Not only was she the oldest, but she was also the shortest of the siblings. Of course that did not deter her in making her point and executing her punishments.

At an early age, she learned how to sew under Mama's teaching. She also learned how to crochet and do embroidering. She was a right-handed person in writing and everything else, except she used scissors to cut with her left hand. I think that had something to do with Daddy insisting that we use our right hand for everything. If we were caught using our left hand, he would make us change to the right hand. My brother started out as a left handed person also. I guess he never paid any attention to her cutting and sewing so that was how she was able to get away with it. I guess that old saying about a left handed person "owing a day's work to the devil" was what he was trying to keep us from having to pay.

Growing up we all looked up to Hazel for guidance and generally followed her lead. During the summers she would make the dreaded trip to Virginia to work on our Uncle's farm. When she came home at the end of the summer to return to school, she was so happy. She used to write letters home to Mama begging to come home before summer ended. Of course their being away for the summer was help to our parents and to our Aunt and Uncle; as they provided extra hands to work on the farm.

Hazel has always been feisty. I guess she inherited that trait from Mama. She would get into your face in a New York minute and will give you a piece of her mind at the drop of a hat. I remember her taking on the neighborhood bullies all by herself when they had started a fight. She sent them home running crying for help. After that the neighborhood kids knew not to mess with any of her siblings. She was our "protector."

After finishing elementary school at Ingram Branch she rode the bus to Beards Fork Junior High School, because that was the closest school for Negro children in Fayette County where we lived. After that she was bussed to Simmons High School in Montgomery, West Virginia, where she became the first in the family to graduate from high school. Mama and Daddy were very proud of her accomplishing what they had been denied. Her reward was her class ring and class pictures. Of course, in those days a high school diploma did not mean as much in a coal mining community because there were no jobs around that required a diploma.

If you did not go off to college, and stayed there your only choice was babysitting for someone. There wasn't even any "well to do" white folks to work for since they were just as poor as the black coal miners. So she settled into helping different people in our community babysitting their children. As the oldest one, and the only one out of school, Hazel was called on to go back to Virginia to help take care of our ailing Grandmother Susie, before she passed.

The time was spent playing with the kids in the neighborhood and attending church activities. She was baptized at an early age and joined Ingram Grove Baptist Church where she was active until we moved to another town.

After we moved to Beckley, West Virginia, Hazel got her first real job working in a dry cleaner. It was while working there that she met her future husband, Lee David Harris, Sr. Hazel would be joined in marriage to Lee David Harris, Sr. Lee's parents were Joseph and Eleanor Harris. His siblings were Joseph, Jr., Ross, Gladys and Octavia. Lee and Hazel are the parents of a daughter, Gladys Yvonne and a son, Lee David Harris, Junior. Their grandchild is Jessica Taylor Harris.

Lee and his family lived in East Beckley, which was another section of our little town. Lee was a military man and I guess Hazel saw him as a good catch and also "a way out of town" and the chance to a better life. Lee wooed her until he got up the nerve to ask Daddy for her hand in marriage. They were married in 1955 and have been living happily together since that time.

We were happy for her to get a good husband, but sad because we were not ready for her to leave the home. They were married at his parent's home and I think the night she got married we were really happy, but when we returned home, we were all sad at the lost of her presence. She was the first to leave home and we felt the lost right away. She went to live with his mother in East Beckley, which was just minutes away but still too far, and Lee went off to his military post.

Lee eventually came back to get Hazel and they went off to live the military family life. It wasn't long before she returned in 1957 to have the first grandchild in the family. I remember when they took Hazel to the hospital to have the baby and Lee called back to get a progress report. I heard Mama tell Daddy "they are going to have to take the baby."

Even at 15 years old, I was very naïve and I did not know what that meant. I was sad because I thought they were going to keep the baby at the hospital. Anyway all went well, and we finally got the news that Hazel had given birth to a health baby girl. In those days, you had to wait for the birth of the child to know whether it was a boy or girl. You can see how things have changed in the last 50 years. They named her Gladys Yvonne. I looked forward to their homecoming, and yes we proceeded to spoil her. At some point Lee got reassigned to a new military base and they moved to Hampton, Virginia, where he would spend many years at Langley Air Force Base. Hazel and Lee would remain there until Lee was sent over seas and Hazel came back to Beckley to await his return.

In 1961 their family was blessed with the birth of their son, Lee David, Jr. They lived there raising their family until Lee's next assignment to Otis AFB in Massachusetts. He retired from the military in 1972 and they returned to Hampton, Virginia, where their children would finish their education, both attending and graduating from Hampton (Institute) University. Lee would get employment with the Newport News Shipbuilding and Dry Dock Company for the next 20 years before he retired for the second time.

Hazel and Lee welcomed me into their home after I graduated from high school, in 1960. I lived with them for almost two years. I guess having a teenager in the household was something new and challenging for them. I was trying out my wings as an adult and I am sure I gave them a few headaches. I did not always pick the friends they would have and soon knew that it was time for me to move on so I could be fully independent. They were very supportive of me and the time spent with them was beneficial to me in many ways.

As I stated before, Hazel has always been the one to look after me, probably from birth. She was the one who walked me to and from my new school when we first moved to Beckley so I would not get lost coming home. She bought me school clothes, fixed my hair and took me to have my first professional photos made when I was in the sixth grade. She also gave me my first birthday party and bought me a pretty black doll. It replaced the doll that had gotten messed up from being too close to the coal stove, while lying on the bed in the living room.

Many years later when I visited them, she had restored the doll that she bought for me and presented it to me once again. It had been so long that I had forgotten about her. I keep her close to me now. I look at her and think about my early childhood days.

Hazel is very artistic. In addition to being a fantastic seamstress, she is a world class doll maker, pottery wear, cook and a maker of beautiful quilts. She came to visit me in DC one summer and I had just completed a quilting class. I had made a log cabin quilt in one day and proceeded to show her how it was done.

She was so impressed that she said she wanted to learn how to quilt. Not being one to procrastinate, as soon as she returned home, she started looking for places that taught quilt making. She joined a quilting club and as they say the rest is history. I like to think that I added a measure of happiness to her daily activities by introducing her to the art of quilting. That is a small gift compared to the gifts she has given me over the years.

Hazel's family would increase again when they welcomed their first daughter in law to the family. Lee, Jr. met and married his first wife, Carol Phillips and I traveled with Hazel, Lee and Yvonne to Denver, CO on the train to attend the wedding. Johnna's daughter, Chanteé traveled with me to be the flower girl in the wedding. My sister Bernice was in a hurry to get there, so she flew out. That was our first trip going across country by train and it was lots of fun. We met Carol's family there and to my surprise, when I met her brother I found out he was a famous TV star, Joseph Phillips, from the Bill Cosby Show. Sadly, Carol passed away a few years later, from complications of Sickle Cell Anemia.

She was such a pleasant person and we loved her dearly.

Lee, Jr. found love again when he met and married the lady who was a prosecuting attorney, Vera White. They gave Hazel and Lee their only grandchild, Jessica Taylor Harris. Lee has been very successful in the digital world. I remember when he was in college and because he had a love for music he wanted to major in music. I told him that music was fine but there were a lot of starving artists out there. I am glad he listened to my words of wisdom for he has traveled the world over with the companies that he has been privileged to work for. He is now the family's "most travelled" member.

Yvonne, my first born niece, continues to be involved in her artistic work and creating unique pieces of art through her company Diva Moon. Both of Hazel's children have successful careers and live in the DC metropolitan area. I remain the aunt in residence. Yvonne has become a "water person" and in addition to working for the Smithsonian Institution, spends quality time on their sailboat on the Potomac River with Myra Cones, who has become a part of our family, along with her family and their friends.

Lee, Sr. has been in our family for so long that it seems like he was born into the family. He has always been there for us and he made many trips up and down the road to take care of his family and ours. He has made Hazel very happy, as evidenced by the life they have shared and the evolution she made, from the petite girl he married in 1955, to the glowing woman she is today.

Josephine Arletha was born in 1935. She was called "Phine" because, as a little child, Mama said Hazel could not pronounce "Josephine."

Josephine was the second child born to my parents. She passed shortly before her 35th birthday, in 1970. She was the first child born at Ingram Branch, after my parents moved to West Virginia. She was always sweet but even as a teenager sort of head strong. She was the favorite of our Uncle Joseph, because she was his namesake and he tried to help her and be very supportive, as she moved into adulthood.

As a child, she was always nervous and timid. She did not like to hear arguments or disagreements when my parents had them. She had been the one who would get jittery at the drop of a hat and very excited easily. She was never one to start a fight and if one was started she never wanted to fight. Hazel, the enforcer, would be the one to defend her. Josephine loved everyone and made friends easily. When they were home during the summer months, she and her friends spent more time trying to get away from me and the younger kids, than they did playing their own games.

She and Hazel were in elementary, junior high and high school together. She graduated from Simmons High School in 1953. Of course that was a special day for our parents because their second child had completed high school. Like Hazel before her, when she was old enough she too was sent to the country during the summer months to work on the farm. She would return at the end of summer and complain about how dark she had gotten from being out in the sun all day long working in the tobacco field. She said she was afraid of the worms on the tobacco leaves and would try to use a stick to knock them off and get into trouble because Uncle Buck said "it messed up the tobacco leaves." She really dreaded when school was out because she knew it meant another trip to Virginia. She said she disliked all the chores assigned to them on the farm.

They would be so tired at the end of the day that there was no time for fun. She did get to meet many of her Virginia cousins during those visits.

As one of the older children, Josephine also had the responsibility of helping to look after the younger siblings. She did not like that so much because it kept her from hanging out with her friends. She had to help with the housework and laundry on wash days. She was always getting into some kind of trouble for not doing what she was supposed to do.

One of their tasks was to pick blackberries and cut up peaches by the bushels. They would get up early in the morning, put on their boots, soaked in turpentine to keep the snakes away, and head out with buckets to pick blackberries. Oftentimes they would come back without blackberries because they would see a snake and by the time they ran home all the berries were gone. That only meant that they would have to go out the next day to pick berries again.

Josephine was a favorite of many of the mothers in the neighborhood because she was always willing to baby-sit and help clean their houses to make spending change. She always loved taking care of the children.

When we moved to Beckley, Phine put her skills learned from working in the home and neighborhood to use by working for the white folks, who were more affluent than the colored folks we left behind at Ingram Branch. She soon got a job cleaning house and babysitting for a family who owned a cabinet making company. She was such a good hearted person and would do anything for you that she could.

One of her first purchases was a couch that she bought for Mama to replace the bed that was in the living room. (We just got rid of the couch in 2010, so it must have been a pretty good one.) In Ingram Branch we did not have a "living room." She also bought my brother his first bicycle. When she moved away, she would send money back to help out with household expenses. One of the special things that she did was she sent Mama money to put down on the piece of land that the first home our parents owned would be built on. She never got the chance to see that dream come true but Mama was so thankful for the start she gave them.

By the time we moved to Beckley, she and my sister Dorothy had gotten to be running buddies. They would sneak out of the house and go places where they weren't supposed to be. They liked to go over to their friend's houses to play cards. The two of them would climb out of the window at night sneaking out after bedtime. Mama and Daddy always had a policy that did not allow us to visit in the homes of many of our neighbors. There were only certain houses we were allowed to go in.

Josephine became active in church after being baptized at an early age at Ingram Grove Baptist Church. She loved to sing and had a beautiful voice. After we moved to Beckley, she joined Welcome Baptist Church and we formed a singing group called "The Evans Family." We traveled with the minister and his wife, who were our next door neighbors, Rev. Charlie and Rosa Edwards. My mother had met them when she was house hunting and they became great family friends and supporters when we moved to Beckley.

Josephine was the lead singer in our family singing group because she had the strongest voice. She had a very unique sounding voice and she could really sing well. Sometimes she would imitate other singers and my Mother was always on her about changing her voice to sound like someone else. She encouraged her to sing in her own voice. She also liked to write songs and poems. Her favorite artist was Brook Benton and her favorite song was "A Rainy Night in Georgia." Her favorite spiritual was "Precious Lord." Rev. and Mrs. Edwards took a great interest in our family and took us along whenever he went to preach at different churches. We were his singers for the services. They always took us out to eat whenever we were traveling with them, which became a special treat. We did not have a car, so getting to go different places with them was also very special.

Because the work in Beckley was limited, when my next oldest sister, Bernice, graduated from high school in 1955, she and Josephine were getting set to leave for the big city. They were moving to Arlington, Virginia to live with our cousin Ernest and his wife Bertha. While living in Beckley Josephine had caught the eye of an older suitor in the neighborhood who was sure she was going to be his next wife. Needless to say, this was not a happy time for Mr. Miller, because by then he was really in love and wanted to marry her. He was pretty well off and he asked my father if he could marry her and said he would support our family financially if she did. At that time Daddy was not working and the money that they could make in the city, and send back home, was needed to help the family survive. My Daddy did not take her suitor up on that offer so plans were made for them to hop on the greyhound to seek a better life in the north.

Josephine was ready to leave the small town for the big city. She had spent time with Ernest when they were in Virginia during the summers and, since he had moved to Arlington, they were invited to come there hoping to get better jobs. With only a high school education, employments opportunities in Beckley were scarce.

In late 1955, she left Beckley for Arlington, Virginia. She stayed there for a period of time working various domestic and hotel jobs, and continued to send money home to help out. It was always nice when she returned home because she would bring me presents. She bought me lots of nice clothes for school and she bought me my first Mickey Mouse watch. Throughout the years she continued to provide clothing for me, including my prom dress and when I graduated, she came home and helped with my graduation expenses.

While living in Arlington, Josephine met and a few years later married John Wright, Sr., known to all as "Big John." John Wright, Sr., was the son of George and Emma Warren Wright. John was from the same hometown as our parents, and he was a self employed business man. John's siblings were Charlie, George, Moses, James, his twin, Henry, Wallace, Adelle, Hazel, Ida, and Mary, who is the only surviving sibling at the age of 98, and who incidentally calls me "Aunt Gearl."

John and Josephine had one daughter, Johnna Marie and one son, John, Jr., and three grandchildren, Chanteé, James and LaShay. John, Sr. also had four other children, Leroy Wright, Raymond Tony, Janice Arviett Walker and Jeanette Euille.

After Josephine and John were married she moved to Alexandria, Virginia. She wrote home and told Mama that they were expecting twins. We were all excited about the prospect of twins being born. She was looking forward to having her twins and she gave birth to Johnna Marie and a little boy, who did not survive.

Recently while going through our mother's old papers, I ran across a letter that Josephine wrote to Mama soon after giving birth and in the letter she said: "I suppose you been wondering why I haven't written. The baby is fine. I sure had a hard time the little boy was born dead, he weight 3 lbs & 2oz. He came first & that's the reason I had it so hard. John is so crazy about her, he fixes her baby formula for me, and she has a head full of hair & straight black. I'll be sending you some pictures of her soon as they are developed." I guess I need to look for answers, to find out what actually happened to the little boy, in the old hospital records from Freedmen's Hospital, now known as Howard University Hospital in Washington, DC.

The following year, Josephine and John had a son, John Jr. By this time they had moved to Washington, DC and she was a housewife with two kids. She was fiercely protected of her children and she doted on them. She carried them with her wherever she went. Christmas Eve she and I rode to West Virginia on the train so Mama and Daddy could see their new grandchildren for the first time. Although living in the big city, Josephine was still concerned about the people she left behind in West Virginia, because she always asked about them in the letters she wrote back home.

Josephine was a good wife, mother, a good cook and a great homemaker. She took pride in her new apartment and was looking forward to the house that John had promised to buy for her and the kids. In their apartment building, she was a very friendly person and very trusting of others. Sometimes she was too trusting of the people who became her friends.

I had recently moved to Washington the summer of 1962 to attend Cortez Peters Business School and Josephine met me at the bus station. I spent my first night in the big city with her. She was a great help to me when I first moved to DC because it was really my first time being away from home on my own. She made life easy for me and my new friends in school because we could always go to her house and eat lots of food when our food and money ran out. Josephine introduced me to many of her friends, and I remember fondly The Hubbard's, Tom and Minnie, and their children, who lived on 14th Street in the same apartment building as she. I made extra money babysitting their children. She also introduced me to Paul "Dean" Harris and his sister Alfredia, who I would share many fond memories with in later years.

In the late 60's Josephine made the decision to move back to West Virginia for awhile. It was there she would have help from Mama and Daddy, with the children, while she made some adjustments. Mama talked about how she would stay up half the night cleaning house sometimes to work off that nervous energy. Bernice says she remembers her coming to her house and cleaning and rearranging everything. She stayed in West Virginia with Mama and Daddy for a short while and later returned to DC.

The time she lived in DC, without the children, she would write letters to them on many occasions telling them how much she loved and missed them and for them to be good for Granny and Granddaddy. Not that she had to remind them to do so. I still have those letters in safe keeping and plan to pass them down to them at some point in time. When Josephine first arrived back in DC she lived with me until she went back to get the children and then they all moved back to Alexandria. We did not see each other as often as when she lived in DC. She never complained about her life although she may have been unhappy at times. We were brought up with the old saying that 'if you make your bed hard, you have to learn to lay in it." In hindsight, I guess that was not always good advice.

When Josephine passed in 1970, Billy and I brought Johnna and John home to live with us in 1971. We did not formally adopt them, but for all intents and purposes, they are our children. I look back on those times and see that we were no different from any other African American family, during that time in history as a family and community. We were brought up to take care of your own and always be there for family. Billy and I had lots of support because during the summer months, to give us a break, Johnna and John would spend time with my sisters and my parents.

Johnna and John lived in our home and attended schools in DC. Johnna always liked school and her teachers. John had more challenges but they both graduated and set out to chart their paths for the journey they wanted to make. They both spent some time in college, but eventually made other career choices. Education was stressed along with being happy at what they chose to do in life. I wanted them to know that education should be used to broaden their view on life socially and economically, but in the end they had to make the choice for their life.

After graduating from Roosevelt High School, Johnna started her full-time career with the government and is now looking forward to retiring in about five years. Johnna bought her first home and has enjoyed living on her own for many years. She did not move too far from home base. She is a very particular person when it comes to her home and enjoys being an interior decorator, always asking for my input when she starts a new project. Nothing like having your own and wanting to take care of it. I can always expect a "show and tell" call when she has completed a project. She also loves plants so I leave mine at her house so she can take care of them and they won't die. She also has a few tanks of special exotic fish swimming around that she loves to take care of. She also loves to cook and entertain family and friends, especially during the summer time and on special holidays. You can always count on her being a good hostess.

Johnna was a good child, as far as I knew. Sometimes now in conversations she will tell me things and I would say: "I am glad that I did not know everything that was going on in your growing up years." I am still proud of the person she has become. Since this book is about me, I will wait until she writes about her life and tell me the things I never knew. She is a loyal friend, and although sometimes moody, like her Aunt Bernice, will always be there for you. As we each grow older, I hope we also become wiser.

Johnna has one daughter, Chanteé Nicole, who is doing well for herself. She has been gainfully employed, since leaving college. She tells me that she intends to return one day to complete her studies and get her degree. I hope she means that. She too lives within walking distance of home base. Each day I see her maturing into a person who will listen, even if she does not agree with everything I tell her. I am glad that she is able to confide in me and seek my opinion on issues in her young life. I pray that my advice will be evaluated and acceptable.

Chanteé was the first grandchild to live in our home, so I guess you can say I spoiled her. We have a connection because I was the first to hold her after she was born. I always tell her that within two minutes of her birth, she was peeing on me.

I was with Johnna through her entire pregnancy and was her coach in the labor room. That was an experience for me because I had not had children of my own. Chanteé also shares a long time friendship with her classmate from school days, Gabrielle Hill, although she relocated to Tennessee. I consider Gabrielle to be one of the special people who became a part of our family. Chanteé, pictured with her father, Gregory Barrow, is sort of a homebody but is a very compassionate person.

Johnna has maintained her close friendships as an adult, with Janis Hill Jackson and her daughter, Melanie, Sonya Hill and her children, and Cynthia Mobley Young (Terry). They have always been like my extra children. I have been privileged to serve as the "Auntie" and "Nana" to many of the children, raised in our neighborhood, especially Cynthia's son, Terrance, who is Johnna's Godson and Sonya's daughter, Jermica, who have been friends with Chanteé, since birth.

Johnna met Harry Gonzales a few years ago. He has been someone to share her life with and who shares her love of travel and fishing. Harry and his family have now become a special part of our family. Harry is always willing to lend a helping hand, and he is always there when you need him. Harry is a caring person whose presence has added to our family. He is a whiz at fixing computers and I depend on him because I am a novice. Even when we depend on him to go with us to family gatherings, he never complains, when he has to do all the driving, since Johnna and I are no longer highway drivers. I am still acquiring new "nieces." After Johnna moved to her neighborhood, I met her next door neighbor, Joyce Washington, so now I consider myself to be her honorary Auntie.

John is my dreamer. He played basketball in junior high and high school and received a full college scholarship after graduation. However, an injury prevented him from pursuing that goal of being a "basketball star." Although even at his age now, he continues to play and mentor young men. John attended Mackin Junior High School, and transferred to Wilson to complete his high school education. He also learned the trade of printing. He has always had a good heart and loves attending church. Even as a child he would be one of the first to get ready to go to church. Mama never had to make him go to church when they were visiting during the summer. He has been very active in the churches he has belonged to and has worked faithfully in them. John has always been like the pied piper where children were concerned. He has a way with them and they all enjoy being around him. I guess that is because he is still a "kid at heart."

John's choice was to be a fashion designer, making clothing items for men and women. He has several patents to his credit for a line of sportswear he created. He had enjoyed a degree of success in the field, and has met many persons that have helped him along the way. He even made his first overseas trip to China in search of manufacturers. He participated in the fashion industry's conventions in Las Vegas, as he sought out new avenues to market his goods.

John also learned the trade of barbering, not knowing that barbering was a skill that many of his ancestors had learned and used to earn a living in their communities. I guess he had seen my father cutting hair during his many trips to visit and while living with them in West Virginia. We were talking once about doing DNA testing to learn something about our ancestors and I said to him, "I wish I had some of Daddy's hair clippings." To my amazement, John said he had some of Daddy's hair. When I said I did not believe him. He proceeded to open one of his old hair clipper cases and tucked neatly inside one of the plastic pockets was hair that he had kept from a time when he had cut Daddy's hair. I have not had the hair tested yet, but it is comforting to know that it is available when I find a reliable DNA test lab that can use hair samples to trace your family roots. John has been a self employed barber and cosmetologist for many years.

John is a people person and values his long time friends from his early childhood, as well as those he has met since becoming an adult and those who have mentored him along the way. I am still waiting to see who the lucky lady will be who gets him down the aisles of matrimony. He has lots of friends but I see he has been spending lots of time with a new friend, Josephine Bynum, so we will see where that leads. She is a very nice mature lady, with a caring heart and sweet disposition, and I like her a lot. I warn all of his female friends that he is known to be rather "spoiled." I like to think he inherited his taste for the finer things in life from me. When he gets dressed he looked like he just stepped off of the front page of Esquire Magazine, and he can give any model a run for their money.

John was late leaving home, which most people attribute to me "babying" him. He recently purchased his own home. He rented it out for a few years, while still living at home, but finally moved in. He has spent many months acquiring quality pieces of furniture and takes great pride in what he had done since moving in.

John has two children; a son James (his mother is Roth Brown), and a daughter LaShay, (her mother is Blanche (Lolita) Dixon), who are just entering adulthood. Jamie, as we call James, has grown up to be a hunk of a guy. Jamie was a rambunctious child and to see him mellowed out is interesting. When he visited us during the summer, he always wanted to stay home with me so he could play all day, but his Dad insisted that he go to work with him each day. His mother Roth has done a great job of raising him and I enjoy looking back on the times he spent with us as a child. I look forward to him becoming more of an integral part of our family.

LaShay, pictured with L-R, her Godfather, Anthony (Tony) Waterman, her mother, Lolita, and her father, has such a sweet disposition. She recently finished cosmetology school, and has her sight on being a business woman. She spent many days with me as a baby. LaShay was very quite growing up and did not talk much. She was shy but has blossomed into a lovely young lady who expresses herself very well. I am amazed at her maturity as we discuss issues in her life. She is determined to be a successful business lady and I look forward to her doing so. From being a shy child to see her take steps to be a model is a real transformation. She recently competed in the local search for the next top model contest. Lolita and her family have been very supportive of LaShay's dreams.

99

I hope that when Josephine looks down from her resting place in Heaven, she is pleased with the way we raised her children. They have added a great measure of pleasure and happiness to our lives. We are so thankful that we were able to step in when she was taken away from us so early. It would have been our wish for her to see them grow into the persons they have become; however God has the ultimate plan for all of our lives, and we have learned to accept his will.

Since parenting is on the job training, I know that I could have done a lot of things differently but I hope the decisions I made for their lives helped them to become good people, with that same love for family that was instilled in me as a child. I tried to firmly plant it in them so that they too will pass it on to their children. I observed the way Johnna and John stood by their father, in his later years as he became frail. John was always appreciative of Billy and me raising them and never failed to let us know how much he loved us for doing so. I also realize that God, in his infinite wisdom, knew that one day their mother would leave them, at an early age, and he had prepared the home and family for them long before they were born.

Bernice Sue was born in 1937. Bernice often called Bern and Neicy never really liked her middle name "Sue." I reminded her that she was honored with our Grandmother and Mother's name. Bernice was the child sort of in the middle of the two oldest and the three youngest. They always say middle children feel left out, but I don't believe that was true in her case.

Neicy spent a lot of time alone growing up. We always said she is like the March weather, very changeable. She did not have to spend as many summers in the country as my two older siblings did. Grandma Susie came to West Virginia to see about Mama after she lost her fifth child and took Bernice and Dot back to Virginia to stay until Mama recovered. Her early memories of the country life were pleasant because she had the good fortune of knowing our grandmothers and our first cousins, who lived in Farmville. Their relationships have blossomed over the years and they remain very close. She said she remembers playing with them and sitting around waiting for Grandma Norma to cook their meals. I wish I had known my grandmothers, but they both passed away while I was still young.

Neicy was baptized in the creek that we used to play in at an early age and enjoyed the times spent with others participating in church activities at the community church, Ingram Grove Baptist. With that being the only church in our community, we all would eventually become members. Neicy went to elementary school in Ingram Branch and then to Junior High School in Beards Fork. She started high school at Simmons, but as she entered the 10th Grade, we were preparing to move to Beckley. This was not a great time for Bernice. She wanted to stay with a family in Ingram Branch so she could finish school at Simmons. Ms. Stevenson wanted her to stay with her also. Of course, Mama and Daddy were not having any of that. She cried when we moved away from her childhood friends. In our family, there was no such thing as breaking family ties, even on a temporary basis. She had enjoyed all the activities of school and church growing up in Ingram Branch and did not want to make the change. She had been with all of her schoolmates from grade school and would have to make the sacrifice of not graduating with them. She knew that moving would mean a big adjustment and she did not like change, and was dreading having to make new friends.

I remember one incident that happened to Bernice as a child, and she still have the scars to prove it. She probably doesn't like to think about it. One of our neighbors, Mr. Helen, had seven hound dogs he used for hunting and she used to feed the scraps from our meal plates every day. On one occasion when the girl was delivering the newspaper, probably helping out her brother, she was afraid of the dogs. Bernice was in the house getting ready for school and because she thought the dogs knew her, she offered to put the newspaper on the porch. Well, Ms. Bernice who was all wrapped up, with a heavy coat and hood on her head, because it had been snowing, didn't realize that the dogs would not recognize her. As soon as she got into the yard the seven dogs attacked her. She was bitten on her right leg and the little ball on the top of the hood on her head was torn off, along with a lot of her hair. Mama was inside the house and did not know she had gone outside until she heard all the screaming. She ran out and somehow they got her away from the dogs. Mama carried her down to the company doctor's office. The doctor did not have the medicine to give her a tetanus shot, and Mama did not have a car, so Ms. Palmer, one of our two school teachers had to leave school to take her to another town to another doctor. That is only one instance where you can see that our teachers were not just teachers, but part of our community and families. Bernice always had long thick hair and she said she was combing out patches of hair for days. After that she said she never fed the dogs again and never had anything to do with them after that incident. That was also probably the last time she tried to help out her friend delivering newspapers.

Bernice had enjoyed taking care of the neighborhood children, especially Carolyn Sue Stevenson, Lawrence (Toots) Berger, and Beatrice (B-B) Hill. As a child Neicy liked being around older people and she always helped out when they were sick. This trait has carried over into adult hood because she still has a soft spot for the elderly. Neicy always was the one to comb all the neighborhood children's hair, so it was natural for her to pursue a career as a cosmetologist. She would braid all the little girls' hair and then practice braiding strands of grass and twine attached to our stick dolls. I remember one of the whippings that took place had to do with a "stick doll" and who it belonged to. I think Daddy ended up throwing it away or in the fire. Neicy would perfect her training by learning how to straighten and curl hair. She says she had wanted to be a beautician since she was a teenager.

She is probably one of the few beauticians who will make house calls to take care of those clients, who can no longer come into the shop for their regular appointments. She is known as the beautician with the growing hands. Her clients tell people with hair problems that they believe she could grow hair on an onion, if given enough time.   Her clients are so dependent on her taking care of their hair that when they die, she is the only one they want to give them their last hair do. She is called to the funeral homes, in Baltimore, to provide them this final service.

Of course before all of these things took place, Bernice put in her time on the farm in Virginia. She only had to go for one summer and she says all she can remember was how hot the sun was all day. She said she was also afraid of the worms on the tobacco and got into trouble with Uncle Buck for using a stick that damaged his tobacco leaves.

Moving to Beckley had one good point; they did not have to go back to the farm in Virginia to work during the summer. We always teased her about not being able to carry a tune while singing, but she was still a part of our group, The Evans Singers.   In Beckley, she joined Welcome Baptist Church and was active in Sunday school as a teacher and belonged to the Baptist Young Peoples Union (BYPU). She never joined the choir though.

After the dreaded move to Beckley, she enrolled at Stratton High School and became the first in our family to graduate from Stratton, in 1955. She never made a lot of friends there because she said most of them had their own little clicks and she did not feel a part of any of them.   One of her classmates was named Bill Withers, who would go on to become a famous singer, with his hits records, including Grandma's Hands and Lean on Me. She and I are featured in a part of the documentary about his life "Still Bill" which was filmed when he returned to Beckley to attend our school reunion in 2008. Of course we are not talking, we did not get paid, and we weren't interviewed, but you can see Bernice on the floor dancing and me talking to Bill. Garnett Mimms was also a graduate of Stratton High School.

While still a student in school, she got a job babysitting for a white family who lived within walking distance of us. They were Dr. James and Naomi Backus. He was a pharmacist and his wife a homemaker with three children, James, Jo-Ann and Jane. She made extra money to get things she needed for school that Mom and Dad could not afford. Years later, in 1995, while visiting in Beckley, during the time that Daddy passed; she would once again see the family she had worked for. While reading the newspaper she saw where Doctor Backus had passed and went to pay her respects to his wife, who still remembered her. She said she learned how to smoke and drink coffee while working for the Backus family.

As stated earlier, after graduating in 1955, she and Josephine would move to Arlington in 1956 to live with our cousin Ernest and his wife, Bertha and her sister Arlene. She found a job babysitting and doing housework but kept her dream alive of becoming a beautician. In August 1961, our cousin Fannie Mae invited her to come to Baltimore for a two week vacation. At Fannie's invitation, she decided to stay and with their help, she enrolled at the Apex Beauty School. It was there she received the training that would fulfill her life dream of being a beautician. She graduated as a licensed beautician in 1962. She liked Baltimore so much that she decided to make that her home. At that time we had lots of relatives living there so she had plenty of family support. She got to know our uncles and aunts on our mother's side of the family. Uncle Joseph and Aunt Nancy were there to offer their help and support.

Bernice worked in many shops under many different mangers, but was finally able to get her own place of business in 1989. It was located on Preston Street, not far from where she lived. That was a great day for her because she could do as she pleased without interference from anyone. She did not have to put up with the envy of other operators who did not have as many loyal clients as she did.

By the time she had moved to Baltimore, I had relocated to DC also and I would make my bi-weekly trips to Baltimore, on the bus, so she could do my hair. I was still in school and she would always give me money for transportation and extra money for school supplies.

She would be joined in marriage to William Taylor. There were no children from this marriage. Her marriage to Bill ended in divorce.

In January 1969, Bernice met William (Bill) Taylor and was engaged in February 1969, and married in June 1969. It was the hottest day of the year, 102 degrees. A friend told her on that day, "I hope your marriage won't be as hot as the weather is today." She must have had a premonition that turned out to be right. Her husband Bill did not turn out to be what she expected and luckily she found out early and as she will tell you, her marriage ended in divorce after 3 years, 3 months, 1 week and 2 days. Bill had one personality in front of family and was altogether different when family was not around. I guess Bernice took seriously what Uncle Joe used to say that "everybody should get married at least once." Of course he did not say you had to stay married. Her decision to get a divorce left her free from his unnecessary behavior and most of all his unwillingness to work.

Neicy joined Mount Pleasant Baptist Church, a large mega church in Baltimore, and has been a faithful and active member since the early 60's. Since she is anticipating a move back to West Virginia, and she is now attending a small racially mixed church around the corner from where she lives in Baltimore. She said she is getting used to being in a small church so her adjustment will be smooth. She really likes her new close knit church family and enjoys their Sunday fellowship. Bernice has spent many hours volunteering her services at nursing homes in the area, where she visits patients and provide services to them, as needed.

After Johnna and John came to live with us, Neicy was a big help to me in raising them. She became their other mother after Josephine's death. She would keep them during the summer months to give me a break and she has always spent holidays, especially Thanksgiving and Christmas, with us. We traveled back and forth to West Virginia together over the years making our annual visits to see Mama and Daddy. We have had a long standing tradition of all of us getting together at least once a year, usually during the 4th of July vacation time.

Bernice is always the first one to suggest that the family get together for special occasions. She is always the dependable one to represent family members at funerals and weddings. She has always been the one to keep in touch with the Carey and Taylor cousins. She is also the one who knew our aunts and uncles on Daddy's side of the family best.

Her independence carried over into her adulthood. Bernice is a successful business woman. In 2002 she became semi-retired and moved her business into her home, where she works when she feels like it. She is known as the "family gambler" because she loves to play bingo and likes to take a chance every now and then with the lottery. She is very free hearted and gives willingly to all. We share lots of goods times together. I can always count on her to help out when Billy and I have our get-togethers. She is always the one left cleaning up the kitchen.

Bernice is a true friend and really cares about those around her. She always says most of her friends in Baltimore have either died or moved away, with the exception of Ms. Lola Mae Davis, who just turned 92 years of age, and her son Clem and his sister Evelyn. With the move to West Virginia, she will also be closer to her long time friend Annette Mussa, who relocated to North Carolina. She and Annette worked together for many years.

Bernice will tell you about yourself though and if you ever get on her bad side; she will put you in your place in a New York minute. She speaks up for herself and will be stubborn if she does not want to do something. She can also be kind of bossy but I have learned to just listen and do whatever I had planned to do anyway. She is not the most patient person and hates waiting for people to do what they said they would do. Neicy likes to know what is going on in your life and has no problem asking you and then giving you advice, whether you ask for it or not. I have learned to accept her moodiness, because that is a part of her personality.

Bernice is now preparing to move back to Beckley, the place she never wanted to move to as a teenager, to settle down and really enjoy retirement life. The only thing keeping her in Baltimore is the need to sell her house. She is agonizing over selling her home in Baltimore with the real estate market going down the drain in so many areas. I constantly remind her that she has the best of both worlds, a home in Baltimore and one in West Virginia.

I sometimes have to be the older sibling when it comes to giving Neicy advice. We have become very close in these later years, with her living in Baltimore and me in Washington. I am going to miss her when she relocates back to West Virginia. Now I will have another reason for visiting more often. She is single and has the choice of getting on a train, plane or bus and heading down for a few weeks whenever the mood hits her. After spending a few days there she can come back and make some money in her beauty shop, while she waits for a buyer for her house. We spend a lot of time on the phone talking about positive things to help her get through this transition. I tell her to visualize herself sitting on the front porch of the home place in West Virginia, counting the cars as they pass by the house on the corner of 8th Street. While reminiscing about the past she can look back to one of her fondest memories, the time when she was treated to lunch in the private dining room of the Oval Office in the White House, as pictured above and below, on her 60th birthday. Bernice remarked that this lunch was a long way from the times we had to sneak and eat those school lunches of cold eggs and fat back sandwiches carried to school in a greasy brown paper bag.

Photo taken in the private oval office dining room with left to right my friend, Helen Robinson, President Clinton's White House Staff Member, Betty Pointer, me and my sister, Bernice.

Dorothy Marie was born in 1938, the fourth child. Dorothy or as we call her Dot, has had a colorful and vibrant life. She was also born in Ingram Branch in the house my parents had lived in since coming to West Virginia. Dot spent some of her early years in Virginia with our Grandmother Susie. She went to elementary school with her cousins there before returning to Ingram Branch to attend the community school and then move on to Junior High School in Beards Fork, West Virginia. When she returned to West Virginia she and my brother ended up in the same grade, until they graduated from Stratton in 1957. My brother was skipped a grade and he cried and told Mama that he did not want to leave his friends and classmates. Of course his tears went unnoticed. He and Dot were the second and third children to graduate from Stratton High School in Beckley.

Dot was always a chubby child. She would always say that Mama had mocked her when she was carrying her. The old folks used to say if you laughed at someone while you were pregnant, the child would be mocked. Mama tells about the friend of hers who used to always make fun of this lady's big belly and how she walked to make her laugh. The lady was slew footed and walked funny so she feels that Dot was mocked by this. Mama also said that when Dot was born, Grandma said she had a veil over her face. In the old days it was said that being born with a veil over your face enabled you to see dead people. We see Grandma Susie still helping to deliver her children's babies. Dot was always afraid of her shadow, and she always slept with her head under the bed covers. It is funny how she will now walk into a funeral home alone to view a body and not be afraid.

Growing up in the summer times meant picking blackberries and Dot was always the one who ended up with few berries in her bucket. If you just said you saw a snake, she would take off running. On one occasion she went off by herself to pick from a big patch of blackberries and as soon as she put her hand in the blackberry patch, she saw a big black snake. That was the end of the berries and the bucket, by the time she finished running home.

When it was time to go outside after dark to get coal or water from the spring, Dot would not go out by herself. She was spared from working on the farm in the country because she was one of the three youngest. Her summers were spent playing outside and getting involved in activities in the community and church, where she had been baptized. She had a really good childhood friend, Margaret Frances Taylor, and they are still friends today. She is probably the only one of us who maintained a friendship in such a close relationship with a childhood friend, after all of those years. Some of it may be due to the fact that Dot never really left West Virginia like all the other siblings did. She always told Mama and Daddy that she was never going to leave West Virginia.

While living in Ingram Branch, Dot was a favorite of our neighbors, the Berger's, Fred and Essie. She was also one of the teacher's pet in elementary school. She went to the same elementary as the older siblings and finished the 7th and 8th grades at Beards Fork. Photo to the left is of me, Dot and our little playmates, Carolyn, her brother and Lawrence.

After the move to Beckley and she was older, she and Josephine became running buddies. They both liked the same things and the same friends. They were the ones that wanted to dance and play cards with their friends. She and Josephine used to slip out of the house at night to hang out in the streets. They would drink home made wine and party with the older neighbors.

Of course, she did not escape from being a part of The Evans Family singing group. She always liked working in church and when we moved to Beckley, she joined Welcome Baptist church where she was a member of the Sunday school and the BYPU. She is still a member of Welcome Baptist Church where Rev. David Allen is the pastor with his wife, Gloria, serving along side of him. They are more than her pastor, but are also friends of our family. I still consider Welcome Baptist my church and look forward to worshiping there yearly. Dot has served as an usher and trustee for many years. She is also a member of the Missionary Society. She does not need to belong to any organization to be characterized as a Missionary, because she is the first to help anyone in the community.

Dot was the first to know everybody in our new home town of Beckley. She was always the one to find out all the neighborhood gossip and news. She has always been friends with the older women in the neighborhood. While in school she did not get too involved in extra activities after school. None of us really got that involved because we were always required to go straight home after school was over each day. She was a favorite with the office staff at Stratton and she worked in the school office helping the school secretary, the wife of the assistant principal, Thomas Evans. Maybe it was because they shared the same first name.

Dot met her first husband, Fred Neal, before she graduated from Stratton High School, in 1957. He was in the army and I think she fell in love with that uniform. His family lived across from the community playground and I guess she caught his eye one day when he was home on leave. It wasn't long after she graduated that she started to talk about getting married. Marriage meant that she would be leaving home, and since she did not want to leave Beckley, this was the choice she made. On December 21, 1957, she and Fred were married in the home of his parents.

Fred's mother and father, Ed and Member Neal, and his siblings, William, Russell, Walter, Sherman, Betty Lee, Ollie, Lilly, Juanita, Linner Mae, and Lou, were one of the larger families in our neighborhood. Dorothy is the mother of three children: Fred Joseph, Teresa Marie, and Clyde Ellis. Her grandchildren are Ashley, DeAngelo, Vaneasha, Damesha, Omara, and Ameera.

In 1960, Dot's first child, a son named Fred Joseph was born. The Joseph was taken from our sister's Josephine's name. She sat up housekeeping and was enjoying being a wife and mother. Dot had two additional children, Clyde Ellis born in 1962 and Teresa Marie, born in 1965. Her marriage to Fred ended in divorce. However, Dot remained close to Fred's family. Among those family members, on Fred's side, are her nieces Patricia and her husband Leon Perry, Sandra, Dorothy, and their families, her nephews, Larry, Milton and their families, and Dell's wife Janice, and their family, who moved back to Beckley, and became part of her extended family.

Her second marriage was to Willie White. Her marriage to Willie White lasted until his death. She recently wed her present husband, Elder James Denson, a friend of the family for many years. He served as the pastor of a neighborhood church, in the early 70/80's, before relocating to Mt. Airy, NC. He is once again living in Beckley, and enjoying retirement as a pastor, although still preaching the word.

At one time Dot moved to Milwaukee for a short time but made her way back to Beckley. Dot was always extra close to Mama and Daddy, since she never left Beckley for any long period of time. She is just a West Virginia girl and you can't take her out of those mountains.

Dot is living a full life in Beckley. She knows everyone in the neighborhood and everyone knows her. Dot loves to cook and will give you the shirt off of her back. She enjoys working in the kitchen preparing the meals that are served at different occasions. She can always be found cooking someone's favorite dish from her own kitchen. Her house is now the house that we gather at when the family comes together at the same time. If you need a good home cooked meal, you need only stop by her house on any given day. She does not like to eat leftovers and the word is out because there is always someone close by to relieve her of them. Leonard (Lenny) Powell, a family friend, looks forward to Dot cooking his favorite pig feet and sweet potato pie. She learned her cooking skills by watching mama cook.

One thing about Dot is she will tell you off in good fashion. She doesn't bite her tongue. If you are her friend you will know it and if you aren't, you will know it also. She is pretty much of a homebody and will not stay away from home too long. She loves to decorate and will change things around in a minute. You can expect to see changes in her home each time you walk in, after being away for a few months. She is obsessive about keeping a clean house. If she ever comes to visit you, the first thing she will do is start cleaning. I guess she got that from Mama because our house was always spotless and clean.

Dot was fortunate to find work with the Webb family early on and since that time she has been part of their family, although they are a Caucasian family. The Webb's were both practicing doctors and when their children were babies, Dot cared for them as if they were her own. John and Joseph (Joey), and their parents have been like members of our family also. Joey was about three months old at the time she started taking care of them and now that he is grown he calls her regularly and never fails to visit her when he comes home to visit.

We can always look for him to be at our 4th of July cookout that we hold yearly, under the big shade tree, in the front yard, that Daddy used to love sitting under.

Dot was in a bad car accident when she was going to see about her son Fred, who was away at college. She still suffers from the effects of that accident. Truly we are blessed to have her still here with us because the car was totaled, and looked like no one could have survived. She was doing what she usually does, when it comes to the welfare of her children, looking after them like a mother hen. She struggled, as a single parent, but with the help of family and good friends, she was able to keep them together and provided the best home for them. They showed her their appreciation when she celebrated her 70th birthday and they surprised her with a wonderful birthday celebration. That celebration came two months after Dot survived quadruple heart bypass surgery. They celebrated with her again in November 2010, at her wedding. After being a single mom for many years, and living by herself when the children were all moved away from home, Dot is now enjoying being married once again and taking care of her new husband. A mother's sacrifices are never forgotten by grateful children.

Dot is a fashion diva. She loves getting dressed up and matching head to toe. She loves to wear her fancy hats and wigs. She will get all of her hair cut off in a minute and is always trying something new on it. When it does not work out she calls Bernice the "family beautician" who in turn scolds her first and then proceeds to tell her what she needs to do to correct the problem.

Dot was the one who was there during the times that Daddy was sick and during Mama's last illness. Dot was the one that could get Mama to take her medicine and eat when no one else could. She was the caregiver who provided loving care during those times when we were not there. Those who don't know think she is the "baby" in the family.

Fred, her oldest child graduated from high school and went away to college. When he left college he made his way to Washington. He lived with us for a short time and worked for a period of time at Canada Dry, where Billy was employed. He met and fell in love with Lorraine (Cutie) Broadwater. Freddie,

Cutie, and her son Andre were spending so much time together, at our house, that I told him it seemed like it was time for him to get his own place. Fred said years later that was the best advice I gave him. It wasn't long before Lorraine and Fred were married, in 1985, and a few years later, they had their own son, DeAngelo.

Fred is presently married to the former Sharon Smith, pictured below. His son, DeAngelo is pictured on the right. Fred is enjoying being a highly sought after tennis instructor, entrepreneur, and personal trainer, as well as step-father to Sharon's sons, Jeremy, Tyranny, Marcus and Sahr Felix.

Clyde, the second child, was a little on the wild side, but not too wild for his Granny to tame, using her switches made of love. When Dot couldn't whip them, she would send the kids down to Mama's so she could straighten them out. She always had something to tell about what Clyde had done. Clyde loved having fun and after graduating from high school, Clyde left home to enter the military service, where he was honorably discharged, after completing his tours of duty. He was married to

Libby Askew and they had one daughter, Ashley. After leaving the military and spending time here in Washington, he relocated to Atlanta, GA, where he is an employee of the U.S. Postal Service. Clyde still resides in Georgia and he is the father of two additional children, a son Omari and a daughter, Ameera. I tease him about still being a "mama's boy," because he calls his mother just about everyday. One thing I can say about Clyde is that he will pay his debts. I loaned him some money once, and although it took longer to pay back than he thought, whenever he talked to me, he would say, "Aunt Gearl, I haven't forgotten that I owe you." He did repay.

Teresa the baby girl is the one who stayed close to home. She was like my Mama and Daddy's newest child. Being the only girl, living close to them, she spent a lot of time with them in their home, and she became like their child and grandchild rolled into one. Teresa finished high school and worked in Beckley, before marrying the love of her life, Martin Staunton. Teresa heard him on the radio, when he was working as a disc jockey, and liked the sound of his voice. She made the call that brought them together. They are the proud parents of two daughters Vaneasha and Damesha. Martin is one of the celebrities in the family, who gets pointed out when recognized by the shoppers in our small town. He is now a news Anchor for WVNX television station in West Virginia. Martin was one of the few African Americans on a network station, in West Virginia.

When they were living in Beckley, as a newly wed couple, they were in the role of house parents to troubled teens. Teresa and Martin relocated to Charleston, West Virginia for a few years, where he was a news anchor for a TV station and she worked for the City of Charleston. Teresa and Martin have recently moved back to Beckley, where she is now employed by one of the local physicians. Cass is still anchor at the local affiliated CBS station. Teresa always was there for her Mother. She and Cass were blessed with many friends around as they were starting to make a new life for their family in their home in Charleston.

It's funny how people end up, years later, in families that their parents were friends with, in another time and another place. Martin's father, John Staunton,

who lived at Ingram Branch, West Virginia, in the 40's and 50's, when we lived there, grew up with Teresa's mother, aunts and uncles. We always joked, as children growing up, that everyone who lived in Ingram Branch was kin to each other, except us. The Peake families and Staunton families were the predominant families living in the community. Now I guess we can say that we are also kin to those families. Teresa and Cass as we call him spend quality time raising their daughters, Vaneasha and Damesha, pictured above, and working with the youth in Welcome Baptist Church. Both girls love to sing, as well as Teresa, who has a gifted voice for singing gospel songs.

Leonard Irie was born in 1940. After losing their first son at birth, my parents were blessed with another one who was proudly named after Daddy. The middle name Irie was added and we always called him that so there was no mistaken who we were calling. Of course, Daddy would have never stood for us calling him by his first name. Irie entered a home made up mostly of females who were more than willing to spoil him. From day one Irie received lots of love and attention from the females in his life. Uncle Joseph used to call him handsome, and not knowing that he was being given a compliment, instead of being proud, he would cry. Uncle Joe would then turn around and on another occasion tell Irie that little girls were made of sugar and spice and everything nice. He would then proceed to say that boys were made of puppy dog tails. I can only imagine what that did to his self-esteem.

Even at that, he was the center of attention before I came along and knocked him somewhat out of the spotlight by becoming the baby of the family. Of course, even today we all still give him lots of special attention.

Irie was always experimenting on things. He got along well with the girls. He had the added convenience of getting his own room as a teenager while all the girls had to share two beds and one room. Irie always had lots of friends to play with. When the Browns moved in next door, at Ingram Branch, he acquired one of his best childhood playmates, Walter. They were both full of adventure. Walter had a sister, Shirley, and she became my best friend.

As the result of these friendships we shared a lot of good times growing up. We were in elementary school together and when he was doing so much better than his classmates in school, the teacher made the decision to skip him to a higher grade.

This decision put a little distance between us and he ended up in the same grade with our sister, Dot. He cried and did not want to go to the next class because he had to leave his best buddy behind. Mama insisted that he be skipped and he and Dot ended up completing the rest of their school years together. Irie eventually got used to them being in the same grade, but I don't know if Dot ever did. He would start junior high at Beards Fork for the first year but then when we moved to Beckley in 1953, he entered Stratton Junior High.

While growing up in Ingram Branch, Irie never spent a summer that he did not get into some kind of trouble. He and Walter Brown used to play Tarzan by swinging on vines from the trees, over the creek and jumping from the rooftops of buildings. It was doing one of those jumps when he got a hole knocked in his head and was afraid to tell anyone. Of course, when Daddy got ready to give him a haircut, the secret was out. One other incident that could have been devastating was the time he and Walter were playing with dry ice in a soda bottle on the 4th of July. When the bottle failed to explode, Irie proceeded to pick it up to put the top on tighter. Well the bottle exploded right in his face and he still has the scar under his eye to show for it. Each time he looks in the mirror he probably remembers how it got there.

Irie liked to "shoot" marbles and was a champion player and he won many games. He had a sack of pretty marbles and a great collection of comic books and baseball cards. If we had only known that one day those baseball cards would be worth money, we probably would have kept them in better condition and in a safe place. Irie's other hobbies were playing dominos and checkers. He and Daddy used to play all the time. He also liked playing cards. He and my sisters would spend hours playing bid whist and tonk. They also used to talk in what we called "pig Latin." I never did learn the language.

Irie and I joined the church during the summer revival with our friends. We would go to revival and they would make all the "sinners" and anyone who had not been baptized, come sit on the front row, which they called the "mourners bench." After the preacher had preached they would pray over you until you decided to get saved and join the church. On the final night of the last revival we attended in Ingram Branch, he and I were the last of the Evans family to join Ingram Grove Baptist Church. We were baptized the following Sunday in the creek that all the other siblings had been baptized in. It was also the same creek that we played in during the summer months. We never did learn how to swim in the creek, but as children during those summer months, we looked forward to wading in the water.

Irie had the responsibility of taking care of the family pet, which happened to be a cat. He also had the responsibility for getting rid of the entire litter of kittens that would arrive during the summer months. Most of those kittens ended up in what was the "white neighborhood" by way of the railroad tracks. He also was responsible for feeding the chickens and collecting the eggs. We played with the chickens during the week and sometimes they ended up on our plate as Sunday dinner. When we went to feed them the next day, there would always be one missing.

Irie was never fond of vegetables, and neither was I. He and I would sneak and put the vegetables in his pocket at the table and when we went outside to play, he would empty his pockets. There was an unwritten rule in our house, enforced by Daddy, that you ate everything on your plate, or you stayed at the table until you finished. Once in our haste to go outside to play he forgot to empty his pockets. On washday the secret was out when the vegetables were found floating, on top of the water, in the washing machine.

Irie was not excited about leaving his friends at Ingram Branch either but he made the adjustment pretty quickly. Entering the 8th grade at Stratton he made friends there and in the neighborhood. I remember his excitement when he got his first bicycle after we moved to Beckley. Josephine had bought it for him. Although it was a used bike, he was still excited.

Irie was the first black boy to play baseball in the white Babe Ruth and Post Lodge 32 Leagues in Beckley. He was a good baseball player and often hit the home runs that won the games. We were excited when we heard his name called on the radio and saw it in the local newspapers the next day. He did not know it but he was making history for the Negroes in Beckley. He said they did not want him to play and insisted that he bring his original birth certificate to prove how old he was. Mama gave it to him, he presented it to them, and he said he never got it back. Recently, I read an article from an old newspaper and it stated "they were waiting to get his birth certificate before they could certify him to play." I guess they were looking for any excuse to keep him off the ball field. He probably could have excelled in the majors, if he had been given the chance.

Irie got a job working at the Tip Top restaurant washing dishes and cleaning up while he was in the 8th grade. He was making $10.00 a week working on Saturdays and after school. He also played junior varsity basketball at Stratton.

In addition to that he was also the bass singer in our traveling singing group, The Evans Family. He later joined Welcome Baptist Church, as we all did, and attended Sunday school and BYPU activities. He was not that excited about sitting in church and would have rather been outside playing with his friends who did not have to go to church.

Leonard Irie graduated from Stratton in 1957 and went directly into the Army Reserve for six months at the age of 17. After he completed his reserve duty time he and the other guys hitchhiked to another town to join the Air Force. None of them were accepted so they came back and signed up for the draft. Soon he received his acceptance letter from "The President." welcoming him into the armed services. With his letter in hand, he left home to begin his military career.

Irie spent his first overseas tour of duty in the Panama Canal Zone. It was there he met Vilma Peterson, the daughter of Efriam and Julia Peterson. Vilma and her family are natives of Panama. Vilma's siblings are Efriam, Jr., Ricardo, Carlos and Veronica. After they were married, he brought Vilma back to the states with their son Ernest and his stepson Dean. Leonard's natural children and adopted children with Vilma are Ernest, his wife Estella, Angela, Dean, Natisha, and Gregory, and his grandchildren are, Raven, Essence, Asanti, Christopher, Jayla, and Nyjason. Throughout Leonard's many years of travel, and the many friends he met along the way, their children and grandchildren became a part of his extended family, but are too numerous to name. He speaks lovingly of all of them.

Although their marriage ended in divorce, Irie and Vilma have remained very close friends and he has been very supportive of their children, grandchildren and great grandchildren. When Irie plans his trips home, he always adds in enough days so he can stop in Columbia, SC on his way to West Virginia, to spend time with his family, and to make the same stop, in South Carolina, on his way back to Georgia. Vilma has raised and taken care of many children over the years and take great joy in being a mother and grandmother to them all.

When Irie returned to the states he went to Drill Sergeant Instructor's School at Ft. Jackson, SC. He spent 18 months there before going to Vietnam, for his first tour of duty, in October 1967, staying there until October 1968.

In May of 1967, Irie spent some time at Edgewood Arsenal in Maryland, before he went to his first tour of duty in Vietnam. He later found out that prior to being sent there, he and other soldiers, for two months, had been used as guinea pigs in an experiment with LSD. They were being tested to see how the drug affected their ability to function. This experiment was done without their consent or knowledge, and they did not find out about it until years later, when some high ranking military officer committed suicide.

After that suicide an investigation was conducted that pulled the covers off of this horrendous breech of liberty. He said that at one point one of the soldiers told them they were giving them LSD, but being naïve and a small town boy, he had no idea what was taking place. He said they would put them in a padded room where they watched their reaction. It is sad when your own government abuses you and then tries to cover it up. He and many of the other soldiers who were exposed to the Agent Orange in Vietnam have had to fight to get compensation for the damage that was done to them, while they were trying to serve their country.

After his first tour of duty in Vietnam, he reported back to Drill Sergeant Duty at Ft. Bragg, NC from 1968 to 1970. It was at that time that he received his next call to serve in Vietnam for a second tour of duty from 1970 to 1971. Before he was shipped out, we experienced the loss of our sister, Josephine. That was a sad time for him and he really did not want to go back to the war. Mama was so distraught with losing her child that she tried everything to get him exempted from serving in Vietnam again. I wrote letters to Senator Robert Byrd for her, but she was told that unless she had lost another son or her spouse in wartime, he could not be exempted from serving there again.

With great disappointment he went off once again to serve his country during wartime. He spent time here with me before he left and told me how so many of the soldiers had been able to get duty, out of harms way, while serving in Vietnam. After his service there, he returned once again to Panama for three years in 1971.

After that tour of duty in Panama, he returned to the States and completed his tour of duty at Ft. Benning, GA in 1980. He retired after 22 and ½ years of honorable service. He decided to make his home in Columbus, GA, where he still resides.

Irie received many honors and awards while serving his country. He is so modest that until I begun to write about him, I had no idea what his military service had been like and how decorated a soldier he had been.

Among his many awards were the Meritorious Service Medal, Republic of Vietnam Silver Action Medal, Unit Citation Badge, Good Conduct Medal (6th award), Army Commendation Medal, National Defense Service Star, and One Bronze Service Star.

While in Vietnam he received the Combat Infantry Badge, Bronze Star Medal (3 Oak leaf clusters with V), Four Overseas Service Bars and the Republic of Vietnam Gallantry Cross, Unit Citation Badge with Palms (3rd Award). He served his country steadfastly and he is humble and does not talk about his service in any great length.

Like most veterans that were in the bush, he never talks much about that period of time in his life. He prefers to keep that part of his military career locked away in his memory. I know that sometimes he has nightmares from those experiences, especially when he suffered the loss of fellow soldiers in his platoon and his life was spared.

Irie had spent most of his time in service in South Carolina and Georgia. We looked forward to his coming home. While in service, he also started to send money back to help out at home, as all the others had done before him. Daddy's time in the mines was winding down and help was needed from all of the children. Irie grew into manhood in the service.

Leonard is now married to Queen Cannon, the daughter of Thomas and Van Esther Cannon. Queen's siblings are Hattie Joyce, Deborah, Donna, Thomas, Jr., Robert, Joseph, Donald, Eddie, Horace and James. They are all natives of Georgia. In February 1981, they were married. Leonard met his second wife, Queen Cannon, in Georgia. She was in the Navy so he became a military spouse. The tables were now turned around for him. They moved to Maryland where she was assigned, and when she got an overseas assignment to Italy, he went there for a little over a year. He returned to the states early and went back to his adopted hometown of Columbus, GA. He would remain there until Queen retired and came back home. Queen is a collector of dolls and their house is full of dolls from all over the world. She probably has every Barbie doll ever made. In addition, she also has another set of valuable Lladro figurines that take up the rest of the empty space in the house.

Leonard and Queen did not have children, but Queen has always treated his children and grandchildren as if they were her own. Queen loves to shop. Leonard can drop her off at the shopping mall and go back hours later and she is still shopping. She also is well read and keeps up with everything happening, so she can give you her opinion of the latest news events. She has always supported Leonard in everything he does. We still call him Irie and I guess that took her some getting used to while listening to us talk.

Since Irie's retirement, he has had more time to spend with his birth family and he enjoys every minute of it. He said he missed out on so much while he was in the military. Every summer we would always try to go home for the 4th of July and he would stay longer than anyone else. He was trying to make up for the lost time. Even today, when he returns home to West Virginia, he comes prepared to stay for an indefinite period of time. He said his greatest joy, during those visits, was sitting down having long conversations with Mama to find out all about her life, especially when she was growing up.

He looks forward to spoiling his grand and great grandchildren and spending time with them. He keeps up with what each one is doing, and if you are doing well, he will praise you, but if you are doing badly, he has no problem letting you learn your lesson the hard way. It's called "tough love." He will help you until you start taking it for grantee and then he puts on the brakes. I have not been around his offspring's much, but look forward to the times when we do get together. Leonard still has a love for playing checkers and spends time with his retired army buddies seeing who can play the best game, while talking about old times.

Irie is very protective of his family and can be counted on when a family crisis arises. If you want to get on his bad side, try to do something or say something unkind about his family. Growing up his big sisters acted as his protector and now he protects us. I guess all the early spoiling is paying off for us now.

He considers himself a very good cook and looks forward to getting on the grill all day long to make sure that the grilling is under his control. He is so loved and I could not wish for a better brother.

LEONARD'S PHOTO WITH HIS CHILDREN AND GRANDCHILDREN

Chapter 6

Memories from My Early Life – 1942 - 1953

Now that I have introduced you to my family, I look forward to having you walk down memory lane with me. Continue to sit back in your easy chair, with your favorite drink, and enjoy the journey. I promise you, you will not get bored as you witness, through words, my life's story.

I must not have been born when this family photo was taken of my five siblings or I was either too small to be a part of this family portrait. I often asked why I was not included in this photo. I was destined to be different and in 1942, shortly after my birth it was evident that my life would be full of change. The first change was my name. My birth certificate was filled out with the middle name "Ann" and my mother promptly changed it to "Geraldine." She said that her friend, who was with her when I was born, gave the doctor the wrong name. I know that my first name is the same as my Mom's but I never thought to ask her where the name "Geraldine" came from. To my knowledge, I don't know of any ancestors or close associates of my Mother who has that name. It was simple to change a name in those days; they just crossed out one name and wrote another one over top of it. My birth certificate reflects how simple legal remedies were in those days. I must have been a special delivery also because my Mom still kept the calendar for the year 1942, along with my baby bottle and a gift box from Johnson and Johnson that contained a box of baby powder and baby oil. The calendar was from the company store, Mary Frances Coalmining Company, Ingram Branch, West Virginia.

I made my grand entrance in the house that would be my home for the first eleven years of my life. Since my father worked for the coalmine company, the doctor who delivered me was the "company" doctor. Dr. Puckett was his name. I was the first of Mama's children that Grandma did not help deliver. After making the trip on five other occasions, I guess she felt Mama could handle this one on her own. I was the seventh child born to my mother, who incidentally was also the seventh child, born to her mother. In later years people would tell me that the seventh child had some sort of psychic intuition. I don't know how true that is but I do know that there have been times when I felt like I knew something before it happened, or I knew someone was going to say something before they said it. This leaves you feeling eerie, when it actually happens, pretty much the way you knew it would.

I was born into an average "colored" family in the early 40's. I am still a "coalminer's daughter." We lived in a segregated community called Ingram Branch, West Virginia. Early on we knew where the line was drawn, because the whites lived at the beginning of the "hollow," and the colored lived on the other side of the railroad tracks. Our part of the community was closest to the entrance to the coalmine, where we had the unlucky benefit of inhaling all the coal dust, seeping from inside the mines. That location was also where you heard the loud noise from the tipple, as the coal was being loaded into railroad cars. The picture to the left is of me and my sister, Dot, standing in front of the house I was born in.

Although separated by the railroad tracks, everyone shopped at the same company store and was attended to by the same company doctor. We all lived in houses that looked the same and were owned by the coal company. Once you were no longer an employee, you had to move. These houses were without running water and inside toilets. We used outhouses, slop jars and got very familiar with the Sears and Montgomery Wards catalog, as our source of toilet paper. You learned early which pages were best for each function. We went to separate schools and did not have white playmates. We went to separate churches and socialized in separate venues, as was the practice for those times. We all knew our place in "society" and made the best of it. As I am remembering about the school system, there was a schoolhouse provided for the black children, but none for the white children. The white children rode buses to a neighboring community to attend school. At this point in time, I can't remember why that was the case.

We had the necessities for life, but were by no means "well off." We probably had more than some families and less than others. Some of the fathers took better care of their families than others. The one thing we had in our family was an abundance of love. We were always close as a family and were never allowed to fight among ourselves.

My father was the "breadwinner" in the family. He worked in the coal mines for as long as I can remember. Mama stayed home during those early years providing the guidance and discipline, as needed. My mother believed entirely in "spare the rod and spoil the child." She was not the Mom that sent you to get the switches for your punishment, she got her own. I never received many whippings on my bare legs because they would leave noticeable welts. However whenever there was a need, welt or not, I got what was promised. The thing that I hated about whippings was the promise of one. I would think that Mom had forgotten the promised one, and as I prepared for bed I would hear that familiar voice saying "didn't I tell you I was going to whip you?" That promise was always kept.

In hindsight, every whipping I got was deserved and I probably would not be where I am today, had my parents not taken their child rearing responsibilities seriously.

As the breadwinner in the family, Daddy never stayed home from work unless he was sick. Each morning Mama got up and fixed his breakfast, packed his lunch pail and saw him off to work. Because he left early, we usually ate breakfast without him, unless it was on the weekend. The whistle from the coalmine was our signal that his shift had ended and we knew that no matter where we were, we needed to make our way home, in time for supper. After he had taken his bath, dinnertime was family time. We all sat at the table in our designated seats and once Daddy blessed the food we were allowed to eat. There was not a lot of conversation at the table, which may seem strange, but that was just the way things were. Daddy would always say, "You can't talk with your mouth full of food." There would be plenty of time to talk after dinner was over. I was a finicky eater and Mom would often make a special meal for me. I was an adult before I learned to enjoy eating vegetables. I still refuse to eat green peas and will pick every pea out of a dish before it goes into my mouth.

At Christmas there was no wondering what you got because everything that was yours was placed on the table at the place reserved for you at mealtime. Of course we always had a real tree that was put up and decorated by all of us. We always looked forward to that time because it was very exciting. Mama and Daddy would go to town on paydays and come back with lots of bags that we were not allowed to open. They found places in the house to hide them, but the older kids always managed to find them. They still did not know what was theirs until Christmas morning. They found a way, using a hair pin, to open the locked wardrobe door, without the key, that had been thoughtfully removed, by my Mother.

We couldn't wait for the next payday when they would go to town to shop and we could ramble once again. I was always happy with what I got because we did not expect a lot and always received more. We always received a new outfit, winter coats and of course boots and shoes. We couldn't wait to go outside Christmas morning to see what our friends had received as presents. Sometimes the younger children received more than their older siblings.

Christmas was also special because we might not have gotten a lot of toys, but everyone received something special, and that evening the house would be filled with the smell of good food cooking. We always went to church on Christmas Eve for the traditional Christmas program and play and the bags of fruit that were given out by the company store. We always participated in the Christmas pageants. We would hurry home so we could go to bed and wait for Santa Claus to come. It seemed that on that night sleep was hard to come and we were always afraid that if we were caught awake, we would not get our presents. I remember seeing in the fireplace what looks like footprints indicating that Santa had come sliding down the chimney. I did not know at the time that Daddy had put the prints there.

One Christmas in particular stands out in my mind because that was the time my brother received a big red wagon as one of his gifts. We had fun riding all through the house. It was usually very cold so a wagon was no good in the snow. Mama had the most fun with that wagon because she said as a child she always wanted a wagon. We rode her all through the house and she was like a child, happy, as if the wagon was for her.

The only time I was afraid that there would be no Christmas was the last year we lived in Ingram Branch and Daddy came home from the company store to tell us that Santa Claus had fallen off the truck he was riding on. There was a tradition that on Christmas Eve the company boss would put someone in a truck and ride them through the hollow singing Merry Christmas to all in the community. It seems that this particular Christmas, Santa Claus had been sampling from the bottle in his back pocket. In other words he was drunk. Luckily he managed to make all of his deliveries and everyone had a Merry Christmas after all.

For a long time I believed there really was a Santa Claus. I stopped believing in him when we moved and no longer had a fireplace for Santa to enter the house. I wrote a note to him and left it in the closet and lo and behold, the next day the note was still there. I guess I failed to let my parents know where I had placed the letter. Nevertheless after finding out that Santa really was my parents; some of the magic was gone. However, I guess it was still a good time to believe in something.

I was a skinny child and was prone to childhood ailments. My daily ritual was taking a dose of cod liver oil to keep me well. The medicine that was to be a cure all was castor oil given with a glass of orange juice. Because we did not have juice in a bottle, to this day I refuse to drink canned orange juice, because it still tastes like castor oil. We also had to wear around our necks in the winter time a mustard plaster bag; one of the ingredients was cooked onions. This was to keep us from catching colds. I guess it worked because we rarely got colds during the winter months. Maybe it was because the smell kept people away from you. Of course, we were not the only kids wearing those "necklaces."

As a coalminer's daughter, I learned what the meaning of the whistle blowing from the mine meant in the middle of the day. It signified that there had been an accident and all the families would rush to the tipple to see who had been brought out injured or killed.

On several occasions, Daddy was one of the injured coming out of the mines on a stretcher. He had had his back broken and legs broken at different times. I remember being so afraid of his crutches that I would not go in the room or get any where near him.

My earliest childhood memory dates back to the time during World War II. I was a little over two years old and I can remember someone coming through the community during the day saying "Lights out tonight." When I asked questions later I learned that was a precaution taken against bombs being dropped during the night hours. I can also remember us having to use Kerosene lamps as a source of light. My mom said I couldn't possibly remember this but I know it is from my memory and not from someone telling me. I also remember when the war was over and the celebrating that took place when the news reached the coal camp. There were people running and shouting "The War is over." Some of them were beating on pots and pans and some of the men were shooting their pistols and hunting rifles in the air. I also remember my parents having to use ration stamps to purchase certain goods, especially sugar. I found some of those old stamps when I was cleaning out my mother's closets. Each person in the household was issued a separate ration book. She, like me, had a habit of holding on to things from the past.

My life growing up those first few years was not complicated as a child. I was allowed to be a child, who had few chores, because I was the youngest in the family. In the summer when school was out we enjoyed playing until dark. We spent our days walking barefoot over the rocks, wading in the creeks, running along the rail road tracks and climbing onto the rail cars filled with sand and coal. In addition to being siblings, my brother and I were also playmates.

We shared the same friends because his best friend always had a sister who was my best friend. We were typical children growing up in the 40's and 50's with few cares about what we were going to do the next day.

Summertime meant a break from school and being able to walk barefoot. The only draw back was when you walked where the chickens were kept and your feet were the recipient of their waste. We enjoyed picking blackberries for pies and picking up the walnuts that fell from the trees to be dried out for eating during the winter months. We always had fruit trees growing around the house so we did not have to buy fruit from the stores. It was our responsibility to pick the fruits in the summer months to be peeled and canned. We complained during the summer, but when winter came and Mama baked a cake and opened a can of peaches or baked a blackberry pie, we were very thankful for the treat. We also raised our own vegetables and spent time in the gardens. In addition, we had a chicken coop under the house where we raised chickens and gathered eggs.

Our meals were healthier then than they are now. We also looked forward to playing in the leaves that fell from the trees in the fall. We would rake them, pile them up and then jump in them, burying each other in them. We would then watch our parents burn them in the end. The summertime was also the time when the house got its final thorough cleaning before winter with new wallpapers being hung to spruce up things. My Mom would take her time making the flour paste to put on the back of the wallpaper, hang it carefully so that the seams were straight, then we would watch it crack at night after the fire was roaring in the fireplace, and the room had gotten too hot.

The end of summer was also the time for the dreaded "forest fires." When hunting season begun in the fall, we could always count on someone being careless with a match and starting a fire. Daddy enjoyed hunting and would bring home the rabbits and squirrels, that I was so afraid of, and would never even think about eating. Sometimes the men would kill deer and divide it up among the families. I did not eat it either, and it was not because I knew about Bambi. I have a vivid memory of the last forest fire before we moved away. Mama was away in Virginia. The forest fire was so bad that the miners were called out of the mines, to help the firefighters fight the fire, and to try to contain it to the woods.

We were surrounded by woods and the houses were always in danger of catching fire when the forest fires got out of control. I remember Daddy coming to the house and taking the water hose to water down the roof and sides of the house so it would not burn. That was such a frightening time and we were standing at the ready to throw things out of the house in case it did catch on fire. We were blessed that time because they got it under control. When I see the fires raging now in California and other places around the country, I know exactly how they feel. Even as a child I knew that a forest fire was dangerous and could change your life forever.

Just as summer presented time for playing, winter time presented unique situations also. One of the worst had to do with going to the springs to get water. In the summer time you did not mind, except for running from the snakes and frogs, but in winter the snow and ice were the culprits. I remember the winters being very cold. Of course we did not have central heat and we gathered around the pot bellied stove and fireplace in the front room to get warm. Most of our evenings were spent around the kitchen table playing cards and board games. We learned to play all kinds of card games, checkers and dominos. My older siblings had a language that they spoke called "Pig Latin." They would hold conversations that no one understood unless they also knew the language. I never did learn it. They would use the alphabets to make up new words. I guess if they had offered foreign languages in school we would have had no problem learning them also.

While we played games, Daddy would often pull out his guitar and play it. He was self taught so he wasn't that good but we enjoyed listening to him play. I think it brought back memories for him of his time growing up in a house that was filled with music and fun. While we were playing games and Daddy was playing the guitar, Mama was spending her time at the sewing machine making clothes for us. There were six of us so most of our clothes were made by her.

We also were the beneficiary of hand me downs. My brother was the lucky one because he was the only boy and did not get hand me downs. Mama also spent her time making quilts to help keep us warm at night. She always used the sacks that flour and sugar came in to make pillow cases and household items. Recycling has been around for a long time and there was nothing thrown away. I guess that is why I always said she was a "pack rat." I have to say I am struggling with that syndrome now.

Wintertime was also the time when it was time to slaughter the pigs and you knew that it would not be long before all the houses would smell the same from the cooking of chitterlings. Daddy and Hazel were the only ones in our family that enjoyed eating them so each winter Mama always cooked a big pot for them. We did not raise pigs but in our neighborhood everyone benefited from them because we all fed them slop to fatten them up for the big kill. This was also the time for making lye soap in the big black pots for washing and cleaning clothes. A fire would be made outside and the black pot put over it and the older children had to stir the pot. We did not know how dangerous a task that was. The lye soap was also used for bathing.

The worse part I remember about wintertime was how cold the house would get after the fire had gone out for the night. We had a coal burning stove, cooking stove and fireplaces, but the fire had to be put out at night. It was then we would stand in front of the stove and try to get warm before running to jump into the bed. Sometimes your legs would get so hot that they felt like they were on fire. Our beds were covered with lots of blankets, quilts and sometimes our winter coats. That was also the time of the year when you prayed no one "wet" the bed, because it was too cold to get up to use the pot, or slop jar, as some called it.

I entered elementary school in what was the primmer grade, at Ingram Branch. School was always fun for me. Our school at Ingram Branch was a two room school that had two teachers, Ms. Palmer and Ms McKinney. As you made progress grade wise you either moved to another row or seat in the classroom, or moved to the other side of the room. We had the same desk every day, but when we were promoted to the next grade, we moved to a different set of desks. Ms. Palmer and Ms. McKinney were early role models because they were dedicated to educating the children, regardless of their economic status. Unlike teachers of today, they stood out because they were dressed professionally, and they wore hats and white gloves every day. The teachers placed a lot of emphasis on good handwriting and cursive was the goal after learning to print. My teachers were devoted to us as students and they were a part of our community. They were given full permission to correct us if we misbehaved and would send a note home to our parents to outline what we did and what the consequences of our actions had merited. Sometimes it was being whipped with a switch or if you were lucky, you just got held in from participating in recess activities or made to stay behind to clean up the classroom at the end of the day.

They rehearsed us for our plays and had lots of activities to keep us occupied, while still teaching us the basics, reading, writing and arithmetic. My memory was always sharp and I could remember my lines before most of my classmates. After learning my lines, because I was competitive, I would memorize their lines and then wait for them to forget theirs so I could tell them what to say.

We walked to school in all kinds of weather. There was no such thing as snow days and closing due to the weather. I was also a little on the mischievous side. I don't know where I picked that up from but I always did like to fight. Of course, we would fight one minute and be playing with each other the next. On many times my teacher would send me home early so I would not fight after school, but I would just wait along the roadside until the others were released from school. My best friend in elementary school in Ingram Branch was my next door neighbor, Shirley (Brown) Wilborne, pictured on the right seated on the bottom row. Ironically as an adult I met someone else with the exact same name and we became good friends. When you read about my adulthood, then you will know that the child and adult Shirley Brown are different people.

Although Shirley, who was my best early childhood friend, and was bigger than me, did not keep me from picking a fight with her after school one day. I have no idea why we were fighting. She went home and told her mother and when her mother came out on the porch and saw me, I did what was unthinkable: I had the nerve to pat my behind at her in front of her mother. Of course, I paid for it when her mother told my mother what I had done. Shirley and I were best friends again the next day and remained so until we moved away. She is one of the few people that I have maintained some kind of friendship with from those early days. When I need to know what has happened to our old classmates, I can count on her for all the answers.

Post Script: I have to insert this here because of a recent conversation I had, a few days ago, with my childhood friend, Shirley. It was so refreshing to talk to someone who had shared so much with me as a young child growing up. She bought back to my memories some things I had forgotten. She told me how she used to get so mad at our teachers, because I was one of the "teacher's pets." She said she remembers how our 5th grade teacher, Ms. Turner, told the class who was "college material" students and my name was one of the three she called. It is interesting how what someone says to you as a child sticks with you. I guess I didn't remember her saying those words because to me it was something positive. However, it was planted in Shirley as something negative. She said we were the group who would be the first to complete our test and be allowed to go outside to play on the playground, while they were kept inside trying to finish theirs. She said we were also the ones the teacher sat at the front of the class. She also reminded me why we ended up going to what used to be the white school in the 5th grade. For some reason they moved the white children out of their school and moved us in. I stated earlier I couldn't remember why they went to school in another town. I left Ingram Branch a few months after I entered the 5th grade, so I guess that is why my memory was kind of fuzzy. She said that she hoped that when we left Ms. Palmer's class, we would not be the teacher's pets anymore, but that did not happen. She told how Ms. Palmer, who had really long hair, would let me comb it and when she would ask to comb it, she would tell her, "No because Martha is going to comb it." She said that would make her so mad that the one time she did let her comb it, she tried to comb all of her hair out.

We talked about how in the summer, to keep the sun from shining on us as we sat on the front porch, we would hang sheets, as shades, from one side of the porch to the other side. She also reminded me how our older siblings used to send us down to steal potatoes and onions from Mr. Baker's garden, and bring it back for them to cook. She said we didn't know any better and ate whatever they gave us. We laughed about how her sister Christine and my sisters, Hazel and Josephine would try to ditch us when they didn't want us to follow them. She told me the day we moved from Ingram Branch was the saddest day for her family. As we were leaving, they all cried and her mother said to them, "don't worry, we are getting out of here too." The next year, as soon as school was ended, they moved to Oak Hill, only a few miles from where we were living. Our families continued to be friends and I am so happy that all these years later, in 2011, we are still blessed to be friends, who can laugh and share those good memories.

There are many things that happen in childhood that make an impression on you, which you carry into adulthood. It could be the friendly smile and pat on the head of an adult who takes a special interest in you, or an event that is so tragic that the picture stays with you forever.

One of those memories was when a playmate's mother died during childbirth and the undertaker brought the body to the home or church before the funeral. As children we were curious to see a dead person so we went to take a look. My memory of the little baby boy lying in his mother's arms is still clear to me. I remember the baby's head being sunken in at the top and it looked like it was covered with some kind of powder. That night needless to say, I did not sleep very well and have had an unnatural fear of dead people since that time. Funny, because as I relayed this memory to Shirley, she said she too could close her eyes and see the little baby lying in his mother's arms. My mother would always say dead people could not hurt you. That may be so, but they could make you hurt yourself trying to get away from them. I guess my fear of the dead is somewhat unnatural.

In those early days, the bodies were brought back to the house for the wake. The bodies stayed there all night before being taken to the church for the funeral the next day. Fortunately for us we did not experience a death during that time so we were never subjected to that scene in our house. We were told that the reason for a wake was a carry over from early days because sometimes a person was not really dead, just in a coma, and someone was assigned to watch over them in case they awakened. That may have been so before undertakers came into the picture, but I don't think anyone would be waking up after their visit to the funeral home.

There was also a longstanding ritual before Memorial Day when Mama would get out the crepe paper to make a flower wreath so we could decorate the grave of the child she lost at birth. We never missed a year going to the cemetery to clean off the grave and leave the home made wreath as we remembered him. He is buried in what is now an overgrown mountain side, along with all the other souls that had that plot of land as their final resting place. May they all continue to Rest in Peace.

I never got to know my grandparents. My father's father died one month after I was born. His mother died in 1952. When Daddy returned from her funeral the only thing he brought back was a pair of her eyeglasses. We used to get the glasses out and put them on trying to see if we could see out of them. If we looked down, it was like stepping off a high step. I found those glasses when cleaning out my mother's house recently and finally let them go. It is funny what people hold onto from their past.

I never got to spend summers in Virginia as my siblings did. However, being the baby in the family, Mama would take me with her on trips to visit her mother and family in Virginia. I was too young to remember much about those visits. When my grandmother passed I remember reading the letter to Daddy that Mama wrote telling him that Grandma had passed. Before she left she had told us that she had received a telegram to come home soon because she was very ill. A few years earlier, when my Great Aunt Ellen passed, I went with Mama to the funeral and I remember being inquisitive about a telephone. I did not know what it was but I would see people pick it up and talk on it. In my curiosity, I picked it up and heard this voice say "number please." I was so frightened I immediately dropped the phone. That was my first experience with a telephone and I guess that is why I spend a lot of time on it now. It would be many years before we could afford such a luxury item.

I experienced my first train rides during those visits to Virginia with my mother. I can remember sitting on the bed with my new white shoes on and new outfit waiting for her to finish packing so we could go down the railroad track to meet the train. Those were exciting times for me because she would always pack a lunch for us to eat on our way. During that time coloreds were forbidden from eating in the cafeteria car. I can still hear the conductor saying "All Aboard" as we rushed to find a seat in the section set aside for colored passengers.

Although death was a part of growing up, the birth of a baby was also part of that time. We always knew when a baby was going to be born because at some point the children in the house would be sent to stay at a neighbor's house. When they returned, there would be a new baby in the house. As children, we did not know where babies came from. We were always told that the doctor bought the baby in the black bag he always carried in the house. And yes, we really believed it. I never heard the word "pregnant" used, but I knew the stork didn't bring the baby.

As I get older some of my early childhood memories are getting dim but I can still see how the house that I spent the first eleven years of my life in looked. There are no photos of the inside but we do have a few of the outside. We always had to go outside with Mama's brownie camera to take photos in the sunlight. That old house, filled with many memories, has been long gone since no one lived in it after we moved. I can still see the big pot bellied stove and the fireplace. In the winter time we had to go outside to dig coal from under the snow and in the summer time we went over to the tipple of the mine to pick up good coal after it had fallen from the coal cars. Sometimes we would be picking up coal after dark and would end up with a bucket full of slate. We did not realize the dangers of playing in those coal cars as children but luckily no one was ever seriously injured.

Our kitchen always had a pot on the stove with something good cooking in it. We would sit in the kitchen and watch Mama mixing the batter for her cake and then fight over who would get to lick the bowl and the spoon. Mama always made a sample cake because the big cake could not be cut until the proper time, after Sunday dinner. Our kitchen was very large because it also served as the dining room.

Sitting in the corner of the room was a wringer washer that was used to wash our clothes. There was a wash tub on the back porch that was used for bathing.

There was a barrel outside to catch the rain water that would supplement the spring water, for laundry. A water bucket with a dipper in it for drinking water was always near by and that water was also used for cooking. The one thing you had better not get caught at was drinking out of the dipper. The #3 tub would be filled with water on Saturday night and one by one we would be put in it for the weekly bath. With six children, by the time your turn came around more hot water, which was being heated on the stove, had to be added to the tub.

On Sunday mornings we got up early to have breakfast and get ready for Sunday school. Church was an all day affair. We were excited because that was the day you got to put on your "Sunday" clothes and shoes. The bad part about having Sunday shoes was that before they could wear out, your feet had gotten bigger and you had to wear them anyway. I guess I was one of the luckier ones because I have not had any foot problems due to wearing shoes that got too small too quick. If they wore out too soon, before it was time for new shoes, you learned how to cut pieces of card board and newspapers to put inside the shoe to keep your feet off of the ground.

Church was always an integral part of my upbringing. The preacher was always someone that you looked up to. In those days they preached fire and brimstone. There was only one church in the hollow for coloreds to attend. We were all saved and baptized by Rev. C. E. Ellis and joined Ingram Grove Baptist church at an early age. Each summer before you turned eleven years old; you were expected to "get saved" and be baptized.

I accepted Christ during the summer revival of 1952. During that revival session all of our classmates were at the age that we were expected to accept Christ and be baptized. We all went to the revival and each night they would

ask all "sinners" to come sit on the front seat. It was referred to as the "mourner's bench." The preacher would preach and the saints would pray and sing over us. Finally on the last night of the revival, we had all decided that day that we were going to join the church and be baptized. I, along with my brother, was the last in our family to be baptized.

I can't say that we knew what we were doing but we were afraid to be left on the bench. The photo to the left is of the church as it looked in 2008, when I made a visit to my birthplace. I was surprised to see that it looked the same as it did in 1952, when on that following Sunday, after we were saved, we were marched down to the creek that we played in, and as the congregation sang "Wade in the Water," we were all baptized.

We had been told by the older kids that if we got choked or swallowed any water during the baptism we had not been saved. We practiced holding our breath long enough to keep from coming up for air too soon. Thankfully, I didn't choke or swallow water. On my visit in 2008, I also found the creek that I was baptized in, depicted in the photo to the left, was still running, a little muddier but still flowing down stream. I marveled at how far I had come through the grace of God.

In the year 2000, when I made my pilgrimage to the Holy Land, I was baptized, on May 31st, by Bishop Milton A. Williams, Sr., a member of the Episcopacy of the AME Zion Church, in the River Jordan, as a symbolic recommitment to serving the Lord. This took place when we visited Yardenit, the Baptism area. This time I was not afraid of the water and I knew what I was doing. It may have been symbolic, but it was real to me. It seems that the circle was complete from my first baptism in a creek in West Virginia to the symbolic one in the River Jordan, on the other side of the continent. Just think a little child born on a coal camp in West Virginia made it all the way to the place where Jesus taught and walked. As a child, I never even dared to dream that such a thing would one day be possible. In fact, I probably had no idea where the Holy Land was located. My daydreams consisted mostly of looking forward to the next play day. I can't say we had low expectations, but the exposure we had in those days was limited mostly to what we read in the local newspaper and heard on the local radio station. If only Ms. Palmer and Ms. McKinney, my elementary school teachers, could see me now. I always knew that I was expected to do exceptional things, but I just did not know how they would be accomplished.

At Ingram Branch we never had a lot of overnight guests or company for dinner. Our favorite guest was Uncle Joseph, my mother's brother. We looked forward to his visit because he always brought us gifts and would give up money before he left. We could hardly wait to run to the company store to spend it on candy, cookies and "pop." For those who did not grow up down south, "pop" is what you know as "soda."

There were a few times when the preacher would eat at our house after Sunday service. That did not happen too often. I guess Daddy felt he had enough to do trying to feeding eight mouths every day. We knew that we would have to wait until after the adult guests had eaten before we could eat. Children were not allowed to eat at the table with the guest. We would just be thankful that they did not eat up all the food. Children were also not permitted to talk when grown ups were talking. In fact, you did not sit in the same room where the grown ups were having their conversations. We were taught to address all grownups with a handle to their name, i.e., Mr. or Mrs. We were taught to speak when you first entered a room for the first time. If you failed to speak, the question would be asked, "Did I sleep with you last night?" Sunday's were usually all day events, beginning with Sunday school. Our manners extended outside the house also, especially in church. All you needed was the evil eye to get your attention. Most of our parents were adept at using their backhand, and we always felt that they had eyes in the back of their head.

In summary, life for the first eleven years of my life was pretty ordinary. I made life long friends and learned valuable lessons that would prepare me for the next phase in my life, which would come when my parents announced that we were moving to another town. I can still remember the times we stayed up late at night listening to the only station that played Rhythm and Blues records, WLAC, with John R as the disc jockey. The station came out of Nashville, Tennessee, and he played the songs of Muddy Waters, Jimmy Reed, Lightning Slim, and Howling Wolf. We did not know until years later that the DJ was a white man who sounded black. Mama brought many records from Randy's Record Shop, as they talked about Royal Crown Hair Conditioner and White Rose Petroleum Jelly. During the day all we heard was what we called "hillbilly" music so we looked forward to nighttime after 10:00, hoping that the tuner on the radio and the airwaves would be clear, so the next day we could tell Mama what 78rpm to order.

Recently I had the chance to reflect back on those times and people from my early childhood and was humbled by how far I had come. When one of those childhood friends passed recently, Bernice and I visited the home of the deceased and were reunited with some of those childhood friends. I saw friends that I had not seen in over 55 years. As I looked at them and saw how they had changed I could not help from making some comparisons. Our family had not been at the top of the economic ladder in those days, whereas some of their families had been. However, I was pleased to see that my sister and I held our own. We were looking good; still having our youthful figures and dressed in the latest styles. In spite of earlier differences, we found a common ground as we talked about old times. We spent the evening remembering things from times past, and in the end we sang old church hymns that we learned as children and thanked God that he had brought us safely to this point. To God is the Glory. I remembered what my Mother always told us, about repairing a fence. You start at the top to take it down and work your way to the bottom. When you are putting it back together, you start with the last rail removed, the one that was on the bottom and work your way back up, ending up with what was once on top, now resting at the bottom, and what was on the bottom now resting on top. That was how she used her knowledge of an every day situation to explain how we could one day be on top.

Chapter 7

Remembering Life in Beckley, WV – 1953 - 1960

Mama and I were the only ones looking forward and excited about our anticipated move to another town. Everyone else was reluctant to leave their familiar surroundings and friends. The coal mines were slowly being worked out and Daddy was no longer employed by the coal company in Ingram Branch. It was just a matter of time before we would have to find housing some place else. All the people that could leave were moving. Most of them were headed north to New York or moving to cities in Ohio. Since we had no relatives in those places, we did not have those choices. There was the problem of Daddy finding work in those strange places because he had always been a coal miner, and had no experience doing anything else.

Mom would leave out many days in search of housing elsewhere. Ms. Essie Berger, her best friend, had moved away to Helen, West Virginia. Mama did not want to move to Helen because it was just another coal mining town. It was almost as bad as where we were living. Ms. Essie introduced Mama to a friend of hers, Ms. Rosa Edwards, who lived in Beckley and Mama went to see her. There was a vacant house next to her that was available for rent. The house was smaller than the one we were living in. Mama did not tell Daddy or us what the house looked like because she was afraid he would not want to move into it.

So sight unseen, he agreed and we proceeded to pack and get ready for the big move. The house we would move into was located at 223 8th Street, in the part of Beckley called East Park. Moving to East Park was like moving from a coal camp hollow to the big city.

The move was chaotic because we were trying to get moved before Halloween. There were also concerns that the bridge leading out of the hollow was about to cave in and the truck full of furniture might not make it across to the other side. The bridge held up and we moved into our new residence. After the initial shock of how small the place sunk in, we had to make the best of our new living arrangements.

It is hard to imagine now how eight people were supposed to fit into that little house. My two older sisters had graduated from high school but were still living at home. The house was so small and we were disappointed to find out that it did not have a bathroom. Of course, we were not used to having an inside bathroom in the house we just moved from. The house did have running water and the outhouse was in the back of the house instead of up on the hill behind the house. There were three rooms and a kitchen. There was no separate room that would serve as a living room. The front room would serve as Mama and Daddy's bedroom and the sitting room. There was a small room off of the kitchen that my brother would occupy. The room next to the front room would be the room that all five girls would have to share. There was only room for beds, with a small closet tucked in the back for storing your clothes. Mama and Daddy always got up early because the only way out of our room was through their room.

There was a small front yard with a cherry tree in it. In the back yard there was a damson tree and an apples tree. The kitchen was located in the back of the house. You had to go through the little room that served as my brother's bedroom, to get to the back yard, and outhouse. The back of the house was high off of the ground, with lots of steps leading to the yard. Our house was not the only one that lacked an indoor toilet, so in that instance, we were not any different from our neighbors. The location was better because we now lived on a paved street instead of a dirt road and there were no railroad tracks to cross. Living on our short street were at least three ministers, two school teacher, a mixture of coalminers, homemakers, and domestic workers. Our street was also the location of the largest Baptist church in the community, Welcome Baptist.

I was excited about the move, in spite of being anxious, knowing I was entering a new school with no friends. On the first day of school my oldest sister, Hazel, walked me to school and helped me get enrolled. I thought that the school would be different from the one I had just left, but we were still in one big room that accommodated two grades. I entered East Park Elementary School in October as a fifth grader. I don't remember too much about those first days but I did meet some new friends. Hazel would come to pick me up from school until I learned how to come home by myself.

I was anxious to let my classmates that I had left behind in Ingram Branch know how well I was adjusting to my new school. I wrote to my best friend Shirley and told her how many blocks I had to walk to school. I did not really know what a block was, so I counted the blocks marked on the concrete street.

This was all new to me and so different from the environment we had left behind. I missed my friends and especially my old teachers. My new teacher seemed real mean. She was a really big lady, who sat behind her desk all day. Her name was Ms. Galloshen (sic). I don't remember her ever getting up from behind that desk, not even to go to the bathroom. She kept switches under her desk and when you misbehaved she made you come and stand by her desk, where she proceeded to whip you with the switch. After witnessing her form of discipline, on the first day, I made up my mind that she would not have any problems out of me. I was wondering if our move to Beckley was the right thing to do. I made the necessary adjustments and after a few days made some new friends.

I had someone to walk to school with. Viola Morton became my new best friend. Our families were introduced to each other by Rev. and Ms. Edwards. We were told that this was a "good" family for us to be friends with. There were five boys and one girl in their family and five girls and one boy in our family. Viola and I became good friends right away. They lived down the hill from our house so playing with her was convenient, because Mama did not allow me to go too far away from home. Our families blended well and as the years went by we became like one blended family. Viola and I spent a lot of time together because she was the first friend I made when we moved to East Park. We became like sisters right away. Our mothers became good friends and I could always go down her house to play. Their house was one that we were allowed to eat food from. The same rules that were in place in Ingram Branch were still in place in Beckley. The only sleepovers for me would come much later when new neighbors moved into the house next door to us. Of course, our house could barely hold my family, so sleepovers were never even contemplated.

My next friend was Betty Lou Holloway. Betty Lou lived one street over from me behind the church so we also walked home together. Betty Lou was an only child living with her mother who was very strict on her. There were not many children that Ms. Holloway would let come to visit Betty Lou. Although we did not play away from her home much, I would enjoy going down to sit on her porch and talk with her. Ms. Holloway took a liking to me and would invite me to come and have lunch with Betty Lou. Although she kept her eyes on us at all times, we had a great time just sitting and talking. Ms. Holloway would serve us lunch and I remember her serving us hot tea with orange juice instead of lemon juice.

Because Betty Lou was not allowed to play on the playground we spent a lot of time in church activities together. Betty Lou was in church every time the doors opened. Sometimes she would be the only child in church. The rest of us would be outside playing on the playground.

I attended Sunday school and weekly church services with my family. We knew that on Sunday morning you did not have a choice about going to church and Sunday school, if you wanted to remain a part of the household. When we weren't attending church services at Welcome Baptist, we were traveling with Rev. and Ms. Charlie Edwards. I was a part of our family singing group and we would go up and down the road singing wherever Rev. Edwards preached. We sounded pretty good for amateurs.

Later the family would join Welcome Baptist, which was located on the same street where we lived. I became active in the choir, Sunday school and the Young Peoples Baptist Training Union. My Sunday school teacher was Ms. Cleo James and she would say in later years that I must have been her spiritual test of faith, because I gave her a hard time. I had not gotten over being mischievous and carried on my antics, even in church.

I was disruptive and agitating to her. I talked back to her, chewed gum and did everything I could to cause problems. When she threatened to call my mother, I told her I would answer the phone and hang up on her. As an adult I apologized to her and she said she was very proud to see that I had turned out so well. She was the first to give me a reference when I needed one for school and employment.

East Park had a separate playground away from the school house and I spent a lot of time playing there. As long as we were home by dark, it was ok. I knew not to miss my curfew. If I ever looked up and saw my mother coming, I knew there was a switch behind her. I enjoyed the playground because I had been used to playing in the woods and in our back yard, swinging from trees and playing in the leaves we piled up in the summer. The playground at Ingram Branch was part of the school ground and we had to cross the railroad tracks to get to it. On 8th Street, where we lived, the concrete streets made it easier to play hop scotch and jump rope. We got plenty of exercise as we played and made up rhymes to jump rope to. There were also lots of kids to pay with on 8th street. Mary Ruth Hale lived a few houses down from me and JoAnn and Frieda Fountain lived in the house below me. They were my next door playmates and we played at the top of the hill, in front of our house, until it was time to go in at night, when we returned from the playground.

When our next door neighbor, Ms. Edward died, I remember going over to the house to see her lying in the bed. She had one glass eye and I remember touching her because someone told me if you touched a dead person, you would not be afraid of their ghost. As I said earlier, I had a fear of dead people from an early age. Rev. Edwards would remarry and his new wife, Bertha Lillard, had children my age. Her daughter Jackie and I became good friends and since her mother and mine were friends, I was allowed to spend overnight sleepovers at her house.

Jackie, standing in the middle of photo to the left, (with her little sister Linda, head peeking out on the right), and me (posing while sitting on the car hood) would stay up late at night talking about boys. That was all I could do because I was not allowed to have a boy friend, although I did have my share of crushes. After Jackie and I became friends, I got to know her cousins who lived on Broadway Street. There were other neighborhood kids but after we finished playing on the playground, we divided up based on where we lived to continue playing until time to go inside. Although her cousin, Lucille (Cookie) Moore, and I were in the same grade we did not become friends until probably in Junior high. Her brothers and my brother were friends and so we started to spend a lot of time together. They had a television and all of the kids would get together at their house to watch American Bandstand and the Ed Sullivan show. Mama's rule still applied and unless she gave the ok, we knew not to disobey that rule, by going inside a forbidden house.

I learned how to ride my brother's bike. I never had one of my own. I never learned how to swim as a child because we were not permitted to go to the park on a regular basis. The one time I was allowed to go to Fitzpatrick Park, I almost drowned because I took a ride in a boat that I was not supposed to be in. When I stepped out, somehow my feet did not find the bottom of the lake and I went down for a frightening moment. Many years would pass before I would feel comfortable in water and finally lose the fear of drowning. As an adult, living in Hampton, Virginia, and working on campus, I finally learned to swim well enough to save myself from drowning.

It was a long time before we could afford a television set of our own so we were allowed as a family to watch TV at a neighbor's house, who lived across the street from us. Mr. Howard Miller took a great interest in us, partly because he had his eyes on my sister Josephine.

He was older and divorced, living by himself in a big pretty house that had lots of pretty furniture, and was the nicest house in our neighborhood. He was a retired coal miner who had been previously married to one of our elementary school teachers. He also had a telephone and since we did not have one, we were allowed to make calls to our friends from his house. When we finally got a telephone it was on a party line and we had to sometimes wait for the other party to get off the line in order to use it. In the meantime, you could always listen in on their conversation. We still have the same phone number that my mother had from over 50 years ago. By the time we got our own telephone, you could dial the number yourself and you did not have to hear the squeaky voice of the operator say "number please."

I had my first birthday party when I was in the 6th grade and my oldest sister, Hazel, had a party for me and invited a few of my friends. We had ice cream and cake and she gave me a new doll baby to replace the one that had been damaged from the heat coming from the wood stove in our front room, as she lay on the bed. Years later, she would retrieve the doll from under Mama's house and restore it. When I visited her she had cleaned it up and gave it back to me. It had been so long since I had seen the doll that I had forgotten how she looked. This doll now has a special place in my home. When I look at her I remember times living in East Park.

Hazel was the one who took me to have my first professional photo taken at a studio. For some reason, Mama did not have pictures of me taken with her other children. I guess by the time I came along, the traveling photographer had moved on to another coal camp. I remember getting all dressed up and even getting curls in my hair. That was a real treat because I always had the worst hair. My hair was sandy colored and short. I never could take good pictures. All of the photos taken with Mama's brownie camera had me making faces, turning up my nose, and squinting with my eyes half closed.

By this time it was time to move from East Park elementary to Stratton Junior High. It was so terrifying because the school was so big and now we did have to change classes. We were all afraid of getting lost and the other kids in the school were so tall. We were like grasshoppers compared to them. We made the transition and soon felt like we were just as grown up as they were. We learned new things and had different teachers for different subjects. We did not have a graduation from Junior High, we just moved on to the 9th grade. I was looking forward to learning new subjects and was sure I would still be able to keep up and stay on the honor roll.

Eventually our family would get smaller after the older siblings started to leave home, either by marriage or to seek better employment opportunities. Hazel was the first to get married and leave home. When she got married we were so sad when we came home from the wedding. We had never been separated on a permanent basis from each other during our growing up years. It wasn't long before Bernice graduated and she and Josephine would move to Arlington to live with our cousin Ernest and his family. In 1957 Leonard and Dorothy graduated from high school. Leonard went into the service, and in December Dot got married.

The following three years found me at home alone with my Mom and Dad. Hazel would come back to Beckley to live before she gave birth to my first niece, Yvonne. I was just 15 years old and looking forward to having a baby to play with because there had been no babies in the house after I was born. I remember overhearing a conversation between my parents shortly after Hazel had gone to the hospital. She said "Leonard, I think they are going to have to take the baby." I was so puzzled and sorry because I could not understand why the doctor would take her baby from her. I did not know she was talking about Hazel having a "C" section.

As you can see no one had spent much time explaining the "birds and bees" to me. As a matter of fact, when I would come into the room and they were all talking, somehow the conversation changed to something totally different. Anyway, as things turned out they did not take the baby and Hazel brought home the first grandchild, who we all proceeded to spoil rotten.

There were some advantages to being the only child left at home also. At last I had a room to myself. There was more money to buy me things and I received more attention from my parents. In addition, Josephine and Bernice would send me different things from the city that the other kids at school did not have. Josephine came home one summer and before school started bought me all new school clothes and my first Mickey Mouse watch. You are probably saying to yourself, am I re-reading what I just read. No, that also was part of Josephine's story. This is mine. There may be other times when you read something twice. I am not losing it and neither are you. You can blame that duplication on the inexperience of a first time author.

In 1956 our class expanded to accommodate the new students who were entering from the surrounding Junior High schools, throughout the county. By this time the East Park group had become a single group that stuck together. The East Park Girls were Viola Morton, Betty Lou Holloway, Aledia Dooms, Lucille Moore, Patricia McDowell, Gertrude Kidd, Mary Ruth Hale, Cornelia Jackson, Marie Thomas, and me. Although we made friends with the other classmates, we still hung out together. The other classmates had formed their groups before coming to Stratton also. There were never any rivalries, although the boys were looking at who was available in their different groups.

During the next four years our class started to bond and we became one big group. At the time of our graduation, we were known as the class that got along well together and the other classes envied our close relationships. The teachers even noticed how well we got along and said that the school was never the same after we graduated.

There were many good times shared at Stratton. I was still relatively shy and did not get too involved in after school activities. One reason was that my mother still kept a pretty tight reign on me. I did get involved in home economics, where I continued to learn how to sew better and cook a few meals. Mama had always had a sewing machine and had started to teach me about sewing long before the home economics classes I took. I knew a little about sewing so I had no problem making the first project, an apron. I was able to complete my assignments ahead of my classmates and looked forward to doing some more challenging projects. We all had to make an organza dress to wear for the May Day activities. We had different color dresses and we used crepe paper to wrap the flagpole as we marched, in difference sequences, around the pole.

The only other activities I participated in were the Thespian Society and I was inducted into the Ralph J. Bunche National Honor Society. The next day my photo was in the hometown newspaper, along with the principal, Mr. Reid and teacher, Ms. Frances Flippen. I wanted to play in the band, but I did not have an instrument. I wish now that I had at least learned how to read music so I could play my piano, instead of looking at it.

I never had a "real" boyfriend in school. I had a few crushes, but my Mama was still kind of strict when it came to boys and me. I hardly ever got to attend sports activities that were held after school. I remember one time she let me go with a school mate to sell raffle tickets for the school representatives in the homecoming parade, and when I did not come home as instructed, she was waiting for me with a switch. I don't know why she was so hard on me because I never gave her any trouble with boys, but I guess because I was the only one left at home and her baby, she was overly protective. I spent a lot of time home alone and learned to enjoy reading books and watching television. Our first television was a used one, but we enjoyed watching it just the same. When the picture would fade out, we learned how to make an antenna with a coat hanger and aluminum foil. If you turned it just right, you might get your picture back before the show ended. We were great inventors and knew how to make do with what we had. We used a piece of colored transparency plastic to watch TV in color.

Sometimes I think Mama would feel bad that she did not let me go out more with my friends and when she would go out shopping, she would bring me something new to wear. I guess this was her way of making up for my not having a "social life." Of course, I was not alone because my friend Betty Lou stayed home more than I did, so I didn't feel too bad.

I got into trouble in the 9th grade and because I was disobedient and did not go to the office as I was instructed to, my name was put into the dreaded "black book." I was afraid to tell my mother what had happened because I would probably have gotten another whipping. One of my teachers, Mr. James Brown, had sent me to the office for failing to do as he had instructed me. When he learned that the principal had put my name in the "black book," he was sorry he had sent me there, and apologized. He knew that was the worst thing that could happen to an honor roll student, who was looking forward to receiving awards upon graduation. I kept this a secret from everyone. It was ironic because some of the dumbest kids and meanest kids avoided the "black book" plague. I never forgave Mr. Reid for that because it was such a minor offense. He must have been having a bad day.

I was determined after that to ensure that my grades would remain at their highest level, in spite of the black mark on my record. Upon graduation I received my gold tassel to wear over my gown and the gold pin that I still keep as a reminder of what hard work and a determined mind could do for you. I enjoyed all of my classes and really enjoyed going to school. I never wanted to stay home, even if I was sick. I had nearly perfect attendance all through school and was very proud to be an academic honors graduate.

The boys in our classes were always doing things to interrupt class, especially when they did not have their homework or if there was to be a test. Their favorite class to act up in was the ones taught by Ms. Ruth Dandridge. They would start something and when she decided to walk around with her stick and pluck them on their head, the fun started. Some of the things that the boys did were unheard of. They would put thumb tacks and glue in her chair and wait for her to sit down to see if she would jump up. I would always sit next to the door so I would be one of the first to run out when the disturbance started. Some of the class clowns were Lewis (Butch) Patterson, Ronald Hairston, Arnold Bush, Jerome Brantley, Joseph Adams, and Theodore Spradley. They would get things started and then sit back to see what was going to happen. We had our share of girls who caused a stir in class also. On the whole, we were still a good class.

I always liked the time spent in physical education. Our instructor was Ms. Lorraine Seay, who was not much older than we were. She taught us how to do gymnastics, play volleyball and she also was in charge of the cheerleaders. She was the first teacher hired for the Negro school to teach physical education. Living through the 50's and 60's was a special time to be growing up. As high school students the girls gossiped about who was "still a virgin" and who was going to have a baby. Most of us were afraid to kiss a boy for fear of becoming pregnant. Sex education was taboo. What you learned came from your peers who knew one thing more than you did. Most of us also were scared to death of being put out of the house if we did get pregnant. There was so much misinformation mixed with threats. The only thing you knew was that if it happened, you would be shamed for life. There was little information on birth control, and even if you knew what it was, you had no access to it. It is a wonder that most of us survived those tumultuous teen aged years.

In those days, they taught our health classes separate from the boys and most of us learned all about the "birds and bees" at that time. Those lessons came too late for some. Pregnancy was the one thing that your mother scared you the most about. I remember how differently the girls were treated, especially by the religious community, and how the boys always got a free pass. No one seems to realize that the girls did not get pregnant by themselves. No one seemed to take that into consideration, as they chastised the girls. They were made to feel bad, and often put them out of church. Before being accepted back in church they were made to come before the entire church and apologize. I don't think I can remember any of the boys having to do that. As I look back over history and families, and talk with my peers, we often talk about the fact that we were not the first generation to be sexually active or have children out of wedlock.

As a teenager, although I was shy, I was also a big tease. That was the extent of my "being fast" as the old folk would say. I always had a knack for wearing tight clothes that showed off what I considered my "good" figure. I would make a lot of my clothes and some of them looked like I had been poured into them. I guess I did not mind flaunting what I considered my best asset. I had a classmate named Melvin Reed who was always chasing after me and nicknamed me "swivel hips." I can remember some of the male teachers, who shall remain nameless, that flirted with their female students. There were also female students who had crushes on the male teachers. We all seem to be alarmed today when we hear about such things, but the difference was that, in those days, most of them never acted on those crushes.

The 50's and 60's was the start of a lot of turmoil arising out of the civil rights movement. We had been living through Jim Crow and the KKK and a new group of leaders were coming on the scene to protest the injustices. As high school students we were not very political and just accepted the status quo. All around us the world was changing. We had gotten used to sitting in the back of the bus, standing at the lunch counters, and sitting in the balcony of the movie theatre. As a matter of fact, we did not mind the balcony seats because it was from this vantage point that we could throw items down on the white people below us.

I grew up with the signs that said "colored" and "whites only." We did not know anything else but segregation. I have to admit that I did not have any white friends. To be honest, as I am presently writing these memories years later, I probably harbored hard feelings towards some white people, just as much as they did towards some black people. Many years would pass before I felt comfortable with whites in my life, other than as co-workers, where I had no choice but to interact with them. I did not know any white people, other than the ones my mother worked for, and the one I worked for babysitting. Upon Bernice's departure to the big city, I took over her job working for Dr. and Ms. Backus. I was making the grand total of $15.00 a week babysitting and doing light housework. The Backus' were a nice family so I had not been exposed to the worse side of racism, on a personal level. My only social time with them was when Ms. Backus and I would stop to talk, and drink a cup of coffee, while smoking a cigarette.

There was a lot of unrest with the stage being set in 1954 to desegregate the schools all across the country. The states in the south were fighting it the hardest. We always knew that our books were used and often came from the white schools and the equipment we had to learn on was inferior. Things had been that way so long that we just learned to live with it. However, when the Supreme Court handed down its decision in 1954, all hell would break loose as students tried to go to the white schools. At Stratton, there had been talk about who would be the ones to integrate Woodrow Wilson, the white high school. Lots of time was spent deciding which students to send and offering moral support while they were there. For the most part, we all chose to stay at Stratton and some of the ones who did go to Woodrow Wilson, chose to return to Stratton, before they graduated. There was little disruption in our sleepy town so most of us went on with our daily lives happy that the unrest was not affecting our community.

Growing up in the early years, I never shopped in the stores because at Ingram Branch, Mama did all the shopping. I do remember her taking a piece of cardboard and tracing the outline of our feet so when she went to get our shoes she could get the right size. We never tried on the clothes before she bought them.

As students, we never interacted with the white kids because we did not play each other in any sports activities. When they finally decided to let students from our school go on the local dance show that was televised, they still went at a separate time. We did get more interested in what was taking place politically across the country and watched the news to see what was going on. During the campaign of 1959, we watched to see if John Kennedy would become the first Catholic president. I remember some of the teachers telling us to tell our parents not to vote for him because if he became President, the Pope would be in charge. Since we were Baptist, we had no idea who the Pope was. It seemed the teachers were the new white folks who were taking over the duty of trying to tell those, whom they felt were uneducated, who to vote for. Most of the Negroes felt that John Kennedy would be the one that would make our living conditions better. We were not old enough to vote, so we did not see what differences this election would be from any other election that had taken place in our lifetime.

For the most part, we were just satisfied to live in our own little world. We enjoyed watching the few Negroes on television and enjoyed watching the singers perform on American Bandstand, because that was about as close as we were going to get to them. We read Ebony and Jet magazines to keep up with what they were doing and, when possible, we purchased their records. Sometimes they were played so much until they were so scratched you could not tell who was singing what. If we were lucky enough to see some of them in person that was an added treat. There weren't too many entertainers who came to Beckley and my mother probably would not have let me go see them anyway.

I remember wanting to see Ike and Tina Turner perform when they were on the circuit that stopped in Beckley. The most I could do was watch Johnny Mathis and Jackie Wilson on television, and swoon and pretend that one day they would be singing to me. I became the student representative for the local radio station to sign up listeners for their radio broadcast. I was elated at having my name called over the radio airwaves and having students come up to me to get their membership card.

In the meantime, as school was winding down and graduation was getting closer my mind turned to school things. The Junior Senior prom was on the horizon and I wondered if Mama would let me go. To my surprise she said yes. Of course I was not going with a "date." Once again, my best friends and I made plans to go to the prom together. My sister Josephine came home and bought my gown, she took me to the hairdressers and helped me get ready. She took my picture before I left the house. I felt so grown up. Viola, Betty Lou, Patricia and I went to the prom together in a cab driven by Mr. Mitchell, the local cab driver. We had fun. None of us had dates and I spent the evening hanging together with them and managing to get in a few dances before the end of the evening. I had spent the week before trying to learn to dance by using the door and a broom as my partner. For some reason, I did not have good foot rhythm then and it is not that good now.

During the last week of school, while working in the office, I met a student from Park Central High School, in Bluefield, WV, who had come by just to visit for the day. I was given the honor of showing him around for the day. I learned that his name was Oscar Lewis and he was what we girls called a "good looker" and what most shy girls like me, considered a "dream man."

We had fun that day and I felt special because here I was, shy me, escorting around this hunk, and everyone wondering who he was. I was excited because he seemed interested in me and seemed to be having a great time also. Before he left for the day, he asked if he could have my phone number and if he could call me. Even though I was about to graduate in a few days, I was still not allowed to have a serious boyfriend. I told him to meet me at the playground in East Park. He did show up but for some reason he went to my house first. Needless to say he received the third degree from my mother, who was not the least bit impressed. You see he was the typical boy that your Mom warned you about. He was considered a "pretty boy" and of course she thought nothing good would come out of a relationship with him. We spent time at the playground and when I finally got home, one of the first things Mama said was "I don't think you need to be talking to him."

Since I was almost finished school and would soon be 18 years old I thought it was time for me to have a boyfriend. He did continue to call me and we would talk on the phone. Of course our conversations were monitored, since we only had one phone, and it was right in the living room, where everyone could hear your conversation. From that chance meeting on the last week of school, I met someone who I just knew was my Knight in Shining Armor and who would be my future husband. I guess it was what I considered love at first sight. We exchanged graduation pictures through the mail and I kept his in a safe place, where I could look at it and dream.

I graduated from Stratton High School with honors in May 1960. I knew what I wanted to do after graduation. I had learned to type very well and knew how to take Gregg shorthand efficiently and very rapidly. I had my own Remington Rand typewriter at home and I practiced constantly. I knew I was prepared to be a top level secretary, and set my sight on working for the Federal government, in Washington, DC. During the last semester in high school, someone came down to administer the Civil

Service Exam. I don't remember if anyone in the class passed that exam. Weeks later when I received my notice of rating saying I did not pass, I found that hard to believe. We had the best business teacher, Ms. Frances Flippen, who had prepared us for many hours before we took the test. I wonder if a little bit of discrimination was at work and we did not know it. Failing to pass that exam, I knew that my parents could not afford to send me to college. They had succeeded in providing each of their children with a high school education, and were so proud when we received our diplomas. They felt like their job was complete. It was a great accomplishment for them coming from an average family. College for me would have to be deferred; I had decided on other goals to pursue.

There was the additional pressure on me to do as all the other had done before me, get a job and help out at home. Daddy had quit working in the coal mines due to health reasons, and finances were pretty tight. My revised goal was to go to Hampton, stay with my sister Hazel and her family, take the civil service exam again and settle there as I worked for the government. I also was seeking my independence from the rules that I had lived under for the past 18 years. I had a vision of getting my own apartment and automobile, although I did not know how to drive. One of my best friends, Viola, and I had talked at length about living together after graduation. I had plenty of dreams that were waiting for the chance to come true.

Things changed and my plans were put on hold until later in the summer. My sister Dot and her husband Fred were expecting their first child and I had to stay home so I could help her with the baby. Fred Joseph was born three days before my 18th birthday and I was the first to take care of him when he came home from the hospital. Dot had a "C" section and needed help in caring for him. Boy did he give me a fit. He had what was called the "six week colic" and he took the entire six weeks to get over it. I spent my nights walking the floor trying to comfort him. The little experience I had gained taking care of the Backus children had not prepared me for this. We got through the hard part and in August 1960, I was given permission to leave for Hampton, Virginia.

My high school days were behind me. I bid farewell to my friends and Stratton High School. The next time I entered the school was in 1965. In 1967, the last class graduated from Stratton, a new high school was built, and the schools in Beckley were finally integrated. That was the end of Stratton High School, as we knew it. Stratton was just a memory to those who were educated there. We can only remember Dear Old Stratton High School every other year as we meet for reunions. There are no new memories to pass on and it is sad to see the class roll of living alumni decrease on a yearly basis.

My class of 1960 would reunite many times over the next 50 years. Friendships that had been made during those formative years have endured the test of time and distance. I left Stratton as one of 116 classmates. Since that time as of 2010 twenty six are deceased, leaving precious memories and the remaining ninety of us to keep the torch burning. A total of approximately 57 have come together at various times to celebrate as a group. These meetings are filled with stories of days gone by and the sharing of new memories since that time.   Our class takes great pride in coming to our school reunions, especially when we started to have our separate "class reunions."

In 1996 a group met at the school reunion, put their heads together, and the next year we were off and running, planning to keep connected. Over the years their spouses and significant others became a part of our group. We were more interested in remembering old times, than trying to find out who did what, or who had what. Most of our guest, who did not graduate with us, consider themselves part of our class and work with their spouses whenever we plan a reunion in their jurisdiction. It is amazing that after all of these years, we still have a lot in common. We put aside any differences we had while in school and just are so thankful that we can still come together as a group and be one.

If I were to call our class roll the following persons would have answered present: Joseph Adams (Judi), Diane Griffin Bates, Barbara Breckenridge, Jerome Brantley (Irene), Betty Holloway Brown, Marie Thomas Chatman, Joan Crawford, Mary Dickerson, Letishia Young Farrish (Robert), Janice Spradley Green, Linda Hairston Green (Robert), Violet Dow Green, Edward Howard (LaRue), Darrell Jones, Lucille Moore Jones, Gloria Hairston Lebby, Jean Moore Mackey, Helen Deering Mashburn, Carnel Mickey, Samuel Morton (Laura), Viola Morton Martin, Gertrude Kidd (Nettles) Waller, Carl Pannell (Evelyn), Elsie Venable Millner, Lewis Patterson (Hazel), Leigh (Loto) Tanks Penny, Aledia Dooms (Melvin) Scott, Lelia Monroe Shorts, Delores Boyden Taylor (Rubin), Evangeline Davis Taylor, John Trice, Leola Flynn Toles, Norval Wooten (Verna), Corrine Thornton Graham, James Griffin, Dorothy Wright Jordon, Russell Manns, Carl Hill, Patricia McDowell, Ronald Smith, Marva Staples Anthony, Anna Hughes Lovett, Naomi Freeman Gill, Dorothy Oliver, Annetta Pannell, Helen Finney Ross, Wilma Schofield Starkey, Joan Powell Edmonds (Jerry), Joseph Tenson, Gladys Strickland Turner, Lawrence

Lawson, Arnold Bush, Ronald Hairston, Patricia Hill Ellerbee, Johnnie Mae Staples Thomas, Lorenzo Turner, and Patricia Webb.

I take the time to list all of these names because in some way each one of them have had an impact on my life and I am honored to call them my friends. Also, as I get older I want to be able to look at the photos taken at these gatherings and at least know the names. Our class reunions, held across the country in places like Cleveland, OH, Washington, DC, Miami, FL, Philadelphia, PA, Los Angeles, CA, Chicago, IL and Atlantic City, NJ, have shown the commitment we have to each other. I have been honored and recognized for my service during these reunions, for what they say I do, but I want to publicly let them know that it has been a labor of love for me. Because I did not have so much interaction while we were students, I take great pride in helping to keep us together now. I love them all because they are part of my life and because of them I am better. Pictured in these group photos are doctors, ministers, nurses, secretaries, teachers, executives, government workers, homemakers and business owners, but the title they hold dearest to me is that of "Friend." I would keep in touch with my core group which I called "The East Park Girls." We bonded and some of us even talk every day although we are miles away. Thank goodness for unlimited phone calls and cell phones with free long distance. These friends have been a part of my life for so long that they are considered more than friends. As the saying goes these are the rocks that keep me grounded and I know that they will always be there.

Left to Right: Patricia McDowell, Gertrude Kidd Nettles Waller, Betty Holloway Brown, Marilyn Aledia Dooms (Melvin) Scott, Viola Morton Martin, Me, and Lucille Moore Jones.

The Stratton High School Class of 1960 at our 45th Class Reunion

Chapter 8

My Independent Life – 1960 - 1962

Summer was fast approaching an end and I was still anxiously waiting to leave Beckley. It has been decided that since I was not going off to college, I would eventually go to live with my sister Hazel and her husband Lee in Hampton, Virginia. I would take care of my niece, Yvonne, until I found a job. I had visited Hampton during the summer of 1958 and was looking forward to going back there to live. I was hoping to get a job with the Federal government either at Langley AFB or Ft. Monroe.

In the meantime, Oscar and I were still corresponding. He called to say he was getting ready to start his military career. We talked about getting together when I left home and promised to keep in touch with each other.

In August I said good bye to one of my best friends Viola and we talked about our future plans to eventually end up in the same town, getting our jobs and sharing an apartment. I was sad to leave but happy that I would be starting my new independent life. I liked Hampton because we lived close to the beaches and the weather was nicer than in Beckley. Although I still had not learned to swim, I enjoyed going to the beach. Segregation was still a part of our every day existence and there was a separate beach for the whites. They enjoyed the sand on the Buckroe Beach side and we enjoyed it on the side called Bay Shore. I guess this was supposed to be another example of separate but equal.

Lee, my brother-in-law, was stationed at Langley AFB so we spent a lot of time on the military bases, especially shopping and going to the NCO club to eat. There were lots of service men to meet but I was still under the "protective" eye of my older sister, Hazel.

Hazel was "Mama" in absentia. At the time I did not realize the enormous responsibility that had been placed on them; looking after an 18 year old naïve young girl. I thought that being 18 gave me the right to do as I wanted to, not realizing that I was still living under someone else's roof, and was not even taking care of myself. In fact, I wasn't even working.

After a short time living there I met Dolores Porter. She and I were around the same age so I had someone to hang out with. I spent time practicing to take the typing part of the civil service exam, which would be my ticket to a government job. I took the exam several times and each time received my notice that I had not passed the typing part, but had passed the general part. I knew that I could type fast and accurate enough to pass the test. I had graduated from high school with the grade of "A" in the typing course and had been one of the best students in the business section. I was baffled again at my inability to pass the test. This was the same pattern that was evident when the examiners came to the high school. Because they did not let you see your test papers, there was no way I could tell if the results they reported were true or not. I started to question if they wanted to hire blacks to work for the government. One of my sister's friends, working as a secretary on the military base, told me not to give up.

I eventually did give up and took a job babysitting for a white family that lived within walking distance from our house. I took care of two little kids and watched soap operas all day. I knew that this was getting me nowhere fast. At some point, I was offered employment with Hampton (Institute) University, as a nanny/helper for the young children of the President, Dr. Jerome Holland and his wife, Ms. Laura Holland. This was a step up and Joey and Lucy were good kids and I was not much older than them, so we always had fun doing things together. The daily housekeeper was named Rosa (Rose) Williams.

Rose was the grandmotherly type and we hit it off right away. From the day I got there, she told me that she did not want me to settle for "this type of work" because I could do better. She said, at her age, she did not have any choice but I did. She was my confidant and my "mother" figure away from home. She had grandchildren my age so she understood my wanting to be independent and able to do the things that young people did, like partying and hanging out with the boys. Rose and I spent lots of time talking when we were alone. Ms. Holland was always trying to find out what we were discussing. Most of the talk was about working there and how some people felt that those of us working in "domestic" jobs should be treated differently from those working in "professional" jobs. Since Ms. Holland was from a well to do family, college educated, and in a different social class, I guess I perceived her demeanor as being bourgeois. I believed she relished her position as "wife of the President of Hampton Institute (University)."

This job paid more and I would have the opportunity to take classes at the University free of charge. This was a good perk, but I did not want to spend years working as a domestic, in order to get a free education. Some people may think that my reasoning was not well thought out, but you can't expect much logic from an 18 year old. The job was easy and I got paid by the week and not by the hour, which I thought was unfair. My days were based on the schedule of the lady of the house, Ms. Laura Holland. When they were away on travel, I lived in the President's residence with the kids. I had my own living quarters on the third floor of the residence. I did not like it when they were gone for extended periods of time and I had to be there twenty-four seven. Those times were very confining and quite boring.

It wasn't such a bad place to live, but it limited my social life. After a conversation with the lady who worked as Dr. Holland's secretary, she encouraged me to keep trying to pass the typing test. I also talked to her about the hours I was working without getting paid and she said I should question them about it. I finally got up the nerve to question Ms. Holland. In that conversation, I pointed out to her that I perceived it to be unfair to work, without additional pay for those hours. She thought that I was not entitled to additional pay and offered to give me more time off in lieu of overtime pay, which to me was not the same. I can't explain how I felt, but I knew that there was something wrong with that picture. I was being taken advantage of and there was nothing I could do about it. I was caught between a rock and a hard place, because on the one hand I needed the job and on the other hand I had no means of correcting the situation. With no viable options to remedy this complaint, I accepted her offer of extra time off. I felt it would be useless and counter productive for me to pursue it further.

This was my first experience at speaking up and questioning those in charge. To this day, I believe if I had gone to the personnel department with a complaint the outcome would have been different. Hampton probably owes me a lot of money for back wages. As I continued to think about how unfair this situation was, I knew then that I would have to get my act together, so I could move on. It was time to set some new goals.

At Hampton Institute (University), I met Chris, a disadvantaged student, who was also working his way through college, at the President's house. On my off days he used to come visit me. My family liked him and thought he was a nice person for me to see. I really was not that interested in him because he was a poor student, who had no money to go out on dates. He was not really my type.

They did not know he spent more time chasing after me than he did doing what his duties were around the house. Just goes to show you can't judge a book by its cover.

I had made it through the summer of 1961 and the holidays were fast approaching. I was still carrying on a long distance romance with the dream man I had met my last week in high school, Oscar. My love life had been stagnant. We communicated with each other through almost daily letters and phone calls. We had not seen each other since I left West Virginia and he was anxious for us to meet again. His letters were filled with talk about our future together. He was now getting used to the army life and stationed at Ft. Meade, MD. He had asked if he could come visit me for New Years.

I finally got up the nerve to ask my family about his coming for the New Year's holiday. They agreed and we made plans for his visit. I was excited and told Rose and Ms. Holland that I wanted to take some time off for his visit. I got approval for the time off. My friend Dolores, her boyfriend, and I made plans to spend New Year's Eve at the club. That was a good plan because they had transportation and we didn't.

When Oscar arrived I was nervous but after the introductions, Hazel and Lee went out for their pre-planned evening. I had agreed to watch Yvonne. After they left the three of us ate a lasagna dinner (frozen), because I could not cook, and watched television. When Hazel and Lee returned Yvonne told them "he was trying to marry my sister." I guess in the eyes of a four year old when she saw someone kissing; it meant they were getting married.

The next day went by quickly as Oscar and I spent time talking and catching up with what had been going on since we last saw each other. That evening, we got ready to go out on the town to celebrate New Year's Eve. I spent extra time making sure that my new green after five dress was fitting right, and when I put on my "mouton" jacket, the mirror said I was looking good. We left and said we would not be out too late. The evening started out fine and we were dancing and having a good time. While talking to my friends at the table, I noticed Oscar had been away from our table for a little while. Thinking something had happened to him, I went to look for him. I found him completing a phone call. I guess because it was New Year's Eve, I assumed he was talking to another woman. Of course he denied it.

At some point during the evening I guess I had one drink too many. I was not accustomed to drinking and did not realize how little it took to get drunk. The events that followed are still blurry but I knew I was afraid to go home once I realized how late it was. I knew my sister was going to hit the ceiling and probably kill me. Oscar tried to convince me to runaway with him, that night, and get married in Maryland. My head was hurting so bad from the alcohol that I couldn't think straight. My friend Dolores was no where to be found and I decided I had to face the music. I knew the minute we hit the door all hell would break loose. Lee had been out looking for us thinking something bad had happened to us.

Once the dust settled, Oscar was giving one option, pack his bag as soon as possible and to never come back. He kept trying to accept the blame to keep me out of trouble, but no one wanted to listen. I think I walked around for the next week still feeling the effects of the alcohol. I am sure that horrible experience accounts for my not wanting to be a "drinker" today.

When I returned to work Ms. Holland was busy trying to find out how my weekend had gone. Needless to say I did not tell her anything. However, I did confide in Rose and she and I talked about what my options were. The following weeks were filled with anxiety and not the best time in my life. I realized that it was time for me to make some hard decisions. I decided that because there was so much hostility towards Oscar, it was best that I stopped receiving his phone calls. I gathered all of the letters he had written to me and decided to burn them. It was quite a barn fire in the back yard. I just wanted to forget everything that had happened and look to the future in another direction. When I finally talked to him and told him what my decision was, he once again begged me to come to Maryland and to marry him. He was asking me to make a choice between him and my family. I knew what to expect from my family but I had no idea what marrying him would bring into my life. I felt torn between him and my family. In the end, my decision was to end the relationship, until I had time to sort out my life.

My choices in my early dating years in Hampton were made out of inexperience. I soon met a man who I would describe as another "Casanova," then there was the older man, who was a skilled liar, and of course Chris, the working student, who was still trying to be the man in my life. My inexperience in the dating game left me utterly unprepared to handle what life was throwing my way. I lived with the constant knowledge that at any time I might be sent back home because I was "out of control." It was not easy to have to make decisions not knowing what the outcome would be. I just had to give some serious thought to what my choices were.

I decided that I needed to reassess my options so I could spread my wings. I was now 20 years old and wanted to go out and party without any restrictions. I wanted to see the bright lights of the big city. I started to think more about my plans for being a secretary and how I could achieve that goal. I made a trip to Baltimore to visit my sister Bernice and decided when I returned to Hampton that I would relocate to Washington and enroll at Cortez Peters Business School. I had picked up the application while I was in Baltimore and I applied, was accepted and started getting ready for the move. The next months were filled with excitement about the move.

Since school would not begin until August, I continued to work for the Holland's. The summer went by fast and they were entertaining at lot of people at the President's house. The most memorable guest I was privileged to meet and serve was Rev. Dr. Martin Luther King, Jr. He was there as the guest speaker for the Minister's Conference, being held on campus. As part of the conference, a luncheon, hosted by the President, was scheduled. At the time I was asked by Ms. Holland to assist Rose with the luncheon, I did not know who the guests were, and I was not pleased because that was not part of my duties. When I found out Dr. King was coming I didn't mind. I had heard and read so much about him and his involvement with the Civil Rights movement. He was a "Negro" who was among the most admired and well-known. I had no idea then how much greater in statute he would become, as he continued his rise as the leader of the Civil Rights Movement, and as he worked to seek justice for all people.

I was left speechless when, before lunch, Dr. King asked Ms. Holland if he could meet the "household staff." We each came in and he shook each of our hands. His hand shake was so soft and warm, but firm. Out of the entire guests in attendance, he was the only one that thanked us again for our service, before he left the house.
Afterwards Rose and I laughed at Ms. Holland's apparent shock that he wanted to meet us, who we thought she considered "the little people." It was at that time I saw how different people view their position in life. It was also my first real confirmation of "colored folks" who thought they were better because you worked for them. I had always been told that most white folks felt that way and now realized that ignorance comes in all colors and social classes.

Recently I came across a glowing article about the Holland's written in April of 2011 about the 11th Annual Dr. Jerome and Laura Holland Youth Scholarship Contest, sponsored by the American Red Cross in Westchester County, where she was described as "a passionate humanitarian." I was happy to know that my earlier opinion of her may have been incorrect.

I am so thankful that I was in a place where our paths crossed and to be able to say that the chance meeting with Dr. King, and the kindness he showed that day, would have a profound impact on my life. He inspired me to go for my dream. I left Hampton in August 1962. I did return to let the Holland's know that I had accomplished something other than what they offered me. When Dr. Holland passed in 1985, I sent her my condolences. She responded with a note that expressed how proud she was of the accomplishments I had made from the shy 18 year old girl from West Virginia, to becoming a competent and successful adult. I lost touch with Rose after Hazel and Lee moved to Massachusetts. I found that I had a voice and in the years ahead I would use it to speak out against injustices, whether it was directed at me or someone else.

As children and young adults growing up in the 40's 50's and 60's, we had a bird's eye view of history, which not always good. We were born into a segregated country but witnessed the doors of desegregation begin to open, as the first recipients of equal rights. We witnessed the assassination of leaders of those decades, starting with President John F. Kennedy, and including Malcolm X, Robert Kennedy and of course Dr. Martin Luther King, Jr. We were the generation who wanted to make a change in our social environment and wanted to make things better for our country and our children. I remember watching the events unfold as the Freedom Riders rode buses through the south, in 1961, and thinking if I could be that brave. Those were ordinary college kids who were not satisfied with the way this country was treating blacks. They were joined by many white people who risked bodily harm and separation from their families to participate. Their brave action made you see that not all white people were bad and racist. It was during those times when I often wondered how a white person could let you work in their house as a domestic, cook their food, watch their children, and then mistreat you. This unfair treatment even spilled over into the workplace, where you were often the person sent to get the coffee and lunch, for the business meetings that you were most likely excluded from.

We also became a part of the Vietnam War era where many of our friends gave their lives for a nation that turned their backs on them when it was over. Our participation then spread out to include, not only the civil rights marches, but the protests against the war in Vietnam.   In the midst of it all we also stood in awe as the first man, Neil Armstrong, a member of the Apollo space team, landed on the moon in 1969. Of course, at that time, some of us doubted if he really was on the moon or in the desert someplace. I had no idea where I would fit, in the scheme of things, as I made my way through this new grown up world I had become a part of.   Not knowing what to expect I made mistakes and missteps along the way in search of my destiny and place in life. I believed that the trials and struggles ahead would be met with confidence knowing that all things happen for a reason. I would learn how to accept some things, try to change some things, and along the way, acquire some wisdom and knowledge to know the difference, as I figured out how to put a positive spin on things that seemed negative.

Chapter 9

A Fresh Start in Washington, DC – 1962 - 1967

I relocated to Washington, DC the last of August 1962. I had enrolled at Cortez Peters Business School and was looking forward to my first journey on my own. I looked forward to it with great expectation and apprehension at the same time. I knew that this would be the start of my real life experiences, as an independent adult.

I spent my first night in the big city with my sister Josephine. I remember the excitement I felt as I stepped off the bus. I retrieved my suitcases and trunk filled with all my worldly belongings and looked around at this brand new place. I had made it to the big city. The next morning Josephine put me in a taxi, to start my first day of orientation at Cortez Peters, where I would get my housing assignment. I was older than most of the students, because I had been out of high school for two years. When we received our housing assignments I found out that my room mates would be Jo Ann Davis from North Carolina and Corrine Frazier from Churchview, Virginia. They were more anxious than I was. I took the lead as we set out to find the place we would be living as young adults, on our own, for the first time.

We were disappointed at our new housing placement. It was located on the corner of 11th and Kenyon Streets, NW, right across the street from a rowdy bar. I wasn't quite ready for that much city life. It was not in a good section of town and the man who owned the rooming house was kind of flirty. He had a bad habit of coming into your room without knocking. The place also had roaches and we later found out the school had placed about fifteen students in this house. We stayed there for less than a month.

Once again I took the lead and complained to the school so they found us another place to live. Jo Ann moved out first and Corrine and I moved next. We lived further away from the school, but we just knew we had arrived when the first day we moved in the man next door was cutting his grass with an electric lawn mower. All the houses on the street were large and many of the families took in students, as boarders, from the local universities.

Our new address was 1622 Allison Street, NW. We later learned that we were living in "the Gold Coast" section of DC. Our new host family was the Witherspoon's. We surmised that they must have been rich, or at least well off. Mr. Joseph Witherspoon was a real estate agent, who owned his own business, and his wife, Ms. Grace Witherspoon did not work. Two of their children lived in the home, daughter, Grace (Madison) and son, Clinton. Another son, Joseph, Jr. (who they called Lovey), his wife Audrey and their family lived nearby on 14th Street. They were the typical middle class Negro family, living the American dream. The house was very large and well kept. We had kitchen privileges and the limited use of the telephone. We were sharing one large bedroom with a connecting bath to the owner's bedroom. We were welcomed by the family. There were few house rules, other than cleaning up after using the kitchen and bathroom, and keeping our bedroom cleaned and organized. We were given a section in the one refrigerator in the kitchen for our perishable goods and a shelf in the pantry for our dry goods. We did not have much money to buy food so that space was sufficient. Many times our food ran out and the space was empty.

There was always something going on in the house. We were finally free to experience new things as adults. Cortez Peters considered us adults so they were not charged with supervising our activities. Since we were paying for our housing, the host family also had no supervisory roles. We were finally free to party, smoke, drink and stay out all night if that was what we wanted to do. Corrine was engaged to be married. Her fiancé, Jimmy Young, would come to town often to see her and we hung out together. Jo Ann was more subdued. She suffered from homesickness and did not always go along with us when we were going out. She said later she always felt like the third wheel in the group. Corrine's fiancé had a car, and when he came to town, we would go to Baltimore to find a party, if there was nothing going on in DC. Ms. Witherspoon would make snide remarks about our conduct.

I had the good fortune of having my sister Josephine living here so she would always invite all of us over to eat meals. I also would baby sit for her and the Hubbard's, who lived in her building. By this time Josephine had given birth to a son, John. Johnna was a little over a year old so I enjoyed spending time with them. The money I received babysitting helped me to buy things that I needed before I got a job. I was the source for cigarettes for the classmates who smoked but could not afford to buy them. I had formed the smoking habit while I was still in high school. Of course my parents never knew it. I would sneak and buy them on the credit account they had established at the neighborhood store. In those early days, you didn't have to prove you were of age to make the purchase. The store owner did not mind because he never gave you an itemized bill for your purchases. Once he did ask me when my father had started smoking Winston's. I guess this smoking habit originated from smoking corn silk, in a corn cob pipe, with my playmates, while we hid behind the outdoor toilet.

After living in the Witherspoon household for awhile, their son Clinton took a liking to me. That was a plus for me because when they had great dinners on Sundays and holidays, I would be invited to join them. As students, sometimes we would run out of food before we got our allowance, and we would sneak and eat some of their food out of the refrigerator. The Witherspoon family probably knew we were doing this, but never said anything to us. We learned how to pool our money to buy groceries and survived on necessities only. We learned the art of sharing clothes, school supplies, and anything else that would save money.

I was excited about going to business school. The classes were easy for me. I went everyday and I really honed my typing skills. I was looking forward to having a job. I was learning how to do keypunching. That was something new to me but it was also another avenue towards employment. We would sit at the machine and punch holes in cards and learned to read what was punched on the cards, according to the placement of the holes. Cortez Peters, Jr., the typing champion, took an interest in my typing abilities, and I was allowed to take daily classes, although I was not supposed to.

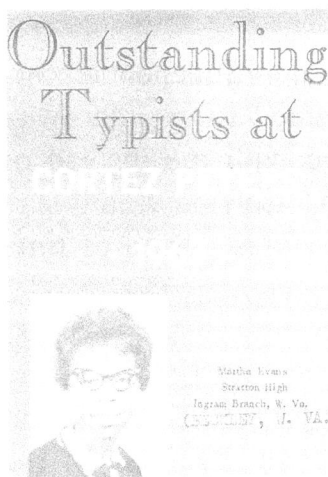

Outstanding Typists at

Martha Evans
Stratton High
Ingram Branch, W. Va.
(BECKLEY, J. VA.

I earned the title of "Outstanding Typist" for the year 1963, for typing 100 words a minute straight copy, without errors. This was a great accomplishment and reaffirmed my belief that there was no way I could have failed all of the earlier typing tests I took in Hampton and West Virginia. I was now being taught by the great Cortez Peters himself. His method of teaching skills still works for me. I have had people stand over me, and watch me type, and try to figure out how I can type so fast. I first learned typing from Ms. Flippen, in high school, who taught me how to keep my eyes on the copy and my fingers on the typewriter. Mr. Peter's teaching techniques were similar.

While we were in school there were always parties and clubs to frequent. I had learned to dance and I enjoyed the excitement of sitting in a club, with a drink and cigarette, pretending to be sophisticated. My drink of choice was Tom Collins. After my "drinking fiasco" in Hampton, I had learned to take one drink and sip off of it all night long. Drugs were not a part of our culture at that time. We were only interested in having what we called "good clean fun."

Clinton and I started to date on a regular basis. He was a very nice person and he was what I considered a "safe" person to go out with. We had lots of fun playing games at home, watching TV and dancing and listening to music. Clinton and I would leave the house to go to the store and come back late at night. His mother was always fussing and sometimes she would put the night latch on the door, when she went up for the night, so we would have to knock in order to get in. His sister Grace would look out for us. She would come downstairs to stay up until we got in. We learned how to walk to the side on the steps, instead of in the middle, so they would not squeak, as we made our way to our rooms, trying not to awaken his mother.

Clinton was a student at Howard University and his mother was always fussing because he did not take his studies seriously. His sister Grace had graduated and was in law school, at Howard University. She had been married, but was now divorced, with a daughter, named Toni. Of course, I was still looking for excitement so I would sometimes go out with other men and that did not go over well with Clinton. He would hate to see Corrine's fiancé come in town because he always brought a friend for me to hang out with, which meant he would not be seeing me that weekend.

I had finished my time at Cortez Peters, and since I was more independent his mother only wanted to rent to students. I guess she wanted to get me away from her son, who she thought was spending more time with me instead of focusing on school. I knew I would be moving out soon. Corrine would stay until she finished school, while Jo Ann would live there for a period of time after she finished.

I was offered a job doing keypunching for a firm in Virginia but I still had my eyes on the Federal government. I passed the dreaded civil service exam and applied for a clerk typist position with the telephone company. When the telephone company called me in for an interview, I was excited. The interviewer was white and, she asked if I had passed the civil service exam. I told her "yes." To my surprise she said to me, "You are overly qualified for our jobs." Upon reflection, I think I had once again experienced covert discrimination. How could I have been overly qualified for an entry level position? She did not know it at the time, but she did me a favor by not hiring me. I did not give up looking and spent the rest of my time keeping my newly acquired skills tuned up.

Shortly thereafter I was hired by the Commerce Department to work in the Patent Office Division in February 1963 as a clerk typist GS-3. My starting salary was $3,820 per year. Boy had I hit the jackpot – from $15.00 a week as a high school student, $62.00 a week as a nanny at Hampton University and now I was making a salary exceeding the salary, of some of the teachers, who had taught me in high school. I had a strict supervisor who was afraid of the top brass and would never speak up for her employees. I learned early on that if I wanted to get my issues heard, I would have to stand alone. The work environment for blacks was to keep quiet and do your work. There were ladies working in that department old enough to be my mother and they were also GS-3s. You started out as a GS-3 and you ended up, after 30 years still working as a GS-3. Considering my supervisor was a "big time" GS-5, there was no place for me to go. There was only one black patent examiner in the entire office, an attorney, working at the GS-9 level.

As an employee in an office with nothing but women, I learned early that there was a lot of jealousy in the office. If you wore better clothes someone always had something negative to say. After I had been there for a while a new employee by the name of Eva Overman was hired. Eva was older than me and since I always got along better with older people, we became great friends. Our friendship lasted until she passed in 1995, from breast cancer. She was the first person I knew personally to die as a result of breast cancer. She refused to have a mastectomy, and insisted on seeking alternative treatments. She traveled all the way across the country to California seeking treatment. Sadly, it was too late to help her. Eva was the one I confided in and shared my secrets with. She always said to me "You ought to write a book." Although she is not here to see that I finally took her up on that suggestion, I will always cherish the friendship we shared and appreciate all the good advice she gave me, while I was trying to find my place in life.

I was now living independently in another rooming house at 1712 Lanier Place, NW. This house also had about ten young ladies living there. Most were recent college graduates who had come from the south looking for employment in DC. The house was owned and run by Mrs. Ruby Blakney, whose main interest was seeing that you paid your rent on time.

Ms. Blakney had some rules about keeping your rooms clean and not letting any boys in your room. It was not the idea place with so many people but it was convenient to shopping and close to public transportation. We shared a small kitchen, bath and in some cases, she had three people sharing a room. We took turns helping each other out with food and money to make it through until our paydays came around. It was in this rooming house that I met Linda (Leach) Truesdale and Rita Howard. They had come from down south after graduating from Livingstone College.

This was just the beginning of the hot summers to come in 1963. The outcry was loud about the Vietnam War and blacks were getting worked up over their lack of civil rights. The summer of 1963 would bring me once again in the presence of Dr. Martin Luther King, Jr. Everyone was talking about this big March on Washington. I had never participated in any sit-ins that were taking place all around the country. Watching the demonstrators being beaten, spat on and killed did not lend itself to me to the point that I could have been non-violent. Although I had been exposed to the injustices of segregation, I guess I was just a silent partner. Just as so many of my ancestors had accepted their fate, as enslaved people, many of us accepted our position as the underclass. We were still carrying our lunches on bus and train trips, because we could not eat in the café car, or even if we were driving, we couldn't order food at the front of the store. When we traveled south, we made sure that we stayed on the main highways, prayed that our car would not break down, and often made the trips so that we would be at our destination before night fall. We saw the signs over the water fountains and on the outdoor toilets that said "Colored" and "Whites Only," and we obeyed them. The only place we did not see the Colored and White sign was in Church, because, in those segregated years, we did not worship together. When it was summer time and we wanted to spend time at the beach, we headed to the beach area set aside for use by blacks.

In many of the areas around the country upper class blacks had their own private beaches, and they too practiced discrimination, among their own race. Most of their discrimination was based more on your social class rather than on your skin color, not to say that color did not play a part in it, to some degree, in the black community and in some families. This is something that many don't like to discuss, but have heard about "passing the brown paper bag" test.

As a young person growing up, living in Beckley, I had stood at the counter in GC Murphy's to eat my hot dogs. Washington, DC was not any better. We were not allowed to sit at the fountains or in the front of the restaurants. We were not welcomed in the exclusive stores downtown, even if you could afford them, especially Garfinckel's and Raleigh's. Woodward and Lothrop, Lansburgh and Hecht Company were not too happy to see us either.

We had our own shopping district in DC on 14th Street, NW and H Street, NE. We had our own movie theaters on U Street named after noted blacks, Lincoln and Booker T. Of course who could forget the Howard Theater? The Howard Theater was DC's showplace where all the black entertainers made their stop to perform their latest hit records. I saw all the entertainers of the day, James Brown, Moms Mabley, The Drifters, Brook Benton, Wilson Pickett, Jackie Wilson and anyone else passing through town. We had our own nightclubs and one of my favorite places was the Caverns located at 11th and U Streets, NW.

My roommate Linda, from Ms. Blakney's house, and I had become great friends and in the ensuing years we would share many memories. I was a bridesmaid in her wedding and when I got married one year later, she assisted me. Life in the Blakney rooming house was fun. We would go out and party all night, come home in the morning, take a shower and head for work the next morning. There were lots of house parties held in basements with the lights dim and the music blaring.

My chance encounter with meeting Dr. Martin Luther King, Jr. the summer before, in Hampton, gave me a real sense of how important it was to be involved and to try to make a difference.

It was early August, 1963, and the day was fast approaching for the March on Washington. The media coverage was furious because they were thinking that with that many people, especially Negroes, in one place there was bound to be trouble. Dr. King kept stressing that this was going to be a peaceful march and that since he was a proponent of non-violence they were instructing the participants to be on their best behavior. I had not planned to attend because I had just started to work and had gotten a sense of how management was feeling about taking off to join the March. My job security was high on my list of priorities.

When I went to lunch earlier in the day I noticed all of the excitement in the streets. Buses were coming from all across the country. People were already marching to the Lincoln Memorial with their signs. I knew this was going to be something big and exciting.

When I returned to work, after lunch, I asked my co-workers if they were going to the "March." Most of them said no. Shortly thereafter, I received a phone call from my other new friend, Rita Howard, who said to me: "This is something that we should not miss." I tried to talk other co-workers to go, but they were afraid of the supervisor, because she had talked against our going. Since I was a new employee, I first thought I should not risk my job by going. I then thought, what the heck, and decided to take a chance on something and be counted. At that point, I really did not care what might happen when I returned. I decided that I wanted to be a part of this day which would probably be talked about in history, for a long time.

Rita and I met and joined the March as it was coming down Constitution Avenue. As we got closer to the Lincoln Memorial the crowd was ecstatic. We pressed our way towards the front so we could get a glimpse of Dr. King. It was late in the day and a lot of people had started to leave, not knowing that the best was yet to come. Although we got in the march late, we were able to get up really close to the stage, and could see and hear all the participants.

When Dr. King started to speak we were mesmerized. I had heard him speak on television, but there was something magic about hearing his booming voice in person. When Dr. King mentioned Lookout Mountain Tennessee, Rita really got excited since that was her home state. Dr. King's speech was so inspiring and that was probably the only time in our recent history that blacks and whites all seemed to be on one accord. It was a great day and we did not know what would come out of the march. We just knew that it had been something happening that day that we would talk about to our children many years later.

We left those grounds with a new sense of pride and the knowledge that we had been a part of history. The newspapers were filled with photos of the crowd and I received a call from Rita the next day saying that our picture was on the front page of the Washington Star. The picture was taken just as we entered the crowd on Constitution Avenue. That is a day that I will never forget, as long as I live.

The day had greater significance to me because we were marching right behind the delegation that had come from Prince Edward County, Virginia, the hometown of my ancestors and the county that had closed their schools rather than integrate them. My Uncle, Willie Carter, had served as the President of the NAACP, in that county. My cousins were part of that school system that denied them their education. Walking along with them had great significance to me. I did not get into trouble, on the job for joining the march, and remained with the Patent Office. I continued to work there knowing that a promotion for me was not in the cards.

During that march I realized how discrimination had really affected the lives of black folks, in the north and the south. We had been so used to segregation that we thought this was how it was supposed to be. I can remember watching the civil right demonstrations of the 50's and being thankful that we did not live in the "deep south." I remember looking at the picture of Emmett Till on the front cover of Jet magazine and seeing how his face had been beaten beyond recognition. It was during those times that we realized that the world was changing and very dangerous because there were people out there who were now willing to come out from the dark and do their dirty work in the open. I realized how bad race relations were in this country. Sometimes I would be walking and pass by a white person, and in my mind I would wonder if they were racist. Even in the workplace you looked at each other differently and you were more aware of remarks having a different meaning from what was actually being said. Black power became more evident as we begun to speak up for ourselves, especially, in the work place. We started to wear our hair in a natural state, as evidence of our newly acquired pride.

In addition to the March on Washington in August 1963, the country would experience yet another tragedy in November, 1963, when President John F. Kennedy was assassinated by Lee Harvey Oswald. It was a warm day in November and I was once again on my lunch hour shopping when I heard the news the President had been shot in Dallas, TX. I could not believe what I was hearing. Everyone was crying in disbelief. I remember going back to work and everyone was sitting around in shock. Everyone started to leave work early and when we got home, we were all glued to the television sets. I can still hear the voice of Walter Cronkite when he came on the air and said "The President is dead." With that he removed his eye glasses and shed a tear, as we all did. The following days were spent with our eyes and ears glued to the television set.

On the following Sunday, we witnessed Jack Ruby shoot Lee Harvey Oswald as they were transferring him through the courthouse. It was hard to imagine how such a tragic thing could happen in the country we were living in. If the President of the United States was not safe, the average person did not stand a chance. The world we lived in had changed and no one knew what would happen next. My boyfriend, Clinton was there with me as we stood in the long lines leading up to the Capitol Rotunda, in the freezing cold, just to have the chance to pass by the body of President John F. Kennedy, to pay our respects.

Nothing would ever be the same. The country was in mourning for a young widow, Jacqueline Kennedy, and her two small children, Caroline and John. We stood in awe as we watched his body being carried through the streets of Washington, in a horse drawn carriage, to his final resting place, Arlington Cemetery.

Things were changing for me also. During those days, Clinton was sick a lot and spent many weeks in the hospital. I learned that he had sickle cell anemia. I did not know anything about the disease, except that it was inherited. I knew early on that our relationship would not lead to marriage, because I did not want to "tie myself down" with someone that was constantly sick. I guess you could say I was selfish. He would always say that he was not supposed to live past his teenage years, so I saw no future there. Once again I had to make some touch decisions.

By the end of summer in 1964, Viola Morton, my classmate and long time friend, had come to live with me in DC and we were looking forward to getting an apartment. I was trying to ease out of the relationship with Clinton. I had never quite forgiven him for intercepting a letter and visit from Oscar, shortly after I moved out of their house. Oscar was on his way to Vietnam and came through DC looking for me. Clinton told him that he did not know where I had moved so he went overseas without our getting back together again. We did start up our correspondence again and for the second time our relationship hit a snag, when he was wounded in Vietnam in an explosion, one month before he was to return home.

Things were never the same for Oscar and me after that. His sister told me that he had received severe burns over 50 percent of his body and I imagined his spirits were very low at that time. When he wrote me from Brooks AFB in Texas, he told me that he would be there recuperating for quite a long time and his healing process was going to take a long time. In addition he had open heart surgery, and we sort of drifted apart and did not correspond with each other for many years. When he did get in contact with me I had married and moved on with my life. He was still telling me that I was supposed to be his wife and had it not been for the fiasco in Hampton, and the missed visit in DC, things would have worked out differently. We will never know. He is now single and has one daughter and granddaughter. The war in Vietnam and the exposure to Agent Orange has taken an additional toll on his health, as it did to so many military men. He is now a long time cancer survivor.

Corrine moved back to Virginia and married Jimmy. I lost touch with Corrine and by chance just recently looked her up on the internet and to my surprise after 46 years, I found her. I gave her a call and she was just as excited to hear from me as I was to hear her voice. Say what you will about the internet, it has its "useful" purposes. Corrine and I spent time catching up. She has two sons and one daughter. Jimmy, her childhood sweetheart and husband passed in 1990; she is still working, but looking forward to retirement. We promised to keep in touch from now on. The bonds of real friendship can never be broken.

Jo Ann remained in DC and we continued to socialize and have remained friends. Their names will probably come up later as I talk about those early days after we left Cortez Peters. We don't see each other often but when we talk we remember the days past. She met Lynwood Coley, through her friendship with me and Billy, the man I was dating. She married Lynwood and they have three daughters and one grandson. Lynwood "got saved" and made a miraculous change in his ways and is now a very active church member. He owns a barbershop and she is now retired, and still keeps mostly to herself, enjoying her family. We do continue to keep in contact, at least on a yearly basis. Just recently we spent a long time talking about those early days and some of the crazy things we did, as newly classified "adults." We talk about the good times spent on Carr's beach and at Pat and GG's in Maryland where all the entertainers made the round, and how when we danced to the music of singers like Tina Turner and James Brown, we had no idea they would one day be famous all over the world. Those were truly the good old days of soul music and yes we enjoyed playing the one arm bandits in an effort to win some extra spending money. Jo-Ann couldn't remember going down to Marshall's Hall amusement park on the riverboat and watching the fights break out on the boat as it made it way back up the river, and the drunks did not have anything else to do, one time even throwing the piano overboard. I remember those times well.

As I started to move on, in December 1963, I was looking forward to meeting new people. I was introduced, by my sister Josephine, to Paul Dean Harris and his sister, Alfreda. This family would be a part of my life in a very meaningful way in the months that followed.

I was getting tired of living dormitory style and since Viola had come to town we started looking for an apartment. This had been our dream since high school days. We had saved up enough money to buy furniture and necessary items for our new place. It was a lot of fun playing grown up and looking for our new home. We found a place and held our breaths waiting for the word that we had could move in.

In 1964, Viola and I moved into our first apartment. It was located at 4014 Kansas Avenue, NW. It was really nice. I enjoyed decorating and was looking forward to showing off my culinary skills to the new man who was coming into my life. After all I was not getting any younger and in those days everyone expected you to be married by the time you reached 21. I had made up my mind to make the complete break with Clinton, after he helped me move into my new place. Yes it was selfish but I needed to explore all my options. The break up was not pretty. I did it over the phone before I went on my date with Dean. Shortly after I returned home, Clinton was standing outside the door begging to come in to talk. Viola was telling me not to let him in because he was upset and may hurt me. It seemed like a lifetime before he left my door, and I really did feel bad for him. We talked the next day and although he was hurt, we agreed to move on and just be friends. My last trip taken with his family was to New York to the World's Fair in 1965. We did remain friends and at various times I went to family gatherings when I was invited. (Post Script: Clinton beat the odds of his sickle cell disease, and lived to be 58 years of age. He passed away in 1996.)

It was time to move on and Dean, another older man, and I became an item in early 1964 and we would spend a lot of time together, either at my apartment or his house. His family was very nice and they really liked me. He was the only person outside of my family that ever called me by my middle name, but he changed it to "Gerri," instead of Gearl. I guess that was because he knew me through my sister, who called me Gearl. Dean was a bowler and I spent many evenings watching him perfect his bowling skills. He taught me how to bowl and play miniature golf. He was in bowling leagues so it took up a lot of his time. On Sunday evenings I would prepare dinner and he would come over and we would spend quality time together. He gave me a special teddy bear that we named "Jerry" representing my middle name Geraldine and his which was Jerome.

It seemed that I was always attracted to older men or vice versa they were attracted to me. Dean was different and as an older person he introduced me to things other than partying. We went to picnics at Haines Point and went swimming often. I was glad I had learned how to swim while I was working at Hampton Institute. I still had a little fear of the water though. Dean had a friend named Howard, and I introduced to one of my classmate from home. She was spending the summer in DC with her parents and we hung out some together before she returned to college. It was good to have someone from home to hang out with that summer.

Dean belonged to a social club and we traveled on many out of town trips with them. He was the first person to take me to Atlantic City. This was way before the casinos made their debut. It was still exciting walking on the boardwalk and swimming in the ocean. The week end was filled with excitement among the club members. It seemed that every couple on the trip had a fight or argument during the weekend, including Dean and me. We patched things up on the way back to DC though. One couple was so mad at each other that they started fighting in their room and it ended up spilling out on the porch, with half of their clothes off. That put everybody back in a good mood as we talked and laughed about it on our way back to DC.

That summer went by fast and Dean started talking about returning to North Carolina A&T State University, to complete his degree in Engineering. Once again in the latter part of 1964, I was put in a long distance relationship. During that time I became very close to his family because his sister Alfredia was very ill. I spent many hours sitting at her bedside keeping her company in the hospital until she passed away. Dean returned from college with his new engineering degree from A&T, but also new problems. He was in a depressed state because he had lost his sister, while he was away, and had not really dealt with his loss. He also felt that he had concentrated so much time on school that he needed some time to get his self together. We tried spending time together but things were strained. I was unhappy and suggested, and he agreed, to give each other some space.

During that period of time, Viola was dating someone she met at work and he introduced me to his friend Walter Booth. Walter was a cook at Sibley Hospital where they were all working. I was still waiting for Dean to sort out some things in his life, so I was not interested in a new relationship. As time passed, I really wanted things to work out for Dean and me. He had asked me for additional time and I remembered praying about it a lot. One night I made a specific request in my prayer. I asked the Lord to show me a sign if I should stay in this relationship or let it go, even though I wanted it. That night I prayed that the sign would be if I opened my eyes the next morning the clock would be at 6:00 AM sharp, I would know then that I should move on. Subconsciously I wanted to sleep until noon the next day.

Sleep did not come easy that night. I tossed and turned for what seemed like forever but finally fell asleep. When I awoke that morning and looked at the clock my heart sank, because the hands on the clock were straight up and down. I lay there feeling sick because I had made a promise to God and knew that although I did not want to follow through; my faith told me that I would be alright. I got up and sat on the bed and I wrote this long "Dear John" letter to Dean.

I did not explain in the letter why I had decided, on this particular day, to move on and had left a little crack in the door. I knew in my heart this was the end. I called for a taxi to deliver the letter to his house, not trusting the post office or myself for fear that I would change my mind. The taxi driver made the delivery and called back to confirm he had personally placed the letter in his hands. Later that day I received a phone call and there was silence on the other end. We didn't have caller ID back then, but I knew it was Dean calling. I hung up without saying anything either.

This was really a difficult time for me. The break up was just before Easter Sunday, 1965, and I did not even want to go to church. I forced myself to get up and get dressed in time to go to the service. At the time, I was a member of First Baptist Church and Rev. Frank Tucker preached a sermon that carried me through that time, and sustains me to this date.

When I went to First Baptist that morning, the pastor preached about the crucifixion and the resurrection. He said that no matter what you are going through look at it as a dark Friday evening knowing that there was a Sunny Sunday morning just ahead. In time the sun did shine again, and I have never forgotten the lesson learned from that sermon. Now I know that the "Son" shines on all my issues and with him helping me go through them, I know I will be alright.

Many years later, Dean and I would become friends again. We had both moved on in different directions, with other people. He was not as lucky – He was on his second marriage. I guess he did not realize what a good catch he had in me until it was too late. I understand from a mutual friend that he suffered from Alzheimer's in his final years and passed away in 2009.

The time between the spring of 1965 and the end of summer in 1966 would present many challenges in my personal life. I would end one relationship, begin a new one, then end it, and then finally start a new one with a person who would be with me on this journey for the next forty five years. It has been one with many twists and turns.

This part of my story gets a little complicated because it involved many lives that intermingled along the way. Three people become prominent; Walter Booth, William (Billy) Montgomery and Virginia Reynolds. They would be a part of this journey for years to come. Of course, Virginia and I would not meet until years after 1966. By coincidence she had known Billy, as a friend, before I met him, and I had known Walter before she knew him.

Sometime after my breakup with Dean in early 1965, Walter was back in the picture. I had just gotten out of the earlier relationship, with Dean, and really just wanted time to find myself. Viola and her boyfriend, who was a friend of Walter's, were still dating. He told me that Walter was still interested and wanted to go out on a date with me. Walter started to call regularly, but I still would not go out with him. He was patient and spent hours talking on the telephone with me. I believed he saw a little opening, and he set out to change my mind. I agreed to see him. It seemed like a good idea since he was my best friend's co-worker and not a stranger.

Walter was also different because he had big ideas and said he was biding his time working at the hospital because he was going places. He talked a lot about the entertainment field and all the entertainers. It was exciting to think that one day I might meet some of these people in person. In May 1965, shortly after we became friends, we all went to West Virginia to a Stratton graduation. This was the first time I had taken someone home to meet my parents Walter met my parents and we had a great time. When we returned from the trip, we started to get closer.

I was still kind of naïve and never asked many questions of the men I dated. We didn't have the benefit of the internet, where with a click of a button, you could view a person's history, from birth to death. I never met Walter's family, but I did know that he had one. He said he was divorced and trying to start over, and I believed him.   Around that time the group called "The Sweet Things" came out with a record.   The lead singer was Francine Hurd, "Peaches" backed up by Dyanne Stewart and Nancy Johnson, singing songs written by Van McCoy of Columbia records. I was young and impressionable and when he was gone for long periods of time, he always explained that he was on the road promoting this group. At that time I had no reason to disbelieve him. I guess sometimes you can be too trusting for your own good.

In the summer of 1965, I had also transferred from the Commerce Department to the Post Office Department on V Street, NE. They had a different pay scale and that meant I would be making more money. I had found out that in order to get ahead in the Government, you had to move on. My co-workers at Commerce kept telling me that I had to stay on a job for three years or I would not become permanent, so I listened to them but later found that not to be true. I stayed at the Post Office for about six months.   There were too many rules there and it was isolated from everything. Lunch time was 30 minutes and I got tired of eating on the run.   I was the only black female working there and there was only one white female working in the office.   We were the only administrative personnel. I knew my time there would be short.

I would soon learn that Walter had big ideas and little money. I remember coming to his rescue at a time when "The Sweet Things" had a performance lined up. They did not have anything to wear. Being the helping person that I was, at that time in my life, he mentioned this to me and said he did not know what he was going to do. I agreed to take them shopping for dresses. This was my first time meeting the group. We met and went together to Capital Plaza Shopping Mall to pick out dresses from Montgomery Wards. Of course, I paid for them. I looked at it as an investment in "our future." I also started to see a pattern in his lack of funds. From that point on, Walter would embark on his journey as a part time road manager, while working part time, as a cook, at Sibley Hospital.

During the times that he would be absent my friend, Linda (Leach) Truesdale and I would hang out together. She had recently moved out of the rooming house that we had shared and we lived within walking distance of each other. We spent a lot of time talking about our mutual problems and going to parties together.   Her boyfriend at the time Chalmers Truesdale was in the navy so we did not have much to keep us at home.   Linda and I had a lot in common. We were both helping out our parents financially. We would budget so we had just enough money left over from payday to payday. We ate sparingly and sometimes walked to work to save bus fare.

We were both from small towns so we felt there was safety in numbers when we went out on the town. We always found a party to attend on the weekend. There were clubs also, but we stuck mostly to the house parties. They were the most popular places to hang out, if you did not have a lot of money to buy drinks at the club, and if you were traveling with a girlfriend.

Since I had not been around this group of Walter's acquaintances I had no idea what his real life was all about. In hindsight I see that he was leading a double life with friends and family that I had no knowledge of. At some point in 1966, I started asking questions. I had found out that he was not always telling me the truth and I suspected him of two timing me by seeing someone who worked at the hospital. Finding out that he was supposedly divorced would only add to my growing sense of insecurity. My earlier misgivings and reservations about a relationship with him kept creeping into my psyche. Paranoia set in and I felt I was being kept in the dark.

As a result of my paranoia, I was not the best roommate during those times. Undue stresses were affecting my work and other relationships. Without much notice, I made plans to move out of the apartment that I shared with my best friend. I moved with mixed feelings because I was leaving my best friend and confidant. We split up our belongings and I moved into a new apartment on the other side of town, where I could make a fresh start.

I moved to Brentwood Village in the Northeast section of Washington. My former roommate Jo-Ann Davis, from Cortez Peters, was also living in the same neighborhood. I was happy to have my own apartment. It wasn't long before another friend from Cortez Peters, Shirley Myers, needed a place to stay and I agreed for her to stay with me temporarily. She was planning to get married so I figured it would be ok for a few months. I had made some contacts through her soon to be husband Calvin Adams, and found a new job. I transferred from the Post Office Department to a secretarial position with the Small Business Administration.

After moving into the neighborhood, I found out that Walter had moved in with his friend Olley Fuller. I guess I thought that being in the same proximity of each other we would spend more time together. At least I would find out what was going on in his life. At that time I did not have a car so I couldn't get around like I wanted to. I had no idea if this move would be the beginning or the end. You know the old saying, "If you look for trouble you will find it." Believe me it is true.

I was not willing to just sit back and see how things would work out, so I started to check things out for myself. Since Walter was living just around the corner, I started to make pop call visits. Sometimes I could sense that things weren't adding up. There were unexpected disappearances, missed or unreturned phone calls, and most of all the little white lies that did not add up. I needed to find out just where I stood and if I needed to move on.

On a Friday night with nothing to do, I decided to make an unscheduled stop at the apartment building he was living in. I had met Barbara, one of his next door neighbors, and I decided to drop by to see her. She had told me about this friend of Walter's who had also moved into the apartment with Olley. I think at the time she had her eyes on him. I had met him on an earlier occasion and found out his name was Billy. When he came through that evening, I did not pay that much attention to him. Barbara and I were talking and having some cool drinks.

Sometime during that visit I found out that Walter was back in town and was next door. Since we had not been in touch for awhile, things were very shaky between us. I figured I might as well find out once and for all what was going on, or had been going on. In the back of my mind I had already decided that this relationship was pretty much over and it was time for me to move on.

It was customary in those days to leave your apartment doors open. Everybody knew each other and it was not unusual to go from apartment to apartment anytime, without being invited. When I finally went next door, I found Walter entertaining a "young lady" at the bar. She could not have been much older than seventeen. He was surprised to see me but I was cool. He didn't want me to come in, but I told him that since it wasn't his apartment, he couldn't keep me out. I proceeded to walk to the bar and take a seat next to the young lady. I asked her name and then I told her mine. Walter was getting agitated and the young lady didn't know what to do. She was trying to explain why she was there in the first place.

Finally, I told her who I was, why I was there and what my relationship was to Walter. In the meantime Walter is not sure what I am going to do. He approached me and said, "Sorry you have to go." I guess that was the wrong thing for him to say because my female instinct kicked in and said this might be your last shot. All these thoughts were running through my head telling me this may be over but you can go down fighting. This may be your last chance to make sure that he will never forget you. At that very instant, I turned around and jumped off the bar stool and my old bad habit, from my childhood days, kicked in. I started to fight. I took him totally by surprise. Somehow I managed to knock his glasses to the floor, and while he was scrambling trying to find them, I was getting in all the licks that I could.

When I looked around the young lady had hauled tail. Billy and Barbara, hearing all the commotion, came in from next door to see what was going on. Walter didn't have time to defend himself. He was still crawling around on the floor trying to find his glasses. In the meantime, I am still swinging with my eyes closed, and he is trying to get me off of his back. I was just getting started. For some unknown reason, I was enjoying every minute of it. I guess it is true that hell has no fury like a woman scorned.

After standing there sizing up the situation for awhile, Billy finally said to me, "Come on, and let's go for a walk." I think he might have been afraid that I would turn on him so he did not try to break up the fight right away. I finally got up, went next door, and had the audacity to call the police to say that I had been assaulted.

Even then the police was slow to respond to domestic violence complaints. I waited around for hours for the police to come. Finally, when it was evident they were not going to show up, Billy and I went out to get something to eat. In one crazy night of events, Walter and I parted and I made a new friend, Billy, who I thought would only be a "friend."

As for the young lady, I saw her at the shopping center the next week and I called out her name and she started to run. I immediately assured her that I wasn't going to hurt her and that if she wanted Walter, she could have him because we were through for good. She kept insisting that they were just friends and she had just dropped by that night. By that time it did not matter to me one way or the other. Walter and Billy would continue their friendship, after our breakup. He was probably one of the best friends Billy had for the next 24 years.

Many years later, Walter and I would become close friends again through, of all people, the man I would eventually marry, Billy. I remember my family saying to me whenever his name and Billy's was mentioned, at the same time, "Is that the same Walter who came with you to West Virginia?" I would say "yes" and explain there was nothing there anymore but friendship. They would just smile and shake their head. We even went on double dates together, traveled together and Walter even spent some nights at our house, when he was in town after Billy and I were married.

The day before Walter passed, in September 1990, Virginia, who I mentioned earlier, his new companion, Billy and I spent that last Sunday evening eating a meal that he had prepared. Our friendship was mended and the wonderful lady he ended up with had become one of my dearest friends. Over the years, we have shared many good times. Billy and I think of Virginia as our sister. I am glad that through Walter's and my ability to move on with our lives, he ended up with a wonderful companion and Billy and I ended up with a friend for life. I remind Billy all the time that Virginia is the only "play sister" that he has. Years later I would meet and get to know one of Walter's children, his daughter Stephanie and her children. Because my relationship with Walter did not last very long, I never got to know them as children. Stephanie and I have spent many hours talking on the phone and I am happy to have her friendship. I had never talked to her, until recently, about her father and me, but I know from conversations we had in later years he loved her and her brothers and was very proud of them.

The night my relationship with Walter ended in a fight, I began a new and lasting friendship with, William Edward Montgomery (Billy), the man who would end up becoming my husband. At that time I had no idea the friendship would end up in marriage. Walter and Billy traveled a lot all over the country, as Walter's dream of being in the entertainment field came to pass. He became the manager for Peaches and Herb and the Manhattans.

More changes were taken place in my life. After I transferred to the Small Business Administration in 1966, I met a co-worker, Betty (Faison) Barnaby, and we became life long friends. That friendship lasted until February 2009, when she passed away. Betty and I would become party buddies and travel buddies. Years later, I was beside her as her Matron of Honor when she married her husband Roy, at the courthouse in Rockville, MD, on Valentine's Day.

My time working at SBA was short. I can remember vividly how the head secretary, who was black, used to insist that we type letters without any errors.

She would hold the original up to the light to see if there had been any erasures. I got tired of having to retype a letter from scratch after getting to the bottom error less only to make a mistake at the closing. I soon became good at using an eraser so perfectly that no one could tell an error had been made. In those days we did not have spell check and we used carbon paper to make at least six copies while typing the original.

My memories are not all bad because I did meet some new people, who would remain friends for many years. Dolores Bailey and Polly (Belk) Buyck and I still talk and see each other periodically. Marie Fields and her husband Bernard would play an important role as they opened their home, a few years later, for my wedding and reception, and asked a minister from their church, Jerusalem Baptist, Rev. R. Clinton Washington to perform the ceremony. Also Douglas Thomas, another co-worker from SBA, was my wedding photographer. Doug was one of the few black males in a professional position at SBA. There were not many chances for blacks to move up in most of the government agencies, where I worked, in the early sixties.

My circle of friends, in 1966-67 was growing. I was getting used to living by myself after Shirley married and moved out and was looking forward to what the rest of the summer had in store for me.

I don't know exactly when I started seeing Billy as something other than a friend. We spent a lot of time during the remainder of the summer of 1966. One of the first places he took me was on a tour of the Franciscans Monastery. During the tour he told he had been studying there at one time to become a priest. I started to wonder what I was in for.

Considering how we really met through his friend, he was slow at pursuing a romantic relationship with me, because he thought things were not really over. He would always ask me if I was considering going back into the relationship with Walter, and I told him that we had both moved on. Being the type of person he was he asked Walter the same question and was assured that we had both moved on. As time went on Billy and I spent more time together. I was once again living by myself and decided to show off my culinary skills to him. Even today he brags that he took me shopping at Giant grocery store and offered to pay for the groceries.

Since I have always been a finicky eater, I was only going to get what I liked to eat and I put a boneless ham in the basket. He said I only did that because he was paying. I was only letting him know that he was in a different social class with me, and he would have to step up to the plate if he wanted to impress me. His favorite song was "When a Man Loves a Woman" by Percy Sledge. He would play that song and say those words said everything he was feeling for me. I don't know if he meant it or not, but it got my attention. Every time that record came on, it was our signal to hit the dance floor. Billy was not much of a dancer, but Percy Sledge could get him on the dance floor, for a slow grind. In our time, that is what we called a sexy dance.

I thought Billy was kind of rough around the edges. I figured I could work with a stone that was a diamond in the rough. He never talked much about himself or his family. He also was not truthful about his age. He knew I preferred older men. He purposefully did not discuss other people in his life, by saying that if I knew too much about him before I got to know him, I might not give him a chance. He told me I was the type of woman he had been looking for because I was "different." I don't know what he or I interpreted "different" to be, at that time.

Billy wasn't as innocent as I had originally thought. We did a lot of partying during the first year. Around that time Linda and I started to hang out together again. Her boyfriend Dave (Chalmers) Truesdale had been discharged from the Navy and had come to DC to live. The four of us would go out to clubs together sometimes. I was slowly finding out things about Billy. There was the incident where he told me he had to go to New York to see his sick Aunt Mary. Since I did not know his family, I believed him only to find out later that "Aunt Mary" was an old girl friend. He was trying to find out what was going on with her since she had moved to New York. I found this out when he told me that this friend was coming in town and he was not going to be available for a few days. Being the nosy person that I was, something did not seem right so when I called his house and a woman answered, I found out that her name was Mary, and she was not his "aunt." That did not go over too well, but I was cool and did not go to the apartment to play boxing games, because we were still early in our relationship. We got through that episode but the seed of doubt and mistrust had been planted.

I also learned that Billy enjoyed playing cards with his buddies. There was this whole group of guys who were mostly from down south and they all hung out in the market area close to where Billy worked at Rock Creek Soda Company. In other words he liked to gamble. In September of 1967, my running buddy Linda got married and I was a bridesmaid in her wedding. My friend and roommate Shirley got married on the same day. With my running buddy getting married, I also had to decide if this relationship with Billy was going anywhere. I wanted to show him a different lifestyle from the one he had gotten accustomed to. We would have candlelight dinners that I cooked; go to movies and hang out at one of our favorite nightclub, the Mark IV, while sitting around having a good time talking about life.

Needless to say I was very skeptical about men due to my failed relationships from the past. I introduced him to my friends who were different from his. They were not "gamblers" and what I described as "loose" women. My friends were trying to get ahead on their jobs and had a different outlook on life. I helped him upgrade his wardrobe and tried to keep him out of the pool hall and the market, which were his friend's favorite hang outs.

Billy had also started to go on the road with Walter who was now managing Peaches and Herb. The Sweet Things had fizzled out after one or two records and Peaches had moved on. I had to decide if this was really what I was looking for. I was spending more and more time alone and he was encouraging me to do things with my friends. Jo-Ann and I had started to go out together and Billy told me he had a card playing buddy who was looking to meet someone. Naturally we introduced her to him and Lynwood Coley and Jo-Ann became a couple. Lynwood became one of the Bryant Street Gang. I now had someone else to party with because all of my other friends were getting married and their husbands were keeping them under tight reigns. Lynwood, Jo Ann, Billy and I hung out a lot together. We mostly partied all night, went to work the next day, only to party again the next night, and repeat the cycle.

I decided I needed to concentrate on moving up in my career. I was looking for a way out of the Small Business Administration, because they already had their "token" black and the rest of us were going nowhere fast. I decided to go back to school to take a refresher course in shorthand so I could at least get promoted from a clerk typist to a clerk stenographer.

I enrolled in a class at the US Department of Agriculture Graduate School and I met Gladys (Tymas) Johnson and Sandra (Briscoe) Powell, who I had met earlier through Betty (Faison) Barnaby, in the class. We completed the class, took the shorthand exam at the Pentagon, and passed with flying colors. That would be my ticket to another promotion. Shortly after that time, Gladys and I would become good friends and hangout buddies.

After receiving my new rating for a stenographer, I asked for a promotion at the SBA. My supervisor told me that I needed to be a little more cooperative, which to me meant "keeping a low profile and not ruffling any feathers." Being cooperative also meant doing more work than the white girls in the office. Not wanting to do this, I started looking for another job. Sandra had moved on to work at the Department of Health, Education and Welfare and told me about a position there. I applied and was accepted and when I told my supervisor, at SBA I was leaving, they were then willing to promote me. Ironically the white lady that worked in the office with me was just as happy as I was when I left. She had some mental issues and they let her get away with a lot of foolishness. When she found out I was leaving she used to walk around the office singing "Happy Days are Here Again." She did not know how happy I was to be leaving her company also.

I was finding out that you had to move around in government to get any promotions. I started working with the Center for Community Planning and at that time the "war on poverty" was a really big social issue. The people I worked with were mostly Caucasian and all together different. James (Jim) Alexander headed up the Department, and Beth Owens was his secretary. The persons I worked under were Natalie Spingarn and Judy Hopkins. Years later, Natalie Spingarn would go on to fame as she became a medical writer who endured multiple bouts of cancer and became a prominent spokeswoman for cancer survivors. She is credited with creating the "Cancer Survivors Bill of Rights" for the American Cancer Society.

We had a really good group of people working together. They were all excited about doing what they could to get rid of poverty. Some of the employees were more sociable than others. This was the first time I actively socializing with white people other than in a work environment. We were on a first name basis, even with the supervisor, and we had lunches and Christmas celebrations as a group.

The first time I tasted caviar was at a Christmas party held at Natalie Spingarn's house at 3212 McKinley Street, NW in DC. Whenever I pass by there I am always drawn to look at the house and recall memories of those days gone by.

Natalie, Judy and Beth Owens were the token "whites" at my wedding. They were very comfortable in our company because they were used to being in mixed environments during the work they did promoting the "get rid of poverty" programs.   They were part of the "new generation" who had been sensitized to the inequalities among the races. They called themselves the foot soldiers for change.   The work environment for professional blacks was beginning to open up in some areas, especially in the area of Community Planning and Urban Development. Our office was staffed with some blacks who had bridged the gap of segregation by educating themselves in those areas. Later I would see some of those names, of people I had worked with in the 60's, mentioned in articles about social change.   James Butts was one of those employees. Affirmative action had finally arrived, or we thought it had. I lost contact with everyone but Jean Smith, who now resides in Las Vegas and Sandra (Briscoe) Powell, who resides in Maryland. We often talk about those early days and wonder where the others are.

The War on Poverty Team emerged out of the rhetoric for change in the form of the great Model Cities Programs and Projects. As a support person, I attended conferences and I had the opportunity to travel with the office staff to conferences, held across the country, experiencing my first airplane flights. The one thing I managed to get out of was living as a homeless person for a week. As employees, we were all required to spend a week in Baltimore living on $7.00 a week, so that we would be more sensitive to the needs of the poor. We were instructed to take a minimum amount of clothes and we were to sleep in sleeping bags for the entire time. That was one experience that I did not have to pretend about, because I had lived the experience as part of my life. I met and made another long time friend, Carlotta Dabney, who worked for the National League of Cities. We interfaced with them in our responsibilities for the Model Cities Program. Over the next years Carlotta and her sister Helen and I had lots of good times hanging out with Metropolitan finest police officers, who loved to party. Carlotta would later marry and divorce Ray Mott, one of the founders of Black Ski. She relocated to Atlanta, GA and we kept in touch while she lived there. After a few years there, she returned to the DC area.

As we moved into the year 1967, I still had not met Billy's family from South Carolina. However, in the early part of 1967, one of his father's brothers died here in DC and his family came up, from down south, to attend the funeral. They sort of sized me up and really did not have a lot to say. I was a little intimidated so I was on the quiet side. I finally got to know who his relatives were that lived in this area. He took me around to see his Aunt Revolla, Uncle Mitchell, who he had lived with when he first came to DC and his Aunt Mary. At that time, I also got to know one of his cousins, Vinson Good, and his wife Elois.

Those family members, that I met, never discussed with me the other members of his family and I never asked a lot of questions. I guess they assumed that I knew everything I needed to know. Later in the year, I would make my first trip to South Carolina when Billy's oldest brother, Vernon, Jr., passed. This was my first trip that deep in the south. I met the South Carolina family and his sister and I sort of connected.

I would soon find out that Billy had kept information from me concerning his past relationships. I was beginning to have some questions and when I pressed him for answers, he decided to open up and talk about his past. During that conversation, I found out he had his first child in 1961, married her mother after she was born and had separated before the second child was born in 1962. Not only did he tell me about those two daughters, Tanya and Vieda, but he also told me about his other daughter. He told me her name was Anita McCoy, but he called her Nee Nee, and that she was born in 1963. He explained to me why he had not seen her after her mother moved back to North Carolina. In my mind I am thinking; He must have really been making up for the time he was studying in the Monastery. We talked for a long time late into the night. Since I found myself more deeply involved with him than I initially believed, I was not willing to walk away. I believed he was a good person who had made some choices with unexpected consequences. I thought he may not have handled them as I would have. He explained that because he had no way of knowing how I would react when I found out his past, he had chosen to be evasive about his background. He felt if I knew everything up front, I would walk away from him, and not get to know him for myself. In my mind I am thinking had he been evasive or had he been lying. I decided to give him the benefit of the doubt and accepted his explanations. I also told him that if we were to continue in our relationship, he would have to sort out things in his past that could prevent us from moving forward. He took the necessary steps to shape up and we made plans for the next year. We became engaged in August of 1967. I went home without him that summer in July and told my parents what my plans were.

The year of 1968 would change a lot of things in this country. On April 4, 1968, Martin Luther King, Jr., was assassinated in Memphis, TN. His assassination caused riots to break out all across the country. The streets were burning and the protesters were filling the streets.

I remember when the first riot started in DC. I was downtown shopping on a payday trying to pick up my lay-away purchases. Everyone in the stores were talking about what was going on outside and the fires were starting on 7th street near the Hecht Company store, on 14th and U Streets, NW, and H Street, NE. I remember hurrying home to watch it on television. I just could not believe what was happening.

I called my sister, Josephine, who was living on 14th Street and she said she, Johnna, and John were out there watching things go wild. I remember wondering where Billy was and was happy when he called to say he was home. He wanted to go out and see what was going on and I begged him to stay home. Things were getting wild. We watched a lot of TV coverage during the next few days. People were afraid to go out and heard that the police had been given orders to shoot if they crossed in to the white section of town, specifically the Georgetown section. It seemed as if the world was coming to an end. Our department stores on 14th Street and H Street were burning down and the looting was in full swing. People were looting and carrying sofas and televisions only to find that their own homes had been burned down so they had no place to put their newly acquired goods.

Race relations in the United States were at a boiling point and no one seemed to have the answers. They even enlisted James Brown to go out and try to talk to the people to calm them down. We all stayed glued to the TV as we watched the events unfold in Atlanta where Dr. King's funeral was taken place and he was being laid to rest. It bought back sad memories of another great American, who had been slain, just five years earlier, President John F. Kennedy.

My mind went back to that day in the summer of 1961, and that chance encounter I had with Dr. King, when I helped serve him lunch. I will forever remember the warm handshake that Dr. King gave me and the kind words he spoke, as he thanked us for our service. I was remembering being at the March on Washington in 1963. We all knew that our lives, as a race, were changed on that day in April, but we had to move on.

I made another physical move to a newer apartment at 1384 Bryant Street, NE. This would be a new beginning. Billy was there to help me make the move. In June of 1968, I guess Billy had gotten tired of walking so he told me that if I learned how to drive, he would buy me a car. I got excited about the prospects of having a car to get around in and decided if he did not buy it, I would. I figured he would at least help me make the payments. I learned how to drive on an automatic after taking six lessons. My first choice for a car was the Volkswagen, but I could not drive a stick shift. My coordination of my feet just did not work out. When I got my driver's license I was so excited about the prospects of finally being able to get my own transportation. I went out looking and put $1.00 down for the salesman to hold it. I purchased my first car July 12, 1968, three days before my 26th birthday, from Eaton Chevrolet. For all of $2,900 I got a white Malibu Sports Coupe. It had everything but air-conditioning. For the next 36 months, I paid $71.18 and Billy and I rode in style.

I became his chauffer and I had no fear of driving. We took our first trip on the highway to see his sister, Eunice, in Morristown, NJ. The trip was fine going up, except that I missed my turn and was headed to New York and panicked when I was about to enter the tunnel leading into the city and downtown. I panicked and I don't know how I did it but somehow I managed to back up and get back on the interstate, without causing an accident. I guess it was a good thing that the traffic was not as congested then as it is now. On the way back, just before we reached the sign on the Baltimore Washington Parkway that says "Welcome to Washington," fate tempted us again and we were almost in a terrible accident. After leaving New Jersey late at night, I was driving along and came upon this car that was sitting in the middle of the highway, with the lights turned off. My life passed before me and I just prayed. There was nothing else to do. My instincts kicked in and I started to pump the brakes to slow down and when the car stopped, it was resting side by side of the other vehicle, with about a foot of space in between, to spare. I know the Lord was in that car with us at that time and I was really shaken up. I also knew that I had to get back on the highway because I had 36 months of car payments to make, and there was no way I could not stop driving.

Even today as I approach that sign, I have a flashback of what could have been. That close call made me stop and think about how quickly things could change.

I knew that I had to get on the right track and was ready to make some serious plans to settle down and start a new phase of my life.

That summer, with transportation, Billy and I stayed on the road. He encouraged me to drive everywhere. We would spend evenings and nights down by the waterfront at Haines Point. I never knew how much freedom a car could give you. This would be my first introduction of him to my family in West Virginia. Up to this point, only Josephine and Bernice had met him. We took our first trip to West Virginia that year, with me driving. Billy joked that I drove so slow that a rabbit was running across the highway and looked up and saw me creeping along, and promptly slowed down to a crawl. Driving down Route 3 along the mountains was not something I had looked forward to doing.

I did not share with my parents everything I knew about Billy, who they had never met. I knew how my mother, and most people in her generation, felt about ready made families. I told them he was a good person and a good worker. I confided in my close friends that I had not shared all of his past with them, but I decided that it was eventually my decision to make.

The family meeting went well and the next time we would all meet would be on our wedding day.

Chapter 10

Start of a New Journey - 1968

When I started writing this book about my search, for my ancestors and family, it was apparent that it would not be complete without the addition of my expanded family, as the result of the union of William Edward Montgomery and me. This link was solidified when we were joined in holy matrimony on December 21, 1968, shortly after 6:00 PM, at 5211 – 11th Street, NE, Washington, DC. The ceremony was performed by Rev. R. Clinton Washington, a minister at Jerusalem Baptist Church, located in the Georgetown section of DC. The two separate families became one on that day.

We had a small intimate wedding at the home of my friend and co-worker, Marie Fields and her husband Bernard. It was not an elaborate wedding because our funds were limited and most of our family members lived out of town. I had a small group of friends that I had made from my various places of employment and from my days as a student at Cortez Peters Business School. My best friend Viola had returned to live in the city, and as she had promised so many years ago, she was my Maid of Honor. Her friendship and support was important to me, as I worked to pull this event together.

We did not plan for months by setting the date early; we just picked that date at random and worked to make it happen. Billy was always afraid of needles and shots, and he nearly passed out when we went to get our blood tests. My physician, Dr. Henry Bell, did not know this and was taken aback when it seemed that he was going to lose a patient.

Our second disaster was averted when we made the deadline for the waiting period to pick up our marriage license. I was not aware that there was a waiting period before we could actually pick up the license, after the application had been filed. Although our wedding ceremony did not have all the whistles and bells that President Nixon's daughter, Julie had, the following day on December 22nd; it was none the less just as special.

I had spent a limited amount of time picking out wedding invitations and favors and held my breath until they arrived. We were working with a short deadline and Billy had failed to give me addresses for some of his family, so they had to be hand delivered. Looking back on that, I can see that was not good etiquette. The date we picked was just before the Christmas holiday and we had already planned to go to New Jersey to spend some time with "my new family."

I was excited at the prospects of getting married and I spent a significant amount of time looking for the right dress. Since mini dresses were in style, I was able to find an after five dress that was suitable for the occasion and me. My dress had a low "v" neck with silver threads braided throughout. It was also the right length to show off my legs. I had the assistance of good friends who helped with the food preparations for the reception. On my wedding day, I was running around all day doing last minute errands. It was a beautiful day and all the out of town guest had arrived safely.

My mother and father had arrived in town earlier, but had gone to Baltimore to my Uncle Joseph's house to spend time before the wedding. I was not expecting any of my siblings except Josephine and Bernice. The group from Baltimore would also include Uncle Thomas, Daddy's brother. Josephine and her children, Johnna and John had come to the apartment earlier in the day to help me get things together. Billy's mother, sister, Eunice and her husband Bobby from New Jersey, his brothers George from South Carolina, and Joseph from Boston, were also expected to come into town. George was Billy's Best Man so he had arrived the night before. Billy had invited some of his card playing buddies at the last minute. Lynwood and Jo-Ann, our party buddies were expected to be there along with Olley, Billy's friend from the day. I did not get to spend any time with them before the day of the wedding and was looking forward to the families meeting for the first time. I had bought outfits for our mother's to wear. I also bought outfits for my sister Josephine and her children. While de-cluttering file cabinets recently, I ran across receipts from my "big" wedding and I think I pulled it off for under $500, which included the cost of everyone's outfits, photographer, cake, flowers and of course my dress.

My photographer and co-worker Doug Thomas came early to take photos before the ceremony. I was a little nervous and sent Viola, who was my maid of honor, downstairs to see if everyone was in place, since the 6:00 PM hour was fast approaching. I found out later that Billy and George had played cards the night before, overslept the next day, and ended up getting dressed in the car on the way to the wedding. I was ready at 6:00 but did not come down the stairs until a few minutes after that time. I was hoping that I would not fall down the stairs as I walked slowly, and pondered the "big change" about to take place. Daddy was waiting for me at the foot of the stairs. The ceremony went off without a hitch as we said our vows and I was waiting to see what Daddy's response would be when he was asked "Who gives this woman to be wed?" Daddy was known to have something out of the ordinary to say.

Now that the ceremony was over, we all breathed a sigh of relief. We had the reception immediately following and then we went back to our apartment, with our families, to continue the celebration. It was getting late and we had to show our guest where they would be staying. I was so tired that as I was driving along New York Avenue headed towards the Baltimore Washington Parkway, from out of nowhere this greyhound bus was right upon me. My new brother in law Bob said that I was so close to the bus that the dog jumped off the side of the bus and hopped inside. I remember him saying, "Did you see that bus Martha?" I was so tired I don't know if I did or not. We finally got back to the hotel so late that the wedding night was just about over and we had to get up the next morning to drive to New Jersey. Since Billy did not drive, Olley offered to drive us to New Jersey. The day before had been sunny and bright but it snowed like heck the next day. Our honeymoon was spent with Billy's family as we celebrated our first Christmas together. After the trip to New Jersey, we returned home and Billy moved in and we settled down to married life.

It took me some time to figure out who all these new people in my life were. Little by little I started to put faces on the names. So that you will know who they are, I will give you a little background on Billy's family. He is not so keen on family history, so I have put together as much as I can to tell you about his ancestors and their descendants. I will talk about his early life, as I share memories of his family throughout the years, before and after we were married. Some things already touched on briefly may be repeated, when I talk about him, in an effort to paint a picture and tell about our complete story and life together.

Photos of the way we looked then and after 35 years of marriage. The photo below was prepared for the anniversary section of the newspaper, in December 2003, but for some reason they ran out of space for that date and we decided not to publish it after the fact. It is good to know that we can still smile. Changes have taken place, but for the most part they have been good. I have realized over the years that marriage is what you make it and that it takes two people willing to listen to each other and "compromise," which is not a bad word, to make any thing worth having work. We have had the support of family members along the way who have embraced us because we chose for the most part to keep our problems between us, as it should be.

William and Martha Montgomery

Montgomerys'
35th Anniversary

Billy and Martha Evans Montgomery of Washington, D.C. were married 35 years ago on December 21, 1968.

Billy retired from Canada Dry Corp. and Martha, the federal government.

They enjoy traveling and visiting their five children and 12 grandchildren.

The couple celebrated at their pre-Christmas open house party.

Chapter 11

Montgomery Family

Billy was born in York, South Carolina in 1939 to Lizzie Mae Tate and Vernon Sylvester Montgomery. Billy was the fourth child born in the family. Billy's mother Lizzie Mae was born September 23, 1914, in York, South Carolina. Her mother was Queenie McKewee. Lizzie Mae was adopted and raised by Frank and Mariah Bryant Tate. She had no siblings but was raised as a sister to Cora, Bessie, Addie and Minnie Tate.

Billy's father Vernon Sylvester Montgomery was born April 12, 1912, in York, South Carolina to John and Mary Vance Montgomery. Vernon's grandparents were John and Elizabeth (Lizzie) Montgomery, and their other children were Will, Charles, Clarence, Jake, Elijah, Buford, Mary, Revolla, and Ponesse.

The Montgomery family was considered well off for Negroes in the south in the 30's and 40. They owned cars, homes, acres of land and farm equipment. Billy said he rcmembers riding to church, on Sundays, in the horse drawn buggy owned by his grandfather.

Vernon Sylvester had one brother; Charles Enmon, who was born on February 23, 1914, two half brothers, John, born in 1924, and Arthur Lee, born in 1926, to his father, John, and stepmother, Addie Tate Montgomery.

Charles was married to Annie and their children were Leonard, Emma Lee, Charlene, and Stella.

John was married to Frances Moore, who was the daughter of Samuel and Fannie Choate Moore. John and Frances had one daughter, Dorothy. Dorothy (Dottie) is married to Foster (Ben) Benjamin, and they have one daughter, Denise. Billy and Dottie were close growing up in York. Years later Billy and I would reconnect with them when Ben retired from the military. They settled in Rock Hill, SC, where Dottie retired from her teaching career. In the early years, we spent lots of times with them when we visited South Carolina and when they visited us in DC. We now look forward to their visits with their daughter, Denise, who lives in Maryland.

Arthur Lee was married to Georgia and he served in the military. After leaving the Army, he spent time working and traveling with the carnival. He was working with the carnival when he died in an accident in Virginia in 1967.

Billy's two great aunts Mary Elizabeth Montgomery and Revolla Odell Montgomery, pictured at left, lived in Washington, DC. Revolla was married to Mitchell Rogers. They were the aunts who welcomed the nieces and nephews from down south to live with them. In the summer time their house was filled with nieces and nephews who were either looking for work in the north or were just passing through on their way to New Jersey where the other family members had migrated to. Mary was never married.

Vernon and Lizzie Mae Tate Montgomery had five children; Vernon, Jr., Joseph Clement, Eunice Wright, William Edward and George Ralph. My father in law, Vernon, was the oldest child in his family. I met him for the first time when his youngest brother, Arthur Lee, passed and he came to Washington for the funeral. I saw him the second time in 1967 when Billy's oldest brother, Vernon, Jr. passed. I would not see him again for many years. In his younger years, he was playing up and down the east coast for the Rock Hill Giants baseball team, in 1939. This kept him away from home for long periods of time. It was his dream for his sons to follow in his footsteps and play baseball in the major leagues.

Vernon, Sr. was a commercial painter by trade and a fisherman by choice. He employed a group of men who he trained to be professional painters. As young children, Billy and George spent time with him growing up in Charlotte, NC, where he taught them how to paint professionally. In his lifetime Vernon amassed a wealth of assets through his business talents, including many rental properties. In the end, he owned fishing boats and a beach house in Myrtle Beach, SC, before ill health forced him to give them up.

He could tell some real fish stories. One such fish tale was about a group he sent out on a fishing trip who never returned. He missed out on lots of times in his children's young lives, but he was very proud of all of them. He loved to brag about them to his friends. Since I never got to know him in the early days, I knew him mostly through the stories told by his children. Billy exhibits a lot of mannerisms like his father, and can also tell real stories that you question whether they are true. I guess Billy takes his love for fishing from his father.

In his later years Vernon came to visit us on occasion and we visited him. On one such visit, he was getting so comfortable, acting like a guest, with me waiting on him, that I told Billy we were going to have to stop or he would never want to leave.

I think he really was sorry that he was not a big part of their lives growing up, but in the end they were there for him, as was their mother. Vernon passed away September 15, 1992, in Cheraw, South Carolina.

My mother in law, Lizzie Mae was born and raised in York, South Carolina. She celebrated her 96th birthday in September, 2010. She did not have natural brothers and sisters, but was adopted by Frank and Maria Tate at an early age and reared as their daughter. She was a devoted mother to her children, often raising them as a single parent. She was too proud to get public assistance, so she worked outside of the house for the white families, as a domestic worker, in York to support her family. With the help of her aunts in laws and other family members, she was able to provide a home for them. She has overcome many health issues and attributes it all to her faith in God. In the early 60's she moved to Morristown, NJ, when her daughter Eunice was pregnant with twins, and remained there for some time, helping to care for their children until they were old enough to start school. She would go back often, in the ensuing years, during the summer months to care for them.

She would eventually return to York on a permanent basis where she was trained and certified as a Nurses Aid. She worked in a retirement home taking care of patients until her retirement.

She has always exhibited a sweet spirit and is so appreciative of anything you do for her. She has been a role model to many young women in her community and church. She enjoyed the summer revivals and would be one of the first on the van as they made the round to all the churches.

She has had the honor of being the Mother of her home church, Gold Hill Baptist, for a long time. She enjoyed singing in the senior choir, as they sang the old gospel hymns familiar to the south. Their style of singing consisted of one person speaking the words, followed by the choir members singing them as they patted their feet to the beat. I believe this type of singing was done when choir members did not, or could not read the words.
My mother in law has come to visit with us on many occasions. She enjoys reading magazines and her hometown newspaper to keep up with what is happening in the community. She loves to read her bible and reads it faithfully every night before she goes to bed.

She lived by herself for many years until her health begun to fail and she would once again move to New Jersey to live with Eunice and her family. For eight years after Billy retired in 2001, he would take her home for the summer months, so she could be in her own home and see all of her old friends. Her best friend, Ms. Lucille Lowery, also 96 years old, is still living in York, SC. When she was in York, they would talk on the phone 20 times a day just like they had done since they were 14 years old. Billy said the part he loved the most about spending summers with his mother was the times they spent talking. He liked to tease her and she could say some of the funniest things out of the blue, like a woodpecker getting a headache from pecking so hard on a tree trunk.

At the last Jefferson School reunion, she was recognized as one of the oldest students that had attended the school.

My mother in law loves to be around all of her grand children and great grandchildren. The years she did not spend in New Jersey, were spent in South Carolina surrounded by her son George and his children.

Billy's oldest brother, Vernon, Jr., was the one I never had the chance to know. He served in the military, lived in DC for awhile, and returned to York, SC, where he resided until his death in 1967. Billy tells me how his oldest brother went into the service to help support him and his siblings when his mother was the head of the household. He said Vernon, Jr. was a good person and loved to have fun. He spent time in Germany while he was in service and was honorably discharged from the military.

His daughter, Betty who we always called Toni, had three sons, Michael, Webb and Antonio. She was married to Webb Johnson and her second son, Webb, is deceased. Michael has a daughter. Toni was raised by her mother Naomi Garvin in DC. I met Toni when she was about 17 years old after her father's death. She has been in and out of our lives throughout the years. We have not always seen eye to eye on issues but we still keep in contact with each other. Toni is the oldest grandchild and provided me with the photo of her father.

Joseph Clement was born in 1936 in York, South Carolina. He was the second child born to Vernon and Lizzie. I first met Joe in 1967 in York, SC. Joe was always very proper. He graduated from Jefferson High School in 1954 and graduated with honors from South Carolina State University in Orangeburg, SC, where he earned a BS degree in Biology.

Joe was very intellectual and had aspirations of becoming a doctor. While he was still in college, he worked in the pharmacy in York, SC. Joe was a Sunday school teacher at Gold Hill Baptist church and he served on the usher board and directed the Gold Hill Gospel Choir. When he left home he continued to help care for his mother and siblings.

He paid for renovations to their home, paid tuition for Billy to attend Mather Academy, a private school, and he always saw to it that his Mom had money to buy gowns for Eunice to wear when she was competing in her beauty pageants.

He completed his ROTC training in 1958 and was appointed 2nd Lieutenant in the US Army. He served until his honorable discharge in December 1961. After his discharge from the service, Joe worked for the Morristown Post Office as a Postal Clerk. He moved to Boston, MA and worked for the Boston Lahey foundation as a Clinical Chemist, Boston Medical Laboratories as a Protein Chemist, and the Boston Public School system as a teacher, where he retired early because of poor health. He was a volunteer for the NAACP, the Theater

Guild, and the National Education Association for Youth and was a member of Alpha Phi Alpha Fraternity Beta Delta Chapter.

Joe spent most of his adult life in Massachusetts. He traveled extensively and in a different social circle. Joe loved to socialize with people, read books, play cards and listen to jazz, classical and gospel music.

Joe and I hit it off right away when we first met. When Billy and I visited him in Boston in the early 70's he enjoyed taking us around to meet his friends. We went to church with him and he was proud to introduce us to his church family. He always liked talking on the phone and would call you at the oddest hours of the day, usually before 7:00 AM.

Sometimes the nieces and nephews did not understand him because he was not the playful type. He was stern but loved teaching children and took pride in seeing them succeed. He moved to the Morristown, NJ area, to be near family, where he resided until he passed away November 26, 2008. Joe was not only my brother in law, but my friend and we shared a unique friendship. He often confided in me and he once told me he had a son whose mother lived in Canada. I don't know if that were true or not.

Eunice was the third child born in the family. She would be the only girl which gave her a special place in the home. The extended family was always trying to help out in tough times. When Eunice was about 3 years old, she went to stay with her Aunt Bessie who lived in New York and lived there for almost 3 years. Her aunt wanted to keep her and her Mom had to threaten to come get her if she did not bring her back home.

Eunice said when she returned home, with a head full of Shirley Temple curls, her brother George did not know who she was and would not have anything to do with her. She said her aunt worked for Phillip Morris and she used to ride to work with her on the train every day. She remembers having lots of dolls to play with. She said Aunt Bessie wanted to take George and Billy to New York also, but George did not want to go and Billy would not go without George.

As a youngster, during the summer school vacation time, she would head to DC to live with her Aunts Mary and Revolla, while the brothers had to remain home. She was very popular in school, always competing and winning beauty pageants. She was Homecoming Queen and won a beauty contest sponsored by

High Point College. Billy said Eunice was always bossy and as children she took great pride in telling them what to do.

Eunice graduated from Jefferson High School and went off to Wilberforce College in Dayton, Ohio for two years. She also studied Management at Rutgers University. During the summer semester break, she went to stay with relatives in Morristown, NJ. It was after one of those summer breaks that she chose to leave college and seek employment in Morristown. Not only did she find employment, she found the man she would marry, Robert Bass.

As the result of meeting Robert (Bob) Bass, Eunice, on the far right, ended up the mother of three lovely children, twins Robert and Robin, and Douglas. She and her husband made a good life for their family in Morristown. They are also the proud grandparents of Robin and Ryan Singleton's two daughters, Bianca and Isabella.

As a child Eunice was active in the home church, Gold Hill Baptist and is very active in the church she joined upon moving to Morristown, NJ, Calvary Baptist Church. She serves as the Finance Officer on the Trustee Board, member of the Usher Board and holds membership in the Women's Fellowship organization. She also provides administrative support to the church.

Eunice loves to entertain family and friends. She made lifelong friends in NJ, among those that became a part of Billy and my life, over our many years of being together, are their cousin Stella and her husband Richard (Dickie) Gray, long time friends, Melvin and Ramona Hubbard, Dot Grant, Robert (Bob) and Arnetha Allie, and the entire Bass extended family.

I met Eunice for the first time when she came to Washington to attend her Uncle Arthur Lee's funeral. I was kind of quiet so we really did not spend a lot of time talking. I guess she was sizing me up, something that she does very well. The next time I saw her was later in the summer when we met in York, SC, after her brother Vernon, Jr., had passed. I think it was then that we made a connection. She made me feel like a part of the family during that time and we have been close since that time. We have had our moments, like the time I had a birthday party for Billy and invited our friends, Mel and Mona, but did not invite her. She really gave me a piece of her mind, but we worked through that and we do still care a great deal about each other.

I think we might have bonded, soon after we met, because she did not have a sister, and since it looked like I was going to be family, we found many things in common; one being we both loved her brother Billy.

In the years that followed we would spend many vacations and holidays together. Our first trip to Nassau was with them. Billy and I made our first road trip to visit them in 1968, before we were married. After we married, our home was always the lodging place for visitors to DC and theirs was the place to stay in New Jersey. We have spent many family gatherings during summer vacations, at Christmas, Thanksgiving and on special trips.

Billy and I spent our second night of married life in their home. Billy and I talked about how cold the house was, and since Bob controlled the heat, we had to wait until they went to work to turn it on. We still kid Bob about freezing people out. He will feed you though. He is the cook in the family. You can count on Bob for good food, good fun and good liquor. Eunice loves the finer things of life, dressing to the nines, and of course she would never drink out of a paper or plastic cup. She insists on eating off of the good china and drinking out of a crystal glass.

During the early part of our marriage, Eunice and her family would come to visit and sometimes Billy would be off on the road. It was during those times that we really got to know each other.

As adults, their children always felt they could come visit us, at any time, and they were always welcome to bring their friends along. They would get a kick out of Billy's story telling. We would get into some conversations and they would say "this is better than the movies." Billy is known for his elaborate "tales." Eunice children always liked being around Billy because he was the one who was more playful with them. They were always timid around Joe because he was not around them as they grew up and they did not always understand his ways. George was also very playful.

Eunice is very protective of her family. Pictured above, left to right, Robert, Douglas and Robin and Ryan and their daughters, Bianca and Isabella. She does not meet many strangers and she always inquires about my family and friends when she calls. She took on the role of part-time caregiver for her Mom a few years ago. Since her mother is not able to go back to South Carolina in the summers with Billy, she is now her full-time caregiver.

Eunice had a successful career with New Jersey Bell, later called Bell Atlantic, where she retired from her Management position in 1998. She and her mother's roles are now reversed. Eunice is now providing the same care to her mom, that she had provided to her earlier.

George Ralph was the youngest child in the family. George and Billy were the two youngest and the closest growing up. They were like twins growing up. When you saw one you saw the other. George attended school in York and graduated from Jefferson High School. He spent most of his adult life in York. He worked for Cannon Mills for a period of time. He moved to New Jersey for a short period of time and worked for Russell's Electric in Madison, as an electrician. He stayed in Washington for a brief period of time, finally moving back to York, where he was a self employed painter, putting to good use the trade that had been taught to him by his father. The white families in York hired him to do their painting and George always got a kick out of telling how he would charge them higher prices, and how they always tried to get him to cut his price. He would give them a much higher price in the beginning so he would end up with what he wanted in the first place. He always gave them their money's worth though. He took pride in his work and came all the way to DC to paint our entire house. George had a love of cars and spent time fixing and racing them.

Because George and Billy were so close, our families had a very special relationship from the first time I met them. George was from the "old school" and felt that you had to keep women in their place and tell them what to do and say. I was from the "new school" and I had to keep reminding him that those days were long gone and were never coming back. George was married to Mae Lawrence, who was very quiet and she always kept pretty much to herself. However, when we became sisters-in-law, and more importantly, friends, we always looked forward to spending time together.

George was a happy person. He always met you with a smile and you knew he wasn't smiling for nothing. He was getting ready to hit you up for something. Billy said George was always the ladies man growing up and the charmer. George enjoyed visiting us because he always knew that he would have conned us out of something before he left. He would make the trip to DC and turn around and drive back like it was nothing. Everyone that knew George growing up said he was full of mischief.

Billy talks often about how he would go fishing and catch turtles to sell and George would be waiting to get his half of the money, even though he had not caught anything. He was put on the baseball field at an early age by his father who had played in the Negro leagues, although that was not his choice. George learned at an early age to help provide for his mother and family. He and Billy would spend summers growing up in Charlotte, living with their father.

George was the first to arrive when the family got together. The only thing I don't remember him doing was cooking. He was the one who felt that "a woman's place was in the kitchen and the bedroom." He was the one who remained in York and was there when his mother needed his assistance. He was also there when his father was in ill health and provided assistance to him in the end.

George was also there when his mother moved back to South Carolina. He provided assistance to her and even took on the challenge of teaching her how to drive. After a little mishap they both decided that maybe it was too risky to pursue that endeavor so he just made himself available to take her where she needed to go. He never did learn how to cook so he would dutifully go to her house to pick up a home cooked meal.

George was married to Mae Lawrence and they had two daughters: Tammy and Veronica. George always wanted a son so he took up a lot of time with the nephews in the family. He was the stern disciplinarian and when he spoke they listened. Tammy has four daughters, Tekilla, Chelsee, Erica and Kieria, and one son, Klye. They live in North Carolina. Veronica has two sons, Alex and Walker, Jr. and they live in Michigan. Mae still lives in York, SC and still has that same quietness about her. Her brother Donald Lawrence is a well known gospel recording artist. I value the friendship Mae and I have shared over the years.

George returned to his Christian upbringing in his later years and loved to debate the Bible with you. He was a bible student who knew the word and of course he always felt that his interpretation was the only one. We spent many hours in deep discussions. He reunited with Gold Hill Baptist Church, where he served faithfully until his passing.

He spent his time sharing the word with those he met along the way. His change in his later years had a positive impact on some of his friends from his wild days. They felt that if George could change, anyone could. He made a dramatic change in his life and never lost his sense of humor during his final illness. George passed away July 2, 1995. The following photos are of his family.

Left to right, daughter Veronica, wife Mae, daughter Tammy

Tammy and Veronica take great pride in her families. They have been single parents at times but have given their children everything they needed. Veronica is a music teacher in Michigan and Tammy lives in North Carolina, where she spends quality time spoiling her grandson, Cameron.

George Ralph's children and Grandchildren with their Grandmother

Chapter 12

William Edwards Montgomery's Early Life

School Days

1948-49

William (Billy) was the fourth child born in the family. He was born in 1939, in York, South Carolina. He attended elementary school in York and he also attended Jefferson High School. He was later sent to finish his high school education at Mather Academy in Camden, South Carolina, a strict private school. His older brother Joe sent him there because he felt he needed more guidance. He learned drafting and many other subjects that were not offered at the Negro high school in York. Mather was the elite school in SC for families with resources. Although his family did not have these resources, through his working on the school campus and help from his brother, he was able to stay there. He washed windows, cut grass and did lots of odd jobs to make ends meet. While a student there he ran track and played football. One of his school mates at Mather Academy, James Clyburn, went on to become a United States Congressman from the State of South Carolina.

Billy loved to talk about growing up. Since I did not know him at that time, he has spent many hours telling me about his early childhood. He said that times were hard and that they did not have many worldly goods.

The first house his mother bought cost $400, which was a lot in those days. Before that they had lived in what was called the "family" house that had been bought by his great aunts. He talks about growing up in the segregated south. His mother worked as a domestic for some of the white families so the white and Negro children often played together. This would be the case until they were entering their teen aged years. It was then that all mothers took them aside and told them they could no longer play with the white girls. He said at that time he could not figure out why and the only answer they were given was "you just can't." He said he remembers riding to church on the back of the horse drawn buggy, dragging his feet on the ground, as his mother was sitting up front. That was a treat because otherwise they had to walk. The buggy was the other forms of transportation for the family.

Billy learned at an early age to work and do odd jobs to help out his mother, in his father's absence. He did spend summers in Charlotte where his father tried to get them to play baseball. He said he played but preferred to play football instead. He would learn how to paint along side his father, who was a professional painter.

As a young boy, he and George learned how to play golf working as caddies on the golf courses, while living in Charlotte during the summer months, so they could have their own money. He talks about getting up at 11:00 PM to go work at the chicken farm and then getting home about 4:30 AM in time to get a little sleep before going off to school. He said at the age of fourteen, he drove the truck, without a driver's license, when the owner of the chicken farm delivered the chickens.

He learned about printing and book binding while working at the newspaper company as part of the clean up crew. As a little boy he was always trying to make money, even if it meant sitting at a pond all day catching fish or turtles to sell. He said he got fired off of his first job, which was picking cotton, because he tried to put rocks in the sack to make up for the 35 lbs. he was supposed to pick. The real cotton pickers in the 1940's could pick up to 400 lbs a day and earn about $8.00 a day. He said, "The white man would drive through the neighborhood, in his truck and round up all the kids, to take them to the fields to work in the cotton fields."

He said he found out where his father used to hide his moonshine money, in the walls of the house, and one day he took a $20 bill and headed straight for the store. In those days if a kid came into the store with $20 they would have to tell where they got it from and when the store keeper told his mother he said he had found it and gave her the remainder. She never knew he had taken it from his daddy's hiding place. He said at other times they would sell the $20 bills for $1. You could buy enough candy to last a week for a nickel. He said they used to watch the moonshine men hide their liquor and then steal it and sell it to the men in the community cheaper. He said someone in town used to hide their moonshine in the church, where the police could not find it. I guess in those days the most lucrative employment was in the "moonshine" and "illegal numbers" business.

One of the strangest stories he tells is when his dog killed a rabbit and he took it home for his mother to cook. He said the rabbit was still warm so he knew it was ok to eat. His mother never knew that they had not killed the rabbit. He said that when you were poor, any kind of meat was a treat. He also tells about him and George killing three buzzards that they took home for their mother to cook, thinking they were wild turkeys. He said he made a vow as a child that when he was grown he would always have food in the house. I guess that is why he is such a fanatic about buying more groceries than he needs and spending lots of money and time in the grocery stores. There is no such thing as a bargain that he does not know about.

Billy said as teenagers, the girls always were after George, because George was the charmer. Instead of chasing the girls, he concentrated on making money, and wondered why the girls gave their money to George so willingly. When he went off to Mather Academy he had a limited social life because the school was very strict, and he did not have much time off from working. The boys were housed in one dorm and the girls in a separate dorm. He did enjoy the school sponsored gatherings that were held, although they were closely chaperoned.

In 1959, at the end of the school year, Billy left Mather Academy and York, South Carolina, headed to New Jersey with some of his schoolmates to look for work. When he arrived at Union Station he called his Aunt Revolla and Uncle Mitchell to say he was on his way to New Jersey. Uncle Mitchell asked him if he could stay in DC, for a little while, to help out because his wife, Aunt Revolla, was sick. He called his mother back in York and she told him it was OK to stay. He got his bags off the train, took a cab to their house, and that is how he ended up making his home in DC for the next fifty two years.

Billy's first order of business in DC was to find a job. He had always worked as a child and now he was entering adulthood with a need to support himself. Since an unexpected detour had presented itself, Billy had to first get accustomed to living in the big city. Aunt Revolla and Uncle Mitchell would take him under their wings. He was reintroduced to cousins he had known who visited or lived in the south, and he would meet new cousins who he had not known. His Aunt Lillie Mae lived in the house behind Aunt Revolla so it was not long before he was hanging out with his new found cousins, Charles,

Vernon (Sonny), and John (JC). Of course he had known his cousin Vinson when he lived in York, SC for awhile, with his father and mother, Leafell and Sylvester Good, before the family relocated to the DC area. Vinson was their oldest child and only son. His sisters were Patricia, Terleta, Deborah and LaNell. He became familiar with the neighborhood and the neighbors.

One of his new neighbors was the Thompson family, whose son John Thompson became famous as the coach of Georgetown University's basketball team. Their families were related through the marriage of his cousin Sonny and John's sister Bertha (Bert). He always talked about how, although he was two years older than John; John was so much taller than he and all the other kids in the neighborhood. He remembers trying on one of John's suit jackets and how it was so long on him, it dragged the ground. Although John became famous his mother remained in the neighborhood, until a few years ago, and John made frequent trips back to the old neighborhood. When Uncle Mitchell passed in 1988, John Thompson was one of the first neighbors to come and pay his respect to the family.

Billy's first job, in 1959 after moving to DC, was working in a Chinese restaurant where he learned a little about cooking. To this day, he does not eat Chinese food. I guess that tells you something about his time in the kitchen. He was paid $32.00 a week for working six days. He brought home $30.00, after taxes. He worked there helping cook and washing dishes for a short time, until the restaurant owner moved to California. It was then he found out about a job at the Franciscan Monastery in Northeast. During the interview process he was asked if he wanted to study for the priesthood. He was told he would have a place to stay and did not have to pay for food or clothing. Being from the south, I guess he was still trying to find his way and he was encouraged by his aunts to take the job. While there, he was given his robe and black pants, which would be his uniform and an allowance to pay for his personal items.

It was about this time that the United States Selective Service sent him his draft notice but because he was studying for the priesthood, they were able to get him a deferment. He went about his way studying and being a part of the brotherhood at the Monastery. He said there was one other black studying there, at the time so he did not feel too isolated. This adjustment would not be too difficult because he has just left a very strict private religious school, Mather Academy, in Camden, SC. He was being taught at the Monastery primarily by Father Paul, Father Rayfield and Father Bonaventure. He enjoyed his family visiting and the tours he gave them of his new home away from home. He jokingly tells about how on one such visit his Aunt Mary picked some flowers from the gardens to take home with her. He later told her that was not allowed.

This too would be a short lived endeavor. He said during their leisure time they often watched baseball games. As they were sitting around watching the Brooklyn Dodgers play and just as Jackie Robinson hit a homerun, one of the white students got so angry he shouted out that damn "N*****" hit a homerun that won the game. He said that being from the south, the thought of someone studying to be a priest using that language, changed his mind about wanting to be a priest. He realized that this was not the place for him and it was not long before he left.

His next job, in 1960, would be working for Peoples Drug Store, located in Seven Corners, VA. He started out making $.90 an hour working as a porter. He was such a good worker that he was offered on the job training by the Manger to be a stock clerk. The manager told him he was the first black they had hired to be a stock clerk. He learned how to stock the shelves, change prices on the items and do the inventory. He said his experience working as a stock clerk taught him how the retail business worked and how they changed prices for sales by marking up the product price first. This early experience has made him a wiser shopper and he never buys anything that is not on sale.

It was while working at Peoples Drug Store that he ran into racism again and realized that he had not left racism in the south. One morning after arriving to work early and sitting at the counter having a cup of coffee, he was confronted by a white customer, who had been let in the store before opening time, and upon seeing him at the counter she told him "N*****" you know you are not supposed to be sitting at that counter. His southern training kicked in and he started to explain why he was sitting there. He did not know the store had been opened for business. Another incident at the store occurred when he was questioned about the price of an item and the white customer refused to take his word for it, telling the clerk, "Are you going to take this "N*****'s" word over mine?" She was not too happy when she found out that he did know what he was talking about because he was in charge of pricing the items. Those incidents did not say much for leaving the south. Since transportation was not so readily available to Seven Corners, Billy went looking for employment closer to home.

Billy was now back in the neighborhood with his relatives, and he and his cousin Vinson started to hang out again. As a naïve country boy from the south, having gone from a strict private school to time spent in a monastery, Billy was now looking to fit into the "worldly" world. Vinson and Billy would become running buddies when Vinson returned from active duty and ended his time in the military. Billy had met Anna Payne, whose parents lived in the neighborhood. When Vinson returned from service, Billy introduced him to Anna's best friend Elois, and there was a natural tendency to hang out together. Billy said since he did not have a car and Vinson did, he saw that as a winning combination. The four of them hung out together and it wasn't long before Anna gave birth to Tanya Elizabeth, in 1961. He said shortly after Tanya's birth they entered a marriage that neither one was ready for. When he realized things were not working out, shortly after the marriage, he made the decision to leave. Anna gave birth to a second child, Vieda Rena in 1962.

Although he left, he realized he had a family to support, and he found new employment with Rock Creek Ginger Ale Company in 1962. Now he was making a whopping $1.25 cents an hour, not much more, but at least he had better benefits. He started out working in the production section. Later, his supervisor, Harry Armstrong, was willing to train him in the operations of the syrup room, in a department that the company had not offered to the black employees. He learned the composition and different mixtures for the sodas. He also learned how to test the sodas, using various testing methods, to make sure the formula did not deviate and that it maintained the same consistency throughout the bottling process. Once the bottling process was completed, he tested samples of the final product to ensure that the product met the standards of the company. Billy liked the flexibility of working at Rock Creek because he could take off whenever he wanted to. Never mind the fact that he was not always getting paid for that time taken off, unless it was for his regularly scheduled vacation time.

I did not meet Billy until the summer of 1966, so I can only assume that during those four years, he lived the life of a single man. Soon after we met, he started to travel on the road with his friend, and my ex, Walter Booth, and the singing group "The Sweet Things. Later when Francine (Peaches) Hurd, left the group, and became the first "Peaches" in the Peaches and Herb (Fame) Feemster duo, he would continue to travel with them. In 1970, he would later travel on the road with the Manhattans, where 17year old Gerald Alston, who they had met while doing a show in North Carolina, became the lead singer for the Manhattans.

In his travels through Florida, he became friends with Gary Clemmons, known as "Iron Jaw Sampson," who would follow them back to DC and perform locally. Sampson's local fame as a strong man, holding a car, while the then Mayor of DC, Walter Washington, was pushing down on the accelerator, led him to an appearance on the Johnny Carson Show. On that show he amazed the audience by picking up Johnny Carson, by his belt around his waist, and walking around the stage with him, as the audience looked on in unbelief. Sampson's other claim to fame included biting silver coins in half, drinking concoction that would destroy a normal person stomach and chewing on razor blades. Billy liked the excitement of being around the different entertainers and the travel to places he had never been before. He has many stories to tell about "life on the road" but I will leave that up to him to tell when he writes his own book. He fondly shares that he knew Patti Labelle, when she was part of the Blue Bells, before she became famous, and that she had a crush on him. His life and travels on the road, away from home, took an enormous toll on our early life together.

BILLY WITH DAUGHTERS ANITA, on the left AND TANYA, on the right
AND SOME OF THE GRANDCHILDREN

Chapter 13

My Life AMTB – After Marriage to Billy

Getting used to married life for both of us created some challenging times. Billy had gotten used to living the single lifestyle again and I was looking forward to living the married lifestyle, whatever that meant. I guess I had the "storybook" version of what married life would be like. We both probably entered marriage thinking we could change each other. During those first years, Billy was doing a lot of traveling with the entertainers, and I wanted to just be a housewife. I was looking forward to keeping house, hopefully having children, to love and rear, and spending time with our married friends. Billy loved to entertain, when he was home. We had many gatherings of family and friends in our first apartment. I took on the role of decorating our first place and doing all the little things that a housewife did around the house. I enjoyed cooking meals for us and planning things to keep us involved. Although if you listen to him, now that he is the cook in the family, you would never believe that I actually know how to cook. I have to constantly remind him that I was cooking before I met him, and before he became the cook in the family. We had different ideas of what a marriage should be, or maybe it was just that we had different expectations.

In spite of his misgivings about my family accepting him, he was welcomed with open arms by my entire family. I knew that once they got to know him as I did they would have no problems. He and my father always looked forward to visiting. They would spend lots of time as Daddy told him about working in the coalmines. Sometimes when Billy is relating a story that my father supposedly told him, I question the validity of it. One in particular is that my father said he was mistaken for a "white" miner in the coalmines, because they were all covered with soot, and you could not tell who was white or black.

In addition to being a married woman, I continued to work. I had decided that I was not getting anywhere in the government, so I left the Health, Education and Welfare agency, in 1969. I had accepted a position working for the International Business Machine Corporation (IBM). I was hired as a Senior

Secretary to one of the Branch Managers. IBM was one of the premiere employers at that time and to secure a position with them was considered a real step up the career ladder. This was a new experience for me and the atmosphere was quite different in the private sector. At the time of my hire at IBM, there was a lot of talk about affirmative action. Although I was well qualified for the position, I also felt that my landing the job may have had something to do with the company needing to reach a "minority quota." At that time they were one of the largest government contractors and pressure was being put on big businesses to hire more minorities. The only other African Americans working in that office was one male employee in sales, Clyde Blassingame, my co-worker, Cheryl Holly, who had also left HEW, and me. They had hired us to fill administrative positions in the division that dealt with government contracts. I settled down to this new position and found it to be very rewarding. Although they were pretty strict on lunch hours and breaks, as opposed to what I had been used to in the government, I managed to make quite an impression on them. As a matter of fact, it was about that time that the "dress code" in the work place for women was being changed. I was the first female in the office to wear a pantsuit to work. All of the other female employees were afraid of getting a reprimand for being so bold, but I was willing to test the waters. Needless to say, there was no backlash and soon afterwards all the females were following the new dress code. Even the men at IBM felt free to leave their neckties at home. One other fringe benefit as an IBM employee was their stock option package. We were allowed to purchase stock at a discount rate made available to employees only. In those days they issued actual stock certificates and I was very proud when I received my first one.

Although satisfied with my job, I decided that I wanted to also focus on having a family of our own. I don't know if Billy was as anxious as I was because he had children and he liked the freedom of the lifestyle we had adapted in our early relationship. We had different interests and different friends and at times that posed a few problems.

As I was adjusting to married life I found it to be a struggle at times. Billy liked to play cards and he spent a lot of time hanging out with his poker buddies. Although things were not perfect in our marriage, I was still interested in having a family of our own. I had a wonderful gynecologist, Dr. Richard Gilbert, who had been working with us on the family issue, as much as he could. All the tests were made but nothing was happening. I think I was more anxious than Billy about having a family. At some point, I made peace with the fact that maybe it was not in the cards for me to physically have a child. It wasn't the best feeling to accept that fact, but I did. Knowing that my branch of the family tree would be empty caused me to focus more on being happy in the state I found myself in. Oddly enough, I never felt that it made me less of a woman, although in some circles being childless was stigmatized. Infertility was not discussed in public settings and most couples suffered in silence. Some marriages also dissolved because of the infertility issues and the "blame" game. I took comfort in knowing that I had lots of nieces and nephews to mother and spoil. I spent a lot of time with my sister Josephine and her children. Billy and I never considered adoption and just accepted that it would just be the two of us. Our families never asked questions about the fact that we had not started a family, so that made things more bearable. I had some friends who were experiencing the same problems so no one made a big deal about it. As a matter of fact the friends that I was hanging out with were in the same position of being childless as I was. It was sort of liberating to have the freedom to come and go and be happy go lucky in a time when there were lots of places to go and plenty of things to keep you busy. We all decided that the only thing we could do was to get on with our lives.

IBM hired another African American, Joyce Austin (Paige), and right away we became good friends. She was such a happy bubbly person all the time. Later as we got to know each other better, she would share horror stories about her marriage. After listening to her, I thought I really did not have it so bad after all. At least Billy had never been physically abusive to me. Maybe he remembered the night we met and the circumstances surrounding that meeting (LOL).

We would remain in our rented apartment at 1384 Bryant Street, NE. He was happy with the neighborhood, but I really wanted us to buy a home. I had always been raised in a house and had lots of problems getting used to the noise coming from the apartment above us. I would continue my search and try to get him interested but I think he just felt satisfied with his old neighborhood and friends from his past. Well I had different ideas and my thoughts were to get him away from his past and his old buddies. To me they were a bad influence on him and were holding us back. Don't get me wrong, they were not bad people, in fact two of his poker buddies were in law school at Howard. One, Woodrow (Woody) Boggs, ended up with a successful law practice and moved in the "DC political circle." As I would drive up and down 13th Street, NE on my way to work in Maryland, I would look at the nice houses and dream of one day living in one of them. While reading the paper one day, I saw a house for sale at the corner of 13th Street and Varnum Avenue and I begged Billy to go look at it with me. I think he was reluctant because we did not have much money saved up and probably felt that we were not ready for a house so soon after getting married.

I was so excited about the prospect of owning a home and prayed that somehow this was the one for us. Each day I would pass by the house and see myself in it. The real estate agent showed us many houses in our search but I knew this was the one for us. Some of the others were either too expensive or not in the neighborhood we wanted to live in. When we finally signed a contract for the 13th Street house, we did not tell anyone because we did not want to be disappointed if things fell through. We needed money for the down payment and at that time had no family members we could ask for a loan. Since I had left the government, I had withdrawn my retirement funds and put it away for this purpose and we were pinching pennies to make up for the rest. Even with all the negatives facing us, we claimed the house and kept thinking positively. We made several trips back to the house and since the family was being relocated to Oklahoma, they were willing to work with us in the purchase. The house was located in a well established neighborhood that was desirable for a home purchase.

In September 1969, less than a year after we were married, the happy day came when we went to settlement and got the keys to our dream home. We purchased the home, in the Northeast section of DC known as Brookland, for $22,500, which was a lot of money at that time. It was located in a neighborhood where "white flight" was taken place. While at my tax preparer's office recently, when he noticed my address, he informed me that he had grown up and lived in the house three doors down from my house, until the early 60's. He also informed me that he had spent many nights sleeping on my upstairs back porch in the summer time, with his friends. He said his parents paid about $9,000 for their house when it was first built, in 1927. In a period of forty two (42) years, between 1927 and when we purchased the house in 1969, the property only increased in value to $22,500. However, before the real estate marked declined, in the 2008-09 time period, those same houses were being assessed at a property tax rate close to $500,000. If the market were still thriving strong, that $22,500 investment would be continuing to rise and represent one of the best investments we made as a young married couple.

When I read the original Deed to the house I discovered that there had been a covenant included, as part of the deed, that stated "…said property shall never be leased, sold, transferred or conveyed to any Negro or colored person or any person of Negro extraction….and this covenant shall be effective until and remain in force until such time as the owners of the majority of the lots abrogate and nullify said covenant…" These words were stricken from the Deed at the time we purchased the house in 1969. I guess by that time the covenant had been nullified and abrogated.

Like our country in the early 60's and 70's, our neighborhoods were going through changes. However, in the late 90's, we started to see another swing in the opposite direction. It was changing from "Chocolate City" to "Neapolitan City." After many years of white flight from the District of Columbia and having the same African American next door neighbors, change was evident in our neighborhood. The Brookland neighborhood was being written about in the newspapers as a hidden jewel in the city. The house next door was sold in 2003 to an investor, who gutted it, renovated it and sold it to a family where the husband Andy was a white Catholic and his wife, Angelique's family was from the country of India. When they first moved in, I did not know what kind of neighbors they would be, but found them to be very likable. We trusted each other and they would leave their house keys with me when they were travelling, and attended our cookouts. In 2008, my newest next door neighbor John Jai who is of Chinese descent, and his wife Milena Durbic, who is from Montenegro, moved in, and now they have added a baby girl, Ksenia, to their household. My longest neighbor and friend is Martha Boxley, who moved in the year after we did, and Carlos and Lucilla (Betty) Arroyos, who are Hispanic and from El Salvador. I can expect a knock on my door at anytime from Betty, holding a tray with some delicious food that she or Carlos has prepared. Carlos and Billy enjoy sitting around talking and complaining about Betty and me.

Our neighborhood, which was becoming black when we moved in, has now been populated with a diverse group of people, including more young white families. Most middle class African Americans have been priced out of the District housing market. When the re-transformation first started it was unusual to see white neighbors walking their dogs and pushing baby strollers. They probably felt the same way we did when we moved into the neighborhood, as they were moving out. These new neighbors of different ethnicity have shown me that race should not be the defining gauge that you measure someone by. As we have accepted each other, we are free to socialize together and share common interests in making our neighborhood a better place. As I was looking out my window recently, I noticed a house with an Israeli Flag and an American Flag flying side by side. Oddly enough, that house sits directly across from St.

Joseph's, a Catholic Seminary that trains men as Josephite Priests. In 2010 a house in the 1300 Block of Varnum sold for $560,000. The neighborhood is holding its own.

Our home is located one block from Providence Hospital, the longest continuously operating hospital in the Nation's Capital. It is also home to many Catholic organizations, including the Franciscan Monastery, the Basilica of the National Shrine of the Immaculate Conception, and two Universities, Catholic and Trinity Washington. The neighborhood has been one of the most stable and well established in the District of Columbia. Many of our friends moved to the suburbs, but we stayed and happily the neighborhood did not suffer from neglect. It has always been known as a middle class neighborhood, home for many professional people as well as blue collar workers. In 1976 when the first metro subway stops were opened, we boarded the first rail cars at Rhode Island Avenue Station and were among the first in the area to ride the newly opened subway system. Since that time the Brookland/Catholic University station has opened and we can walk to it, or we have the luxury of a metro bus stop one block from our house. So many District residents talk about gentrification in racial terms, but I think of it as more of a social trend where any middle class person decides to move into a neighborhood that is up and coming. I wish more of our friends had chosen to stay in the city so that the Capital City would have continued to be a melting pot, with varying political views and ideas.

Sorry for the digression, but I wanted to paint a picture for you about the early neighborhood we started our married life in. We had finally told family members and were trying to get things ready to host Thanksgiving for Billy's family. My sister Josephine came over to help us move. She was a big help and was so happy for us. Billy and I cleaned, painted and packed until we were worn out. It was a good feeling though. Most of his buddies who had promised to help us move managed to disappear when they were needed. We managed to get moved in and set up in record time and were looking forward to filling the house with family and friends. On Thanksgiving, we had our first of many family gatherings, when Billy's family came to spend the holidays with us. We had enough furniture to put in all the rooms and those that did not have a bed to sleep in were happy to sleep on the newly carpeted floors. At that time we did not know that for many years to come our home would be the lodging place where all of our out of town guests would stay when visiting.

I had my hands full right away getting used to cleaning an eight room house. It was a big difference from the one bedroom apartment we had just left. I figured that with the four bedrooms we would have plenty of space if at some point we did have children. At least we had plenty of space to entertain family and friends. We had a large basement that served as the hangout place for the parties held, with the red light low and the music pumping.

Billy was still going out on weekends to play cards and I was still afraid to stay in the house alone at night. He was working during the day and home at night until the weekend came when it was gambling time. I used to complain so he would take me with him and I would sit up all night while he and his friends played cards. I finally decided that it was time to get used to staying by myself. At first I would sleep down stairs until he came home late at night, but I finally got comfortable enough to stay alone upstairs. It was during one of those weekend card playing nights that I got this frantic phone call from Billy. It seemed that someone had found out about the house where the poker playing was taken place and sent a young lady to the door. Being "men" they opened the door to her and right behind her were two guys with guns. Needless to say they were in for a rude awakening. In addition to taking all of their money they were made to strip naked and were locked in the bathroom. Somehow one of the guys got away and called the police. When the police knocked on the door they thought the robbers were coming back and they were all in the bathroom trying to push the wall out so they could escape. I am not sure which one was last seen running down Bryant Street naked as a jay bird, but I think they all learned their lesson that night – you can't trust a young lady knocking at your door, especially if she was not invited to the party. The guys teased Billy afterwards and told everyone that I beat the police there. I think Vinson and Lynwood were the only ones who gave up poker after that incident.

For the next year, we both went about during separate things and having different friends and interests. In June 1970, our family suffered a great loss when my sister Josephine passed. I had just returned home from the Memorial Day weekend, and on the 6th of June all of our lives changed. My sister Josephine passed away suddenly and nothing would be the same in our family for a long time afterwards. She was the youngest person in our family to die and it was such a shock that we walked around in a daze for many months. I remember the sadness that my mother and father and whole family felt. There is something unnatural when a parent has to burry their child. It was too painful to talk about and we all sort of shut down. My brother was preparing to go to Vietnam and his wife Vilma and children had moved to the DC area to live while he was away. They stayed with Billy and me for a few months before she got her own place. That first summer was a sad time for all of us. Josephine's children, Johnna and John, remained with their father. Their older half sister, Janice moved in to help take care of them. When she moved back to Baltimore, Billy and I stepped in and I would pick them up on weekends. In 1971, I decided that I would leave IBM to return to the federal government. It was at that time John, their father, Billy and I decided that the children would live with us, in our home full time. I knew that my whole family would be there for them. It was then I realized that the home we had been blessed with was really for us to raise children in, although we had no knowledge at the time they would not be our natural children. I have learned that giving birth is not the only way God intends for a woman to be a mother.

We knew that more changes would be coming to our lives but we welcomed them and it also meant that I would not be spending so much time alone. It has been a blessing to have them come into our lives and I always give Billy gratitude for opening our home and his heart so readily for children who had been a part of my life from their birth, although he was not raising his natural children.

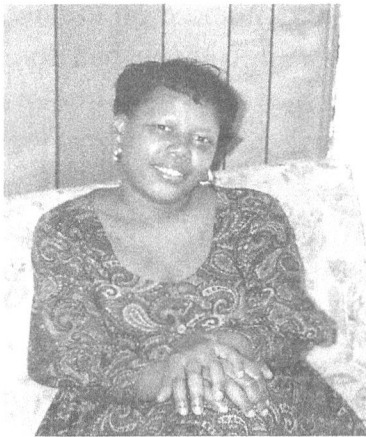

My (step) children, Tanya and Vieda, pictured at left, lived with their mother, Anna, who was the custodial parent. In those early years, my contact with them was minimal, usually when they visited on some occasions, when Billy's family came to town, or when we picked them up to take them shopping for school clothes or at Christmas time. Billy had told me earlier that he had another daughter, Anita, who lived in North Carolina with her mother, JoAnn and her husband, who was raising her as his daughter. We had no contact with her in the early years of her life either.

Our blended family would not come into being until many years later. In the early years, my (step) children did not get to know my side of the family because they were living with their birth mothers. When Billy and I traveled to see my parents, they never accompanied us. This was not something that was done on purpose, it just happened that way. As they grew into teenagers, Tanya and Vieda got to know Johnna and John and some of their extended family. At that point we sort of let them decide what type of relationships they would have with each other.

Years later Tanya married and had her first two children, Gary and Antoinette. Her first marriage ended in divorce and she later married Carlton Smith. They have three children, Lakia, Carlisa and Carlton, Jr. They have 4 grandchildren. Tanya and her family live in Baltimore, MD, where she has spent most of her adult life. Vieda also got married and she also lives in Baltimore. She does not have children.

In the meantime, the years between 1971 and 1980 would bring many changes. Johnna and John settled in to a new school and met new friends and got accustomed to a new neighborhood. I returned to the Federal government to work for the Department of Transportation where I worked for the Special Assistant to the Secretary. It was there, once again, that I saw subtle discrimination. I was passed over for higher positions in favor of incompetent while females that I had provided on the job training to. When I requested an explanation as to why I was not being promoted to a higher position in a different division, I was told that they needed me in the position that I was in, because I was more competent. Things were changing but not for me. DOT brought in General Benjamin O. Davis, Jr., one of the original Tuskegee Airmen, as Assistant Secretary of Transportation. At least I had the privilege of meeting him through my co-worker and friend, Gloria McCain, who was his secretary. African Americans were still not being given the opportunity to move up through the ranks. A few tokens were supposed to make us think things had changed. We knew better but there was little we could to change things.

I did make another lifelong friend there; Nancy Moore. Nancy and I soon found out that our maiden name, Evans, was the same and that our families came from the same part of Virginia. We decided that we had to be related. We often joked that my grandfather, Sam Evans brother, Thomas, who was said to have left Virginia for Massachusetts, probably only got as far as Powathan, where he settled there and started her family. My other coworker Dolores Bailey, who I had met at the Small Business Administration, had transferred there, and was working in the front office of the agency. She had been one of the people who had been so helpful, at our wedding reception, when Billy and I married, in 1968.

In 1972, my dreams of living happily ever after were dimming. I was happy with the children that had been added to our household, but I guess I was not quite prepared for all that married life required. I had not mastered the art of give and take too well and four years into the marriage, Billy and I were spending more and more time going our separate ways. During the summer months, the children would go to visit relatives and I would once again be home alone. I started to think that life was leaving me behind so I hooked up with some of my single friends and I started to go out and party again. I thought I had been missing out on the good times that Billy and I used to share. As I begun to meet new people, Billy was more than willing for me to go places with them. He was more and more into his gambling and I admit that when he won the atmosphere in the house was quite different from the times when he loss. There were times when his family would come to visit and he would be off with his buddies, or traveling with the entertainers. We sort of had an understanding and drifted in different directions, while still living under the same roof.

I was dissatisfied with my job and really did not care. I wasn't going anywhere at the agency career wise so I saw no need to apply myself. My supervisors made promises that they did not keep so I drifted along for the next few years not really caring about the job. I looked forward to the weekend because there was always a party going on.

As long as the children were home during the school year, we did things together. Their summers were spent with their grandparents and aunts. I drifted for sometime without going to church on a regular basis, but realized that I needed to go back to my Christian roots, especially for the sake of the children. I soon returned to First Baptist Church on Randolph Street, NW, and Johnna and John were baptized. One of my running buddies at the time was Barbara Barnes. We both had children around the same age so we spent a lot of time together. Barbara and I had become friends through Ken, a songwriter out of New York, who Billy had met during his travels in the entertainment world. Billy was still hanging out with that group. We did find time to go to many shows and spent a lot of nights in the clubs. We got into some joint ventures with investors who thought we had money. I had learned to be quite a manager of my finances, even if I had to be creative at times. I can remember charging a $100.00 gift card at Hecht Company or Woodward & Lothrop, making a minimal purchase, and receiving the change in cash, which would carry me over until the next payday.

In the summer of 1974, my old Chevy was about to quit on me. It picked a time when I was on my way to a party to meet my friend Betty Faison, who had become one of the first women to join the DC police force, and some of Metropolitan's finest police officers, and two of my still dear friends, Harold Herndon and Arnold Wiggins. I was in the middle of Florida Avenue, NW and heavy traffic, when the Chevy decided it was not going any further. I managed to get it to the side of the road and called for a ride to the party. That was one of many evenings we all spent going from house party to house party, searching for a good time. In later years we all decided to settle down. Harold and I were working in the same building and car pooling together. We also were attending the same church, and I was still trying to hook him up with a nice young lady. Although I did not introduce him to Minerva Lawrence, who he later married, I was his coach, encouraging him to take the plunge. She was attending Howard University, and in medical school and he was a little intimidated. On her first birthday after they started dating I went with him downtown to pick out her first present; a bottle of expensive perfume. Harold and I have remained friends and are now attending the same church once again. We sometimes talk about some of those crazy times and the people from the past. Arnold moved to Atlanta, GA and still keeps in touch. I can say that I made lots of friends in those days, who have remained friends over the years. Most of those who are still alive have settled down and like me probably think about those crazy times when we were young and wild. We were all in uncomfortable circumstances and shared time either trying to forget something or trying to find something.

Before all of the settling down took place, I knew that I needed transportation to hang out with my new friends. I set out to visualize my next ride. In October I purchased a new red 1975 Ford Elite. This time it had all the bell and whistles, including air conditioning. I didn't have two nickels to rub together but all of the reading I had done in my self help books had taught me how to visualize what I wanted. I paid $6,051.65 and I did not put one penny down. I even got the $5.00 deposit back when I picked up the car. I was rolling once again. Billy was shocked when I took him with me to pick up the car. He couldn't imagine how I had been able to get it with no money down. I learned that a good credit rating would also get you what you wanted.

In 1975, I soon got tired of playing games with the Department of Transportation group and I moved on to what I thought was the promise land. I started working for the Cost Accounting Standards Board, as a GS-7, in a quasi government element of the General Accounting Office. I had only managed to move up the career ladder by four grade levels in about a nine year span of federal employment. This office was the envy of the agency because we had more money allocated to us, worked in plush offices and had higher grade levels, at least for that time period. We also had many problems. Number one, the job was an excepted position with no career protection. I started to wonder soon after I arrived there if I had jumped out of the frying pan into the fire. I learned that they had just cleaned house of "what they considered incompetent employees." Needless to say they were all African Americans. I did not have the fear of losing my job from being incompetent because I knew that I was a competent employee. I learned that I had to stay on the good side of the head administrative person because, although she was not the Chairman of the Board, she had the Chairman's ear. I learned early to know who your enemies were. The old saying "keep your friends close and your enemies closer" had a lot of truth in it in this particular office.

I worked for the General Counsel and the Assistant General Counsel and had a good working relationship with management until they went out of business, due to lack of congressional funding. I was very good at taking shorthand, but sometimes I would sit for hours taking dictation from the attorney, who was reading from notes. By the time he finished my fingers would be numb, as well as my mind. He would read from his notes and then throw them in the trash. When he left the office, I sometimes had to retrieve them, make a copy and compare my notes to make sure they were correct. I soon learned that I needed to go back to school if I really wanted to move ahead in my career. The agency had a strict policy of not paying for college classes if they were not job related.

When I decided to go back to school, in 1975, it was soon after the whole world had spent hours watching the miniseries Roots. Each day I went into work there was an eerie feeling in the office. All the African Americans were walking around with a new understanding of just how bad slavery had been and the whites were walking around tip toeing, for fear of setting off an explosive reaction. This was probably the first time that we all had to face that dark part of our country's history. It was not an easy time for any of the races to face the realities of how racism had destroyed families. I guess I decided to play the "race" card when I told them I wanted to go back to college and wanted them to pay for my tuition and books. They did not even ask me what my field of study was going to be – they just signed the paperwork and for the next four years they paid for me to get a degree in "social work." I also saw first hand how that agency had kept African Americans at the lowest grade levels. There were black males with degrees working in the mailroom as GS-3's and GS-4's. We all ended up at the highest grade level – GS-8. My office hired one African American female, Jacqueline Cook, who became one of my best friends. Jackie started out in a GS-12 accountant/auditor position. She was the one exception, as an African American, who had been able to secure a higher grade level, working at the GAO in the 70's. Years later, I am still friends with Catherine Thomas, Princetta Roane, Helen O'Neal, and Ida Wesley Young.

As I alluded to earlier about becoming a "creative money manager", I also got hooked on playing the illegal numbers during that time. We had a white male who was the number runner working in the General Accounting Office main building. I still believe that management knew about him and what was going on, because to my knowledge, I don't believe he even worked for GAO. It was rumored that he had a relative who was part of the top management in the agency. We knew where he would be waiting each day and would drop off our number slips and hope we had a winner the next day. I don't know how he did it but he knew everyone that played numbers and when they had hits. He also would let you play on credit, which probably was not such a good idea. My tab had gotten so high and I had a hunch for a number one day but couldn't put it in. As luck would have it, that day the number came out and I decided that it was time for me to just give them up. I needed to find another way to get money for the bills and necessities of life. Jackie was instrumental in getting me back into church when I joined Mt. Zion Baptist Church, the church she was attending, and I really learned about tithing and depending on God to supply my needs.

I was still trying to raise the children and spend time with them in addition to going to school. They would go to camp on a few occasions but the trips to WV during the summer were coming to an end, much to their delight. There were some rough times and money was tight. I saw to it that they had the necessary things for school. John was going to private Catholic school after Junior High and I was paying the bill. He was playing basketball, but not doing as well in his studies. I finally had to transfer him back to public school in his last year since I was paying for summer school, at DeMatha, where he could make up his classes. In 1978, Johnna got her first federal government job and was able to help out with her school expenses.

Johnna graduated from Roosevelt High School in 1979 and after transferring John to Wilson High School, he graduated in 1981. We had finally accomplished one milestone for them. They had been really good children and that had made our early parenting job much easier.

In 1979 I graduated from the University of the District of Columbia with a degree in Social Work, while working full time. I made the Dean's list while carrying a full course load. I met new friends in college and we had great study groups and parties afterwards. I started out majoring in Criminology but switched my major to Social Work, at the chagrin of my law professors, who tried to get me to concentrate on studies that would lead to a degree in law. Truth be known, I was getting tired of school, but at the urging of my good friend Betty (Faison) Barnaby, I did not quit. I was not that active in school activities but was a member of the National Association of Black Social Workers. I also worked as a counselor with runaway children at the SAJA Runaway House in Washington, DC. When my kids would act ungrateful I would tell them some of the horror stories I listened to at the Runaway House and remind them just how blessed they were. Working there was a real drain on me emotionally. I took so much of what I was exposed to in the runaway house home with me and thought I got too involved to be effective. I wanted to change the world they lived in, but soon realized that the system only allows you to do so much.

Instead of transferring to a position in the social work field, I decided to just use my educational experiences in my private environment, where I could control how involved I became. That training helped me to not only understand myself but more importantly to be able to help others while counseling them. I think that having the ability to listen, and not be judgmental, made it easy for others to share their feelings with me. I have taken great comfort in knowing that after listening, sometimes for hours; to someone I was able to finish our conversations positively. It was during those times that I realized that there is nothing wrong with using your education for personal fulfillment and that it does not always have to translate into career advancement or more money.

In 1979, Billy and I were about to get back on the right track. I think he was tired of gambling and hanging out in the streets. Times were getting bad and the card games had been held up on a few other occasions. He always managed to call me to pick him up after the stick up men had gone. For so long he had been under the mistaken assumption that when he had left to play cards, I had stayed home. That was a big mistake he made. He also came to the realization, as did I that we could have accomplished so much more had we been willing to work together all of those wasted years in between. I guess we were both finally growing up.

During those years I had met a lot of so called influential people and was moving in a different circle of people. In 1979, I worked for President Elect Jimmy Carter's Inaugural Committee as a Public Information Specialist. Billy and I attended our first Inaugural Ball at the Sheraton Hotel. That was a big night for us because we dressed up in formal wear, mingled with the "in crowd" and were close enough to get pictures of the President and First Lady. I think Billy was beginning to see what a good time we could have together.

After working with President Carter's Inaugural Committee, I had made a few contacts and in January 1980, I left the Cost Accounting Standards Board and moved once again back to the Department of Health Education and Welfare. I went to work for a wonderful supervisor, who turned out to be more than that, we became good friends. Patricia Schoeni (Pat) was a career executive who was so competent that she did not mind promoting others competent people to higher positions. Our time at HEW was short lived because six months after I started working with her, she was offered a high level position with the General Services Administration. Because we had gotten off to a very good professional working relationship, Pat asked me if I would move to GSA with her, once she got established. She became my mentor and my friend. I always joked with her that I was her "token" black friend. Of course, nothing was further from the truth, because she had always had African American friends.

We were both born under the sign of Cancer. Some of the other employees in the office called me her "clone" because we had so many ways that were alike.

Working with Pat was so different. She had complete trust in me and pushed me to my highest potential. I used to get a kick out of employees from the Regional offices coming in for meetings and asking for "Ms. Montgomery." When I would say I am Ms. Montgomery, the look of surprise would be on their face because for some reason or another, they thought I was "white." Pat worked at GSA as the Acting Deputy Administrator and held the permanent title of Associate Administrator for Administration. I was her staff assistant in all of the positions she held. I had the opportunity to move into other professional areas under her guidance, but because we had such a good working relationship, I felt that being satisfied on the job was more important than making more money. My decision to stay with her was rewarded with Outstanding Ratings and lots of big cash bonuses. When she left GSA for the private sector, there was a void felt by me in the workplace.

Things were getting better in my home life. Shirley Brown and I had become friends through our mutual friend, Betty Faison. We formed a social club in the early 70's and called ourselves the Sylvanites. We had fun in the club because we would sponsor trips and Saturday night card games. During those times I didn't mind Billy card playing because it was in a controlled environment, and our club got a cut out of the house take. We also sold dinners on weekends to raise funds. Our last big function we held was a New Year's Eve Cabaret at the Stadium Armory. Shirley and her husband Charles (CB) and their daughters, Kim and Crystal continue to be part of our social group. Shirley is one of my confidants and offers good advice. She enjoys being Grandmother to Kim's son, Chance. In the early years, we got into exercising on a regular basis and would spend time during the week at the Harambee House Hotel, managed by Howard University. This was a training facility for students who chose the hospitality field, as their major. At the time it was one of the meeting places for government workers who were looking to meet people or just to socialize. We would spend time exercising and in the spa and swimming pool and then go down to the restaurant and eat a hearty meal of good old soul food.

I bought my third car in 1979. It was a yellow Toyota Corona. I paid $6,451 for it. Billy and I were beginning to focus more on our marriage. We started to do some traveling together. He had always wanted to stay behind if his "friends" were not going with us. Our first real vacation was in 1980 when we went to Nassau with his sister Eunice, her husband Bob, and their friends from New Jersey, Melvin and Ramona Hubbard, pictured to the left, who have become part of our family too. That trip was the start of many vacations that we would take together. Mel is a minister at Calvary Baptist Church in Morristown, New Jersey, where he is responsible for the senior's Ministry. He devotes lots of time ministering to them in the nursing homes. He and I spend hours discussing the Bible and life in general. We consider them our brother and sister.

In September 1980, Billy received a permanent layoff notice from his employer of almost twenty (20) years, Rock Creek Ginger Ale Company. At first we were wondering what we were going to do knowing it would be hard to find employment elsewhere. The new owner, Canada Dry Corporation, needed someone with the knowledge required for mixing the syrup formulas for Rock Creek sodas and the operation of the bottling equipment. Since Billy had been trained in production, as well as in the syrup room laboratory, he was offered the job with Canada Dry. He reported to work the following week as the night production supervisor and syrup room operator. The company was moving from its location in the market district of DC to Silver Spring, MD and since Billy did not drive, he was fortunate to be close to public transportation. Our next challenge would be his work schedule, which changed from day shift to night shift. That took some getting used to. It was during those days at home with nothing to do that Billy took a greater interest in cooking. I would soon get used to coming home to dinner waiting for me. He turned out to be a good cook so I decided to turn over the kitchen to him.

In November, 1983, I met Anita; Billy's other daughter, who was about twenty years old. Billy had only seen her from a distance, after her mother, JoAnn Sanders McCoy, returned to North Carolina. He had agreed to stay out of her life until they felt it was time for her to meet him. That time came on a visit to South Carolina for the Thanksgiving holiday. Her grandmother brought her to my mother-in-law's house to meet us. Anita, who was called Nee Nee at the time, was introduced to Billy as her father and me as his wife. She came to spend her first Christmas with us that same year. From the beginning we made every effort to blend her into our already established household. I wanted her and Billy to get to know each other and although she did not know it, I had accepted her as my (step) daughter, long before she even knew me, because I had always known about her. In the following years, our families did blend, even to the point that her family was always welcomed to stay with us. During a visit, sometime later, her grandmother, aunt and uncle stayed with us and spent a day touring the sites, memorials, the National Zoo, and the attraction most locals fail to visit.

Sometime after that first meeting, Anita joined the Navy where she met and married David Johnson. Their first child, Alesha was born while she was stationed in Italy. When she came to live in Washington, after her discharge from the Navy, she and their daughter Alesha spent those first weeks with us. Alesha was so active and would cry a lot. It took her a little while to settle down and get used to us and her new environment. They lived in Maryland until she and David transferred jobs to Atlanta, GA. After she and David moved to Atlanta, they had another daughter, Naomi and their son Isaiah, who is in high school where he is thriving well. Anita still lives and works in Atlanta, while attending Bible college part time. Alesha is a recent graduate of Howard University. She is now attending Duke University to work on her Master's Degree. Anita's family on the Sanders and McCoy side, and David's family, the Johnsons, all came to DC for Alesha's graduation from Howard University and celebrated together at our house, with Billy doing the cooking and me being the hostess. We really have become a blended family. Naomi is attending college in Atlanta and working part time. As the saying goes, "We are Family," all of us.

My first European trip was a 3 week stay in Italy in 1984. My brother was living there with his new wife, Queen, who was in the Navy. He had decided that he was coming home early so if I wanted to visit him I had to make up my mind to go soon. Johnna was pregnant and since I was her birthing coach, I had to postpone my trip until after her baby was born. Being her birthing coach was a real experience that I will never forget. I walked the floors with Johnna waiting for her to give birth. I was in the delivery room when her daughter, Chanteé was born. Johnna told the doctor to give her to me after she was born and I was the first to hold her once the doctor checked her out. I always tease Chanteé that she initiated me by peeing on me and I guess that is the bond we share. I experienced through my walk with Johnna, as she prepared for the joys of childbirth, the miracle of a new life – since I had not had the opportunity to give birth.

I waited until August and set out on my first transatlantic trip. It was very exciting. It was my first time flying for such a long period of time and I looked forward to seeing all the places I had read about. We almost did not make the trip because the travel agency we had made our arrangements with filed for bankruptcy and cancelled the flight the day before we were to leave. Lucky for us, my sister Bernice had a friend who was a travel agent, and he was able to book us on another carrier and saved the day. He was nice enough to get us on a regularly scheduled flight, paid for our tickets and let us file insurance claims when we returned to reimburse him. From that time on I have always taken out travel cancellation insurance to prevent such a disaster from happening again. My travel companions were my sister Bernice, friends Brenda Robinson and Vernita Hall. We landed at the airport in Rome, Italy and right away we saw armed guards patrolling the airport with Uzis. This was an unexpected sight to see.

The trip was very interesting. We did tours that were sponsored through the Sheraton Roma Hotel where we stayed. We almost went on a tour with one of the employees that had befriended us, but better judgment told us not to trust strangers, even those who worked for the hotel. We surmised that he probably had a group waiting at a certain point to rob us and leave us stranded. Since none of us spoke Italian, I think we made the right decision. He had promised to take us to Naples and after we cancelled the trip, he was very cool toward us the rest of our stay. I guess he was thinking about all the American money he could have had.

We visited all the sites of Rome. It was amazing to see the ruins from years ago. We walked and sat in the coliseum, where all the chariots races took place, visualizing how and where the gladiators fought.

We walked through St. Peters Square and went inside to tour St. Peter's Cathedral and marveled at the splendor associated with the Vatican. I rubbed the feet of the Black St. Peter statute that was supposed to be for good luck. Vernita was the only Catholic in our group so she knew more about the workings of the church. She was given the opportunity to go to confession. There was so much gold inside but as soon as you walked out the back door, the streets were filled with gypsies and children begging. It was so sad to think that some of the wealth inside could not have been used on the poverty stricken outside. We visited the site of Trevi fountain and threw coins in so that one day we would return, and we climbed the Spanish steps.

Our trip did not end in Rome. We made our next stop in Verona. We managed to understand enough Italian to make sure we did not miss our flight. The people were friendly although they stared at us a lot. We found out later that it was unusual to see Black Americans traveling in Italy, who were not military people, in the early 80's.

When we arrived in Verona, Leonard and his friends were at the airport to meet us. We were happy to see some friendly black faces. Leonard and Queen did not live on the base, so we got to see how the locals lived. We met a nice Italian couple who lived next door and they had us all over for dinner. One thing I learned early in Italy was that they loved their wine and it is served daily. I bought two bottles of wine back to keep as souvenirs. I lost one bottle when Eunice was visiting, and she and my sister Bernice opened a bottle, to my dismay. After opening it they said it really wasn't that good. At least they left the other bottle untouched.

We had lots of fun sightseeing. We went to Verona and toured the building where Romeo and Juliet leaped from the balcony. We also spent a lot of time shopping. One day on a shopping trip, we thought we might get detained by the police when one of our drivers hit a bicyclist. Luckily he was not injured and was not interested in shaking us down for money.

I made my first large purchase there when we went looking for a grandfather clock. Instead of purchasing the clock, I ended up purchasing a "one of a kind" autographed sculptured brass bed. I also purchased a sofa, two chairs and a coffee table to go along with the bed. Prices were very good there and the dollar was very strong against the lira. I would not have been able to pay for the shipping but my brother was able to have an additional shipment sent to the states when he returned. I am happy to say that the furniture was well worth the money and I enjoy it daily. We spent time with the locals at a nude beach. Of course, we did not take our clothes off. I found out that the Europeans are much more liberal in their thinking and life styles. Of course we got to sample the great wines of Italy at every meal.

Our last stop was in Milan. We were going to take the train but Leonard and his friends decided to drive us. That was really an experience riding on the autobahn highway. It seemed that all the drivers thought they were racecar drivers and boy did they drive fast and crazy. I was very happy to get to the city of Milan. We only spent one night there but we did get to do some sightseeing. The month of August was vacation time for a lot of the shopkeepers, so we did not get to do much shopping. The trip was a real eye-opener to be able to see how other people lived outside of the United States.

Before that trip I had only visited the Islands and it was quite different when you see people as they go about their normal daily lives. My friend Vernita did not enjoy herself that much because it was her first trip abroad and she had a hard time getting used to their "laid back" attitude. The old saying "When in Rome do as the Romans Do" was hard for her to adapt to. I think she was miserable most of the time, especially when she said her roommate Brenda snored at night and she could not get any sleep. Needless to say she has no desire to go back again. Vernita was born under the sign of Gemini and I got to see that other "twin" on many days. I am happy to say we are still friends although it has not always been easy. I can always tell when she is having a bad day by the way she answers the telephone. When she refers to me as her "mommy" I know she is having a good day. Over the years, she has mellowed out to some degree. I tell her all the time that she has come a long way. She probably feels the same way about me. If she is reading this book, she knows everything I am saying about her but probably won't agree with it. That is what real friendships are all about. They can stand the test of time and disagreements.

Billy and I took our first cruise to Bermuda in 1985 with Winston and Angela Thames. Billy and Winston had been friends for many years, but Angie and I had never met. It was nice to finally know that Billy had some friends that did not hang out in the market, playing cards, and that they were interested in the same things that I wanted him to be interested in. When Angie and I finally met, we found out that the four of us got along really well together and we started hanging out together. This relationship has blossomed over the years and we still do things together and look forward to our periodic trips that we still take. I have watched their children, Amber and Gmerice grow into adulthood, and I am now watching their grandchildren, Michael and Giana grow up.

I liked cruising so much that I went on my second cruise to Mexico in September 1985 with my GSA co-workers and my social club friend Shirley (Montgomery) Brown. It was a hastily planned trip but it was nice to hang out with male and females who were just trying to have good clean fun. My first two cruises were on ships that looked like they had been converted battleships. Billy did not like to fly so sometimes I went with a girl friend. My first trip to Las Vegas and Los Angeles was in 1988. While I was there, we lost Uncle Mitchell. Billy and I were more in tune with each other then and we had sort of been Uncle Mitchell's caregivers after Aunt Revolla passed. Billy would visit him regularly and do his grocery shopping and I handled his finances. He left us in charge of his estate, upon his death to ensure that his sister would be taken care of. He also rewarded us for our faithfulness to him and Aunt Revolla by bequeathing his home to us, after her death, in an up and coming DC neighborhood, Trinidad/Ivy City. Being an executor for his estate was a real learning experience. Not knowing much about the legal system in handling estates, we hired an attorney to walk us through the maze. Uncle Mitchell had worked as a cook at DC General Hospital and on his salary he had amassed a pretty good size estate. That goes to show you, it is not how much you make, but how you spend/save it.

John recently purchased that home from us and is now living there. We are seeing a new beginning in that neighborhood, after so many years of blight. The H Street Northeast section is becoming like the famous U Street area of DC became, years before, with sidewalk cafes and sit down restaurants and nightclubs, and expensive condos. This area is now home to the movers and shakers who want to be a stone's throw from the Capitol. This section is often now called "Capitol Hill Extended." Of course those of us who have lived in DC for a long period of time know where the boundary lines are.

In the meantime, this cruising thing was getting good and in 1987 I helped plan a cruise with my new fellow church members from Reid Temple AME Church, on Michigan Avenue, NE, that took us to Caracas, Venezuela, Grenada, St. Thomas and San Juan. In 1990 we went to Nassau with some of my new found church friends, Howard and Betty Pointer, and upon our return I planned our first family cruise to Nassau in 1991. The travel bug was pushing me to explore lots of new places. Finding the money to do so was the challenge.

Before I joined Reid Temple AME Church, where I am still a member, I had been a member of several churches along the way, including my first church as a child, Ingram Grove Baptist Church, in West Virginia, Zion Baptist on Blagden Avenue, First Baptist on Randolph Street, NW, Isle of Patmos on 12th Street, NE, and Mt. Zion on Georgia Avenue. I left Mt. Zion with Rev. James Harris, who was the Assistant Pastor there, when he organized and founded Faith Community Baptist Church, on Layhill Road in Silver Spring, MD. I was among the founding members and very active at Faith Community. We were just a few servants who were trying to start a new place of worship. It was hard work but we kept the faith. In the beginning we met in other churches and at the home of Rev. Harris, when the church we were meeting in was condemned. We were finally able to purchase and establish our first sanctuary on Layhill Road, in what was part of a building that had been used as part of a kennel.

Rev. Harris had a vision and we worked hard and were blessed to eventually move into a brand new sanctuary. We were bonded together as family. I was a member of the choir and served as a Trustee, until I turned in my resignation in 1985. I guess reading this it looks like I was a "church hopper" but nothing could be further from the truth. Some of my memberships were due to the proximity of where I lived and my wanting to be close to the church location.

When I left I always left in good standing, and remained friends with the membership. Tamara Blanc (Tammy) and Evelyn Swan, who was the mother of the church, were two of the members who were at Faith Community with me. We prayed a lot as we struggled to start a new church.

The spiritual journey that led me to Reid Temple, photo to the left, was through John and my nephew Fred. Once John was old enough to make his decision of where he wanted to worship, he chose Reid Temple AME, because it was the neighborhood church and his friends attended there. When my nephew Fred Neal joined and was married there, I had the opportunity to meet some of the members and the pastor, Rev. Dr. Lee P. Washington. John and Fred had been telling me about this dynamic young preacher who was the new pastor, and they kept asking me to attend with them.

After coordinating Fred's wedding and meeting Rev. Washington, I decided that maybe I would check the church service out. After I listened to him preach that first sermon, and felt the warm welcome from the members, I started to think that this might be what I had been searching for and where I wanted to serve. Mind you, when I first moved into the neighborhood in 1969, I had visited the church, but the service was more "traditional AME" and quiet, unlike the emotional Baptist services I had been used to. I never imagined that their style of worship would ever change. Boy was I wrong. Being born into the Baptist tradition, baptized and raised in the Baptist faith, as were my ancestors, who founded the family church in Prince Edward County, VA, in 1867, presented a big decision for me to ponder. Sometimes a lack of knowledge can be your worst enemy. I soon learned that we were all worshiping the same God and shared the same beliefs.

My neighbor and friend, Ruth Hill, kept after me until I finally joined. I attended for a year to make sure this was the church I wanted to be in for the duration and I finally joined in 1986. I was eager to learn about the AME doctrine and Ruth Hill gave me my first Discipline. I wanted to know as much about the church and their beliefs and structure so I was encouraged to attend Annual Conferences and the General Conferences.

At Reid Temple, I found a new church family that included Howard and Betty Pointer. Betty was my first class leader after I joined. I also got to know Dorcas Hart, Lillian Hill, my present class leader, Mr. and Mrs. James Parker, and Alphonso and Elizabeth Brooks, who became my adopted parents, as part of the "adopt a senior' program of the Lay Organization.

I was encouraged to get involved and I became a member of the Lay Organization, serving for many years as their Historiographer, Pastor's Aid (Agape) Society, Bereavement Committee, Resource and Development Committee, and was elected to serve as a Trustee at Michigan Avenue, serving there and at the Good Luck Road location. I was privileged to work with the committees on each of our relocations, from Michigan Avenue to Good Luck Road, to Glenn Dale, MD. When the decision was made to start a second location in Silver Spring, MD, I started to worship there and presently serve as a member of the Capital Campaign Committee. The Committee took the lead in helping to coordinate the search, planning and eventual move to the new location, on Tech Road, under the direction of Rev. Matthew Watley, Executive Minister.

In 2011, as I look back over the many years at Reid Temple, I still value the relationships that came out of this church family. That family has grown to include many other members who I met at the Michigan Avenue location, who have been supportive over the years, including John and Susie Oliphant, Richard and Willie Prather, Robert and Katherine Fisher, Gladys Jefferson, the late Winifred Cameron, Annette Stratford, Thornton and Jean Little, Avis Pointer, and all those from that location too numerous to name. These people have been there for me and when we get together, it is like a family reunion. Although I don't see them often, it is so good to know that we are part of a caring church family. We have a senior pastor, Rev. Lee P. Washington (Anna), and Executive Minister, Rev. Matthew Watley (Shawna), who boldly preach and teach the Word with conviction and continue to lead souls to salvation telling us to "Have Faith in God."

Under their capable leadership, I have been blessed and have grown in my Christian walk with the Lord. I can truly say that the things I used to do, I try not to do anymore and that it is my desire to continue to grow and be all that the Lord wants me to be. With God all things are possible. I look back knowing that only God brought me to this point. I have found new friends to add to my circle of church family at the North Location, where Gerald and Michelle Francis, Frank and Vivian Wilds, Carolyn Armstrong, and my old friend Harold Herndon and his son Reggie and a new friend, Linda Brown are among the faces I look forward to seeing on Sunday morning. After Sunday service you can find me, with my other church friends, Shirley Rivens-Smith, Ursula Kennedy, Sharline Reed, and sometimes Patricia Anderson, relaxing at McDonald's talking about the wonderful worship experience we had, before we discuss the current events of the day.

When someone asks me how I have grown as a Christian over the years, I use the analogy of the physical size of the two church buildings that I have shown in photographs in this book. I tell them to look at the physical size of the little church that I was saved in as a child, and then look at the size of the one I am now worshipping in. In doing so, you can readily see how I measure my Christian growth. The illustration does not have anything to do with the physical size of the churches that I worshipped in, but they are only used to represent the expanse of my growth, as I strive to become a better Christian. Although there has been a lot of growth since that time, I continue my journey believing and having faith in God's word and his promises. I know that I am far from where I need to be.

I can't remember exactly how Betty Pointer and I became such good friends, but if you know Betty, you know she does not meet any strangers. I think she invited me to go on one of the bus trips where the church members accompanied Rev. Washington to a service held on the Eastern Shore. On the trip down we were seat mates and we talked and got to know each other better. Later, when Howard and Billy met we found ourselves spending a lot of time together. It wasn't long before they became part of our extended family. Arnetta Scales, who also attended Reid Temple on Michigan Avenue, also became another one of my long time friend. She and her husband, Leon, are the proprietors of Mr. T's Beauty Salon. Arnetta is a published author and has encouraged me as I write this book. She has kept me from making some missteps she made as I searched for a publisher.

Howard soon became our family dentist and the friendship between our families continued to grow over a period of time. Billy had just about cut his ties with most of his buddies and was spending more time at home. During one of our conversations, Betty started to talk to me about joining the Investment Club she, Howard and his sister, Avis, belonged to. At their next meeting, I met James Chandler, Loretta Thompson, and Wanda Smith and Jessie Parker, two of Howard's dental schoolmates. I would later meet Jessie's wife, Paulette and another of his dental schoolmates, Fred Harris, when they joined the Investment Club. This was a new joint adventure for Billy and me and we took advantage of this new club to learn more about the stock market. We attended investment seminars, enjoyed investing in the stock market, and attending the social gatherings sponsored by the club. We went on ski trips and other fun adventures. I enjoyed doing the research and recommending the stocks. Our Investment Club was doing very well until a fateful day in April, 1994, when Jessie, Paulette and Fred were on their way from North Carolina, to our house for our monthly meeting. As we sat waiting for them to arrive at the College Park Airport, I received a call from Betty saying that she had heard on the radio that a plane had crashed and Howard was on his way to the airport. When we saw Howard and Rev. Washington coming into the house we knew the news was bad. No one survived. The next week we had to get the strength to attend four funerals. It was a sad time for all of us, especially the families and young children that were left behind. Our Investment club never recovered from that great loss and in 1999 we cashed in our stocks and Kollective Kollections II ceased to exist.

I think one of the most powerful lessons I learned from that tragedy was that life is so short and we never know when our time is over. I have learned to live each day as if it were my last and to never hold a grudge that keeps me from having a good relationship with the people in my life. I have learned that it is good to tell people that you love them.

It was doing those early days, spent at Betty and Howard's house on Sunday evenings, that I also met Helen Robinson, who since that time became a very good friend. Helen had come to town from Little Rock, Arkansas with President Bill Clinton. She was one of the African American staff working closely with him in the Oval Office of the White House.

Through my friendship with Helen, I really did get a chance to see how the other folks lived and socialized. I was privileged to have lunch in the President's private dining room, next to the Oval Office, on several occasions and spent many evenings watching performances at the Kennedy Center, sitting in the President's Box. Not only did I tour the public rooms in the White House, but had the privilege of seeing and taking photos in some of the private areas that are off limit to the general public. I proudly signed my name in the register for the Oval Office.

I got to know President Clinton's secretary, Betty Currie, when we attended functions that the President attended. I have stood behind the "gold" ropes with the other VIPS when the President welcomed foreign dignitaries to the White House, at their arrival ceremony. The last time I was at an official arrival ceremony was when the Pope was received at the White House, by then President George Bush.

Photo below provided Courtesy of the Official White House Photographer.

To William and Martha Montgomery
Happy New Year · January 1, 2000
Hillary Rodham Clinton   Bill Clinton

My most memorable moment was when Billy and I stood in the Oval Office, listened to the President give his final Radio Address to the nation, and then have an official photo taken with the President and First Lady, on the 1st Day of January, 2000. That day was a long way from the company owned house, located in a segregated coal camp in a West Virginia hollow, called Ingram Branch, where I entered the world in 1942, as the seventh child of a proud coal miner and homemaker, and the great-great granddaughter of former enslaves ancestors.

Life was good and I continued to work at the General Services Administration, now looking forward to retirement in a few years. When my mentor Patricia Schoeni left the agency, I ended up working in personnel as a personnel security specialist, for a short period of time. I was then assigned to work for the General Services Board of Contract Appeals, where I retired as a Contract

Appeals Specialist and Assistant Clerk of the Board, in 1996. I was featured, along with my co-worker, Beatrice Jones, Clerk of the Board, in a profile of the Board published in one of the first issues of the national publication, Federal Computer Week.

While working at GSA and the GSA Board of Contract Appeals, I met more new friends, who have become a part of my life. When I first arrived at GSA, Brenda Short was the first person I shared an office with. She and I got to be good telephone buddies. We worked together all day and talked half the night on the phone. The other good co-workers, who still remain close friends, are Brenda Robinson, Fannie McDavid Jackson, Arnetta Cook, Joy Brown, Marcia Baisden and Vernita Hall. When I first arrived at the Board, I was not welcomed with open arms, but I let them know that I did not come there looking for any new friends. I was only interested in making time pass by until I was eligible to retire. At the Board, when Cheryl Hilton came on board, I immediately took her under my wings and she became my "adopted daughter." She and her husband Stanley, daughter Keyonna and son Kevin, and grandchildren, Jaden and Jayla, are now part of my extended family.

Work had become a means to an end as an employee of the GSA Board of Contract Appeals. I missed the close working relationship I had with Pat. I did my eight hours and only socialized with my co-workers from my previous offices in GSA. I played with the GSA softball team after work during the summer months and we had many after hours get together. The Board was not always a happy place to work but I had learned to tune people out and say what was on my mind. I did not experience any major problems with the other employees, other than the usual things that go on whenever you are working with a "group of women."

I got along great with the Chairman and Chief Judge, Leonard Suchanek. Leonard was blind, brilliant and tough to work with. He had known about my competency from my days working in the Administrator's office and he had campaigned to get me into his office. The Board was not my first choice, but in hindsight it turned out well. Leonard was Chairman until some of the Judges set out to get rid of him. They succeeded and once again I remembered the old saying about keeping your enemies close by and as my Mom would say, "Feed them with a long handled spoon." I saw firsthand the cutthroat mentality of people who would stop at nothing to get rid of you. Some of his trusted Judges were the very ones who turned on him. At least with Leonard, you knew where you stood.

Working for the government was changing. We had spent over 30 years working to get to the $50-$60,000 salary level, in 1995. The new kids on the block were coming in at that level and we were expected, in many cases, to train them to do our jobs. There was a new work environment that lacked trust and the dedication of civil servants was falling by the wayside.

I was starting to count down the time until I would be able to retire. I had been working in the Government since 1962, with a three year break for private industry, and was looking forward to doing other things. In 1995, the agency offered a new "buy-out" package and I decided to take the money and run. We could work until December 1996. I thought of another old saying: "It is better to run and fight another day, than to stand and lose the battle." My temperament and patience was getting shorter. There had been an incident where two of the female employees had a shoving match that reached the attention of the security office and the front office. This prompted the new Chairman, Stephen (Steve) Daniels, to decide that we needed to take a course on "Conflict Resolution and Anger Management." It was then I noticed that they were trying to single out the female for disparage treatment, especially the African Americans, because we were the first one set to go to the training. So that it would not look racial, they included the few white females to cover their "assets." Beatrice Jones and I, who worked in the Clerk's Office, were included although we were not a part of the legal staff assistants working group.

After working for almost 35 years, with a sterling work record, I could not leave with something like that on my record. In all those years, I had never had anything negative in my personnel folder and was not about to allow this to happen. The evening before the meeting I walked down to see the Vice Chairman, Robert (Bob) Parker, and I told him I was offended that I had been pulled into this dispute and I had not decided whether I was going to call in sick the day of the meeting or come to work and boycott the meeting. He said to me, "don't worry, it is not about you, just go along with the program." By the time I got home that night I was so furious that I had decided that I was not going to participate and proceeded to draft a letter to management pointing out their discriminatory practice. They had said in the memo that all employees were being required to take this training, but I knew that the Judges were never going to go. They would have accomplished their goal by having the administrative personnel attend first and then as management always does, decide that it was no longer necessary. The next day I arrived at work early and proceeded to write the final version of the letter and hand delivered it to Steve's office. I went back to my office and sat back and watched the doors opening and the scurrying around by the Steve and Bob going in and out of the General Counsel's office. I told the other employees that I had decided I was going to the meeting anyway and see what came out of it. I guess my early militant side was peeking out and I knew that I had nothing to lose.

At the appointed time, we all went down to the conference room and then Steve came in to start the meeting. Bob, the Vice Chairman, who I had known from the time I worked with his father at the GAO Cost Accounting Standards Board, and up until that time had had a very good working relationship, came into the meeting after it had started. We were having a good discussion until Bea asked the question as to why the administrative employees, in particular the African Americans, have to attend this training, since there were only two people involved in the conflict.

After some back and forth discussion, I guess the Vice Chairman was feeling superior and made the statement that we had to do it because "he was the boss" and he said so.   Those were fighting words. I don't know what happened but the mere fact that he was putting himself above us, not only because he was Caucasian, but because he felt he could dictate to us what to do just hit me the wrong way.   I don't know what happened but I sprung to my feet in such a manner and loudly told him "you are not my boss, my husband is not my boss, and I only have one boss and that is God Almighty and you certainly are not God." I also let him know that just because he made more money than I did, and may be considered my supervisor, the same person (Uncle Sam) signed his check that signed mine.

I was moving towards him with finger pointing and body language that made him feel that his best bet was to make a hasty retreat out of the conference room. At that, the meeting was adjourned and I immediately went back to my office, got on my computer and found the largest font I could and typed in bold letters "I AM THE BOSS." I placed the sign on my desk for all that had not been in the meeting to see. Needless to say, before we could get back to our offices, the word was out.

When he uttered those words about "being the Boss," all I could hear in the back of my mind were those words I think were uttered so many years ago by Fannie Lou Hammer, "I am sick and tired of being sick and tired." I was demanding the same respect that I had shown to them and for the remainder of my time at the Board, my former friend did everything he could to avoid contact with me. He had finally shown his "true color" - Ignorance. Cheryl told me later that when I stood up, she was reaching for my coat tail because she thought I was going to attack him. I guess old fighting habits die hard. She asked me later was I on some type of medicine or had I forgotten to take my medicine.

I don't know who was the happiest on January 3, 1997, my last official day working for the Federal Government, them or me.   When I saw Steve, who is still the Chairman in January 2011, at the funeral for the mother of my friend and play daughter Cheryl, photo on the left, he asked how I was enjoying my retirement. I told him it was the best decision I made. He admitted that I looked like retirement had been good to me. I in turn asked him, being factious "Are you still working?" He said yes and that he was now enjoying work and not taking it so seriously. I bet he still remembered that day in his conference room more than 14 years ago, when the other side of me came out. I still smile whenever I think about it. There comes a time when you have to stand for something or fall for anything. I am glad I took that stand. Life has been good during the past years of retirement life. Whenever someone asks me what I do since retirement, I usually answer by saying "whatever." To some that may not be a good answer but to me it is the best answer. When you can look back over your life and see how you have grown and how far you have come, it is truly a blessing. I have spent so much time exploring this world through travel and meeting so many new people and making so many new friends.

Chapter 14

Life after Retirement

Retirement is a new phase of life that I have faced with great expectation and excitement because now I was able to pursue other interests. However, those interests would have to wait because within days I had received my summons to serve on Grand Jury Duty for six weeks. I got to see first hand how the judicial system really works. We ended up hearing the evidence in one of the biggest cases to come before the DC Grand Jury, known as the Starbucks Case. I did make a new friend from those days of being cooped up behind closed doors, Helen Glenn. Helen and I always call each other when we see news events that name those attorneys who spent hours presenting their cases before us. I guess my name must be on the list of potential jurors who are willing to serve, because faithfully every two years, I get my dreaded summons.

In 1997, I became involved with my high school classmates as we initiated plans to meet every other year to celebrate our life long friendships. As students, we had bonded and now we were looking forward to strengthening those bonds to include all of our extended families. I had the privilege of chairing the committee when we hosted the reunion in DC in 1999. My retirement afforded me the time to really work towards some goals that I had set for myself while working. I learned how to quilt, took some advanced computer courses with a group of retired employees, who not only learned new computer skills, but spend time giving back to the community.

We were blessed to have as our head instructor, George Woolridge, who was a retired private sector executive, and had as his mission to give back something to the community. I cannot thank him enough for allowing me to be a part of those classes and the group. I was a novice when I entered but accomplished enough afterwards to impart my knowledge to other "seniors" who are struggling with learning how to use a computer. These classes were a gift to me. I learned desktop publishing; Microsoft Access, and Excel, courses that had been foreign to me prior to the classes. My knowledge of desktop publishing has enabled me to create wonderful personalized business cards and greeting cards for friends as they celebrated special days. The only downside is when friends ask me to do a project for them and I have to say no, only because what I do is for pleasure, and when it becomes a job, it is no longer a pleasure. My ex-computer classmates will be happy to know that I am completing this book that I started while a member of their class. George and his wife Ella moved back to Texas but we still keep in touch. I got him interested in genealogy and the last I heard from him he is still tracing his ancestors. Claude Brame keeps in touch through e-mails.

In 2001, Billy joined me in retirement. I encouraged him to retire before he turned 65 so that we could spend more time together doing things that we had put off in the early years. We had to put our plans on hold because within a week after he retired, he headed down to South Carolina to assist his mother. He spent his first three months of retirement in South Carolina. When Christmas arrived, I journeyed to SC so I could help him get his mother ready for her move to New Jersey for the winter. This would be the beginning of an eight year ritual. We both knew it would be a sacrifice but agreed that we had to do what was necessary for his mother. It had been decided that he would take her home for the summer months, so each May we would start to make plans for his absence. Those were difficult times for us but we managed. The telephone company made a lot of money off of us during those summers away. There were some family and class reunions that he had to miss, but it was worth it to be able to spend time with his mother. I stayed here in DC to take care of our home and at the end of summer made the journey to SC to help him lock up for the winter. This would continue until it was too much for him to handle and last year, 2010, was the first summer we had spent together since 2001. His mother turned 97 in September and still asks Billy when she talks to him, "when are we going south?" Billy has really made a 360 degree turnaround and so have I. When I need someone to shape him into place I call on our long time friend Melvin Hubbard. His work as a minister has equipped him to help him see the light. Mel, Mona, Billy and I just spent our vacation on the West Coast.

My travel, in 2000, with a friend, Linda Pettaway and the AME Zion Church, to the Holy Land and Egypt was one of the most memorable highlights in the last few years. For me to be able to walk through the holy land, be baptized in the River Jordan, swim in the Dead Sea, ride through the Sinai Dessert along beside the Red Sea, travel through the Suez Canal, and most of all visit the places where my Lord and Savoir lived, performed miracles, died and rose again, is so humbling. The miracle for me is that so many people thought I would never get to this point, but only God had the plan for my life. I set some goals but I am thankful that God still holds the plan in his hands. As a descendant of enslaved people, I have been able to see places in this world that my ancestors never knew or dreamed about.

In 2004, I traveled with Linda, Dottie Benjamin, and my friend Virginia Reynolds, to Paris, France and London, England, two of the remaining places I had on my list. In addition, I have traveled to all the States in this country, with the exception of Hawaii, Oklahoma, South Dakota, Utah and Wyoming. We will hit Mississippi and Texas this year, and hopefully next year we will take a cruise to the Panama Canal Zone. In 2005, Billy and I traveled across country, by train to Los Angeles, CA, to attend my high school class reunion and cruise to Mexico. We stopped along the way, having lunch in Albuquerque, New Mexico, before continuing on as we marveled at the beauty of the rolling countryside. Again in 2007, Billy and I traveled to Seattle, Washington by train, to meet Foster, Dottie and Denise Benjamin for a cruise to Alaska. We took a side trip to Portland, Oregon and then headed for the great state of Alaska, where we rode the railways along the White Pass and Yukon Route. We visited the Mendenhall Glaciers, went panning for gold, attended a salmon bake and crossed the Border where the United States and Canadian flags were flying side by side, as we made our way to Victoria, British Columbia. We saw a lot in Alaska, but regretfully "we could not see Russia from our cruise ship balcony."

In 2009, we traveled again with Foster and Dottie, as we visited all of the New England States; stopping along the way to admire the beauty of the mountains and fall foliage of Vermont and New Hampshire. We took the ferry to Martha's Vineyard, where we toured the small towns that make up the well known compounds of the rich and famous. We then headed for the State of Maine, and before the fog came in, drove to Land's End, where the land runs out and the only place you can go is out to sea. We took photos standing at the edge of the water and since we did not have a yacht, we returned to our car in search of Maine lobsters and their famous lobster rolls.

I can truly say that I have visited most of the places I dreamed about and am satisfied to look back at the pictures and remember the journey. There are many more places that I will probably visit, but even if I don't, I can say that I am satisfied with what I have seen. The experience of traveling here in the United States and abroad opened up so many opportunities to see how other people live. I have looked at the lifestyles of the rich and famous, without envy, and have been humbled when I saw the slums, inhabited by the poor. In the back of my mind I say a little prayer of thankfulness for all that I have been blessed with.

The greatest gift I have been given was to have family and friends to share this journey with. From the time I started writing this book, there have been so many changes that have taken place and so many loved ones who are no longer here to share in the culmination of this dream.

The dream started over thirty (30) years ago when I wanted to know who my ancestors were. I have learned a lot about them and in doing so have learned a lot about me. I still have so many people around me that are important in my life and for that I am thankful. I only wish that my mother and father were still here so I could share their history with them. In 1995 I lost my father and in 2006 I lost my mother; two of the most important people in my life. I hope that I have made them proud in the choices I have made and that my siblings will join me in honoring them as we live our lives the way they always wanted us to, loving and caring for each other. This book is a gift to their descendants and all the future descendants who will come out of the great tribe of ancestors who paved the way for us to be what we are today. I will always be thankful for my family members who have always been there for me and who continue to inspire me. They are the real heroes in my life. I hope that everyone I wrote about in this book knows that what I have written about them is coming from my memories and from my heart.

Along the way I have been privileged to meet well known people from all walks of life, who have contributed in so many meaningful ways to our world, among them President and Mrs. William (Bill) Clinton, Dr. Martin Luther Kings, Jr., Dr. Dorothy Height, National Council of Negro Women, and Dr. Joseph Lowery, Southern Christian Leadership Conference. I have also met many every day people, too numerous to name, who continue to make a difference in our world. The photos with Drs. Height and Lowery are special because I know I benefited from their contributions to our race.

Former Resident Attends Inaugural Ball

A former Beckley resident and her husband were among attendants at the inaugural balls for President Jimmy Carter and Vice President Walter Mondale Thursday.

Mr. and Mrs. William E. Montgomery attended the ball as host and hostess with the Diplomatic Corps and special guests from Vice President Mondale's home state of Minnesota at the Shoreham-Americana Hotel.

Mrs. Montgomery is the former Martha Evans, daughter of Mr. and Mrs. Leonard Evans of 203 8th St., East Park, and a 1960 honor graduate of Stratton High School.

The Montgomerys also attended a party for members of the President's Transition and Inaugural Committee staffs Wednesday evening.

Mrs. Montgomery has been working with the Inaugural Committee as an information specialist since early November. She is employed as secretary to the Assistant General Counsel at the Cost Accounting Standards Board in Washington and is presently completing her degree work in social services at the University of the District of Columbia. She plans to pursue a career in rehabilitation counseling.

Montgomery is employed by Rock Creek Ginger Ale Company in Washington, where he and his wife live with her niece and nephew, Johnna and John Wright Jr.

I was privileged to work on the Inauguration Committee for President Jimmy Carter and Billy and I attended our first Presidential Inaugural Ball in 1979.

After volunteering and working to help elect the first African American President, Barack Obama, I was privileged to work on his Inaugural Committee. It was truly a day that we had all prayed for and hoped that we would live to see; an African American taking the oath of office as President of the United States. I celebrated for all my ancestors who paved the way for a change to come in America. I attended his Inaugural Ball in 2009, celebrating his victory with my husband Billy, my children, John and Johnna Wright, my other family members, Harry Gonzales, Dorothy and Denise Benjamin, and my friends, Kimberly Spencer, Helen Mashburn, my high school classmate and David Minton.

Early in 2009, I felt the need to try reconnecting to things that had been dear to me. So in January I checked my address book, made a phone call to some old friends and invited them to become a part of a new venture, a Book Club. As a result of those calls, the Metropolitan Literary Society (MLS) Book Club was organized. The group consisted of ex-government employees, the owner of a small business, a former President of a publishing company, and the owner and operator of a child care facility. The original members of the MLS Book Club and more importantly my friends were Angela Thames, Brenda Robinson, Marcia Baisden, Angela Thompson, and Betty Faison Barnaby, who passed away in February 2009. We welcomed our newest member, Bertha Luster, in 2010. We are a group of diverse individuals who enjoy reading and sharing our opinions, however varied on a monthly basis. I think, as retirees, we all missed having that everyday challenge of "adult conversations" in an environment where we interacted and shared opinion on a regular basis. We meet and while eating a delicious meal prepared by Billy, discuss our book for that month and then set out to solve the problems facing our world.

I have experienced a tremendous amount of growth in my personal life. I have seen my immediate family grow by leaps and bounds and I can see the future in the new generations who will be around to finish telling the story. I hope this book will give them a sense of satisfaction of knowing who their ancestors were and that they have a lot to be proud of for the struggles they endured to make a better place for all of us.

Billy and I are at a place in our lives where we are content to share the simple things in life. We can spend an evening with family and friends, or we can spend an evening with him watching his favorite TV sports show, and I can spend hours on the computer, knowing that we are both here together. I can spend time on the phone talking with friends from all over the country, and he does not feel left out. He can go to the kitchen and make a meal for me, bring it to me and say he does it all out of love. I can go outside and rake the leaves or shovel the snow, and tell him I did it out of love for him. Some people don't understand us, but we understand each other. We have come a long way and we keep asking for God's guidance.

In a recent conversation, my granddaughter, Chanteé said to me, "Nana why don't you all ever do anything? You all always stay home. When I come over you are on the computer and he is watching TV alone." I tried to explain to her that we were content at this stage in our lives. When we want to travel, we do, when we want to visit friends, we do, when we want to go to a club to listen to some music with friends, we do. In other words, "been there – done that." I don't know if she fully understands that your life and priorities change as you get older and what used to be important takes a back seat to peace of mind and contentment. Just because we don't agree on everything and because we have different opinions, that we don't mind expressing, does not mean that we don't love and care about each other. I asked her how many couples she knew who have spent over 45 years together. I know a few and we all pretty much do the same things.

On August 19-22, 2011, the Carey/Evans families have plans to meet for a reunion in Williamsburg, Virginia. This will be the first major gathering since 2005. This will also be the first time that the younger generation has taken the lead in planning for the reunion. We are looking forward to seeing the old family members and meeting the new ones. We hope that the lessons we learned from our parents, about family unity, will continue to be passed on to the new generations. These lessons will be worth much more than any material things we can pass on to them. The torch was successfully passed.

In 1960, after my parents had successfully raised us, and one by one sent us out into the world to pursue our own interest, we started a tradition of returning home to West Virginia each 4th of July.   These early gatherings had been the place where we remembered old times, and enjoyed the family cook out in the little house that was home to eight people for many years. It would not be long before those gatherings were hosted in their new home, surrounded by a big lawn with large trees for Daddy to sit under, watching his descendants, while Mama was busy inside preparing all the favorites dishes we loved.   After my father passed in 1995, we continued to make the pilgrimage back to the home place. It was not the same with Daddy gone, but we knew it was important for Mama to see that we were still a united family. After Mama passed in 2006, we made a promise to each other that we would continue to meet at the home place as long as we could.

This years I knew going home would be different. Last year, in 2010, my sister Bernice had started to make plans to relocate back to West Virginia.   In preparation for this, as a family, we finally let go of some of the material things that belonged to our parents. Because some of the items could be used by family members it made letting go easier. At the end of last year, Bernice moved her furniture into the house and we agreed to rearrange the rooms. When I walked into the house this year and did not see the things that I was accustomed to seeing, I realized that our parents were really gone and we had to move on.   They will never be forgotten because the memories are still in our hearts. The sadness of their loss is still there but there is also joy in knowing that we are still that family who love each other, and still honor them.   As this chapter of the story concludes, my wish is that you have enjoyed this journey as you traveled with me in search of my ancestors, and down memory lane.

I was reminded of the importance of family and friends on August 23, 2011, when DC was hit by an earthquake. Arnetta Scales and I was in a taxi headed home after we had viewed the Martin Luther King, Jr. Memorial, took pictures to document the day, and I had said hello and posed for a photo with Mayor Vincent Gray. I was thinking how Dr. King had changed the conscious of a nation when the taxi started to shake for a period of time. It was not until we arrived home and Shirley Brown called to ask if I knew we had had an earthquake. Chanteé called and said "Nana, my whole apartment building was shaking." I was trying to call Johnna and John was calling me. I was praying that Billy, who was not home, was ok. In a short period of time everyone realized what was important. It wasn't how much money you had or what you were gong to wear that day; rather it was if you would see another day and get a chance to get it right. I thank God for keeping us safe and giving us another chance, for He is the God of many chances.

Billy and I just returned home after spending seven days traveling over 6500 miles across country and back enjoying the beautiful countryside. We spent eight days in between travel having lots of fun with old and new friends, and made many new memories. The story will continue......

PICTORIAL SECTION

Billy and I have been blessed to visit many parts of the country and the world and have had the privilege of sharing those trips with family and friends. Many memories have been made on those trips. In recent years, Billy has not been flying so most of my trips out of the country have been without him. He wants to go to Australia and I want to go on a cruise to Panama, so we will see who gets to their destination first. Our last trip across the United States carried us to Las Vegas, NV and Los Angeles, CA. We had a wonderful time meeting new friends along the way. For the first time out of all my trips to Las Vegas I really got to see something other than the strip. I had two classmates, Joseph and Judi Adams and Jean Moore Mackey, who hosted us in a wonderful way. We toured the sections of Las Vegas that the tourist never gets to see. Jean carried us to the section of Las Vegas where African Americans first settled and we also saw where all the rich and famous live and play. My ex-coworker, Jean Smith, treated us to a tour of her new hometown, Henderson, NV. The economy has hit Las Vegas very hard and people are beginning to look for someplace else to retire. Las Vegas is still the place for "fine dining" at a reasonable price.

EARLY TRAVEL PHOTOS WITH FRIENDS AND FAMILY

Wilson/Joy Brown, Mel/Mona Hubbard and Robert/Eunice Bass – 1994

Week-end with Winston/Angela Thames, Mel/Romona Hubbard and Robert
and Eunice Montgomery Bass

L-R Billy, Me, Roy and Betty Barnaby, Chalmers and Linda Truesdale

Cancun with GSA Co-workers, L-R Arnetta Cook, Beatrice Jones, Brenda Robinson, Bill Tillman, in the back and Shirley Brown, next to me far right

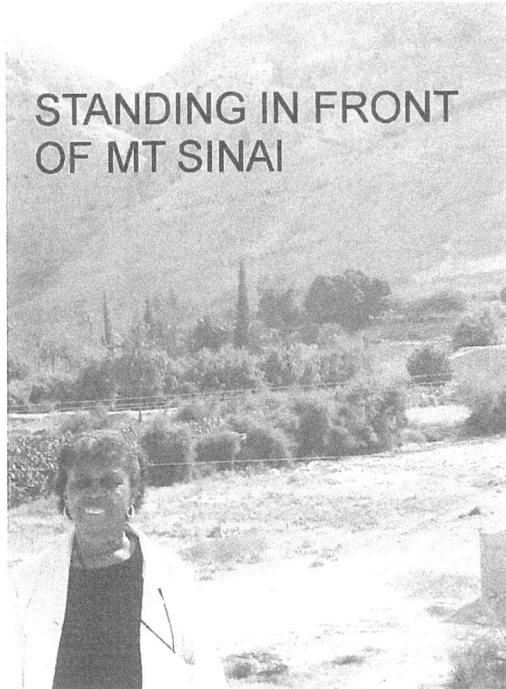

Top L – R – Cruise with Reid Temple Church 1988, Trip to Holy Land and Egypt with AME Zion Church and Trip to Paris, France with AMEZ Church

St. Peter's Square
Rome, Italy - 1984

L-R – Bernice Taylor, Vernita Hall, Brenda Robinson and Me

Bermuda Cruse 1985 – L-R Angela and Winston – Far Right Billy and Me

CANCUN CRUISE 1985 .GALILEO

London - Barbara L. Shaw, National Chair of Nat. Council of Negro Women

Doing a Little Shopping at Harrods Department Store in London

SOME OF MY REID TEMPLE AME CHURCH FAMILY

Rev. Dr. Lee P. Washington
Senior Pastor

Betty Pointer, Dorcas Hart, Me, Lillian Hill

Me with Bishop Cornal Garnett
Henning, Sr. AME Church

Dorcas Hart, Lillian Hill, Bishop
Frederick C. James, AMEC, Me

Me and my travel Partner, Betty Pointer, 2nd photo – L-R Susie Oliphant, Alphonso and Elizabeth Brooks

Katherine and Robert Fisher

Willie Prather & Betty Pointer

Susie Oliphant/ Arnetta Scales

Winifred Cameron and Avis Pointer

Linda Brown & Harold Herndon

Howard and Betty Pointer

EARLY FAMILY PHOTOS

Mother, Johnna and Chanteé

Me and Mom Christmas 1995

Photos of Mom Summer at my House and First Christmas after Daddy Passed in 1995

Diva Chanteé and Johnna Wright

Me holding Olympic Torch 1996

EARLY YEARS WITH VEIDA, TANYA AND FAMILY

Billy and Me With daughters Vieda and Tanya and her family during Christmas visits during the early years

McCoy/Johnson Family having breakfast before going to President Obama's Inauguration- L-R Naomi, Jo-Ann Sanders McCoy, Anita, Alesha, Isaiah

Billy, George and Mom B'day

Billy with Mom, Nita and Children

MORE FRIENDS THROUGHOUT THE YEARS

Me and Virginia Reynolds

Helen Robinson, me, Betty Pointer, Dorcas Hart

Winston and Angela Thames

Gladys T. Johnson and Me

Levi & Marcia Baisden

Brenda Short/Lolita McIntosh

C-R Arthur and Linda Pettaway, James Chandler and Nancy Moore

Fannie McDavid-Jackson
And Wayne Jackson

Walter Booth and Virginia
Reynolds

L-R Arnetta Cook/Helen Glenn
Patricia Harrison

Josephine Bynum

Leon and Patricia Wright Perry

Virginia Reynolds
And Tamara Blanc

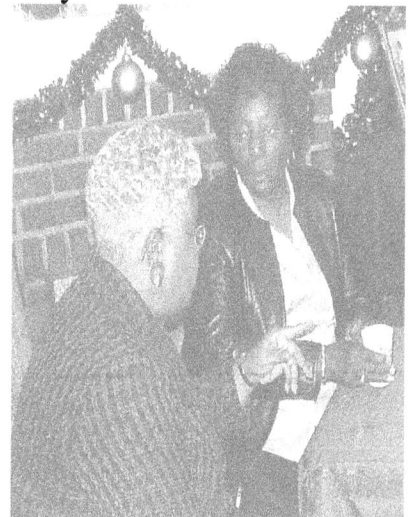

Dolores Bailey and
Shirley Montgomery-Brown

Alesha with Aunts (Sanders side), Grandfather, Mother and Siblings

Alesha Celebrating with Family after Receiving Her Degree

ALESHA'S Graduation Party With her Father, David Johnson, Grandmother Johnson (On Right) Aunt (On Left), Mom, Anita, siblings, Naomi & Isaiah

WHO COULD FORGET SEPTEMBER 11, 2001

This was the day the world stood still. I remember what I was doing as if it happened yesterday. I was in bed watching the morning news on NBC. There was a pause and the news anchor stopped to say that it looked like a plane had hit the Twin Towers at the World Trade Center in New York. Everyone thought it was an accident until we looked on in disbelief to see another plane heading toward the same buildings. It was at that moment that the anchor said something was wrong and we all knew something terrible was happening. Those pictures will remain in my memory forever. I ran downstairs to tell Billy to turn on the news. He had just come in from work and I was so relieved to know he was safe because the next few minutes we heard that a plane was headed for the Pentagon. The Pentagon metro stop is where he transferred to catch his train home. I immediately started to call family members in the area to see if they were safe and my phone started to ring from out of town friends wondering the same about us. We then heard that another plane had been heading for the US Capitol. It was taken down in a field in Pennsylvania. For the rest of the day I sat glued to the television as things unfolded and I thanked God that all my family and friends were safe. I said prayers for the victims and their families and realized that our country would never be the same again. Later that week, Johnna, Chanteé and I went to see the damage to the Pentagon, where we took photos to document that terrible day in our history.

PHOTOS TAKEN FROM MEMORY HILL WHERE MEMORIALS TO THE
VICTIMS HAD STARTED TO PILE UP

For a short period of time our country came together as one. I look forward to the day when we can do so again, not as the result of tragedy, but because we all want what is best for each other and our country. I am preparing to work again on President Obama's reelection campaign and I hope he will be successful. I believe that if God has a plan for your life no one and nothing can alter that plan. I continue to pray for his safety and success during his term in office. We are all called to make a difference. Sometimes it takes you awhile to find out what your calling is and how best to accomplish it.

As I close this book for the second time, I do so knowing that I have tried to carry out one of the goals I had on my "bucket list." This book is our family history, my history and the history of our country, from the eyes of one of its citizens. I have traveled all around the world and I still think America is still a great country. May God continue to bless each of you, our country, and the entire world.

Peace and Love to All.

BIBLIOGRAPHY

Following are genealogical and historical references, including works cited in the text.

Ancestry.com website: www.ancestry.com

History of New Hope Baptist Church, Keysville, Virginia

Library of Congress American Folk Life Center, National Public Radio's Story Corp's Project

National Archives and Records Administration, 1860 – 1930 U.S. Census Records

Social Security Death Index

State of Virginia Death Record Index

State of Virginia Vital Records Division, Library of Virginia

The Church of Jesus Christ of Later Day Saints - Family History Library

Virginia Slave Birth Index – 1835-1865, Alexandria Library Local History/Special Collections, Leslie Anderson Morales, Editor, Jenifer Learned, Assistant Editor, Beverly Pierce, Assistant Editor, published by Heritage Books, 2007

ABOUT THE AUTHOR

Martha Montgomery, (formerly Martha Evans), the seventh child of Leonard and Martha Carey Evans, was born in Ingram Branch, West Virginia. She was educated in the public school systems of Fayette and Raleigh Counties. She graduated with honors, in 1960, from Stratton High School in Beckley, West Virginia. She completed her studies at Cortez Peters Business School and earned a Degree in Social Work from the University of the District of Columbia. This is her first book.

She started her career as a clerk-typist with the Federal government, in Washington, DC. She was also employed as an Administrative Secretary with IBM Corporation. She completed 32 years of Federal service, retiring as a Contract Appeals Specialist, in 1996.

She and her husband of 43 years, William, reside in Washington, DC, where they raised her niece and nephew, Johnna and John Wright. Martha is the stepmother to three daughters, Tanya, Veida and Anita, and fourteen grandchildren.

She became active in church as a child and presently worships at Reid Temple AME Church, One Church in Two Locations, Glenn Dale and Silver Spring, Maryland.

She has travelled extensively across this country to forty-six States, Europe, the Middle East, South America, and the Caribbean.

www.ingramcontent.com/pod-product-compliance
Lightning Source LLC
Chambersburg PA
CBHW080954130426
PP18130600001B/6